LAURA
INGALLS
WILDER

W9-CAD-579

SOUTH DAKOTA BIOGRAPHY SERIES

Laura Ingalls Wilder
by Pamela Smith Hill

Wild Bill Hickok & Calamity Jane
by James D. McLaird

Seth Bullock
by David A. Wolff

LAURA
INGALLS
WILDER

A WRITER'S LIFE

PAMELA SMITH
HILL

South Dakota
State Historical Society
Press *Pierre*

Boca Raton Public Library

© 2007 by the South Dakota State Historical Society Press
All rights reserved. This book or portions thereof in any form
whatsoever may not be reproduced without the expressed written
approval of the South Dakota State Historical Society Press, Pierre,
S.Dak., 57501. Excerpts from the published and unpublished literary
works of Laura Ingalls Wilder and Rose Wilder Lane, as well as their
correspondence and related quoted materials, are used with the
permission of Little House Heritage Trust, the copyright owner.
All rights reserved.

Laura Ingalls Wilder is Volume 1 in the South Dakota Biography Series.

This publication is funded, in part, by the Great Plains Education
Foundation, Inc., Aberdeen, S.Dak.

Library of Congress Cataloging-in-Publication data
Hill, Pamela Smith.
Laura Ingalls Wilder : a writer's life / by Pamela Smith Hill.
    p. cm.—(South Dakota biography series ; v. 1)
Includes bibliographical references and index.
ISBN 978-0-9777955-6-7 (alk. paper)
1. Wilder, Laura Ingalls, 1867-1957—Juvenile literature.
2. Authors, American—20th century—Biography—Juvenile literature.
3. Frontier and pioneer life—United States—Juvenile literature.
4. Children's stories—Authorship--Juvenile literature. I. Title.
PS 3545.I342Z665 2007
813'.52—dc22
[B]   2007030827x

Printed in the United States of America

The paper in this book meets the guidelines for permanence
and durability of the committee on Production Guidelines for
Book Longevity of the Council on Library Resources.

Please visit our website at http://www.sdshspress.com

18 17 16 15 14   7 8 9 10 11

Cover and frontispiece: Laura Ingalls Wilder in 1906, courtesy of
the Laura Ingalls Wilder Home Association, Mansfield, Mo.

Design and set in Arnhem type by Rich Hendel

FOR RICHARD,

who encouraged me to write through my grief

Contents

Acknowledgments

In many ways, writing this book has spanned a life time, and so I begin my acknowledgments with family and friends in my home town, Springfield, Missouri. I am deeply grateful to neighbor Opal Scott, who recommended that I read Laura Ingalls Wilder in the first place, when I was ten years old. My thanks to my mother for driving me to the bookmobile, where I checked out my first Wilder book, *Little Town on the Prairie.*

During the 1970s, my long-time friend Jean Maneke supplied me with a file of Laura Ingalls Wilder clippings from the Springfield newspaper morgue when I first started writing about Wilder for the South Dakota Division of Tourism. I have referred to those materials often in the writing of this book, especially the columns by reporter Lucille Morris Upton.

Another long-time friend, Dr. Kathy Pulley at Missouri State University, recommended that I discuss the economic history of the Ozarks with one of her colleagues, historian Dr. Stephen McIntyre. Thank you both for your able assistance.

I am indebted to my father, who became my "local color" expert on the Ozarks and responded to endless e-mail queries quickly and tirelessly. My sister Angela has enthusiastically promoted this project.

Cheryl Palmlund, executive director at the Laura Ingalls Wilder Memorial Society in De Smet, South Dakota, gave me complete access to the archives there. Her staff, particularly archival assistant Rachel Clendenin and tour guide Sara Madison, made my visit effortless and productive. I extend special thanks to my tour guides at the Laura Ingalls Wilder Home and Museum Association in Mansfield, Missouri, especially Janice Bennet, who measured the exact height of

Wilder's kitchen cabinets for me at Rocky Ridge Farm, and to Director Jean Coday, who graciously allowed me to xerox an article on Wilder from a vintage book in her private collection. Archivist Spencer Howard at the Herbert Hoover Presidential Library kept me well supplied with box after box of materials from the Lane Papers, and visiting Herbert Hoover presidential scholar Glen Jeansonne made sure I always broke for lunch.

My sincere thanks to Elizabeth Engel at the University of Missouri, who responded promptly and thoroughly to my request for microfilm materials in the Western Historical Manuscript Collection. The library staff at Washington State University Vancouver helped me figure out the workings of their new microfilm machine and were especially helpful when it overheated. I am grateful, too, to research librarian Linda Frederiksen. She tracked down all the obscure books and early twentieth century magazine articles I requested.

Peter and Milena McGraw graciously granted me permission to quote from an unpublished manuscript by children's book author Eloise Jarvis McGraw. Margery Cuyler, publisher at Marshall Cavendish Children's Books, and Regina Griffin, vice-president and editor-in-chief at Holiday House, provided relevant insights into the working relationship between children's book writers and their editors.

I am indebted to the work of Wilder scholars William T. Anderson, William Holtz, John Miller, and Rosa Ann Moore. Their scholarship made my own work possible.

My critique group in Portland, Oregon, offered careful and instructive suggestions that strengthened this book, especially biographer Dorothy Nafus Morrison. Monthly Chez-Day lunches with writers Susan Fletcher, Cynthia Whitcomb, and Laura Whitcomb fueled my creativity. My agent Emilie Jacobson wisely encouraged me to think of this book as a labor of love. My thanks to children's book authors Carmen T. Bernier-Grand and Carolyn Digby Conahan for reading and critiquing the entire manuscript.

I am deeply grateful to my friend of thirty years and editor Nancy Tystad Koupal, who entrusted Laura Ingalls Wilder to me in the first place. She offered me this project when I needed it most and, through this book, helped me rediscover the joy of writing.

Finally, I thank my daughter Emily, who has never lost faith in me, and my husband Richard, the generous ghost looking over my shoulder as I wrote every word.

Introduction Not the Whole Truth

"All I have told is true but it is not the whole truth."

Laura Ingalls Wilder delivered this line in a speech she gave in 1937 during Detroit Book Fair, marking the release of her fourth book in what we now call the Little House series. She was fast becoming a celebrity within the world of children's books, though not yet a legend. Perhaps that is why this line from her speech did not get much attention. The truth, as Wilder defined it in Detroit, went beyond a simple definition of historical fact. She chose not to tell the whole truth in her books, she explained, because some of the stories she wanted to tell were not appropriate for children.[1] What she did not say, however, is that throughout her career as a novelist, Wilder shaped the history of her life for the purposes of her story. In a letter she wrote to her daughter, author Rose Wilder Lane, as they discussed character, theme, and historical accuracy in the first of her novels set in South Dakota, *By the Shores of Silver Lake,* Wilder admitted, "I stretched a point when I had Laura go with Pa to see the work [on the building of the railroad]. I never did. He would not have taken me."[2] In a later letter, also to Lane, Wilder explained why she stretched this point: "I did it . . . to have Laura see it first hand and get her reaction."[3]

She altered the truth to create a better story, and for some Wilder readers, this idea is uncomfortable, even disloyal. After all, she maintained that her books were "autobiography, true in every detail," and her reading public came to believe that as well. A newspaper headline from 1949 described Wilder's books as "True Stories That Read Like Fiction."[4] But Wilder was first and foremost a storyteller. She quickly embraced what most writers of fiction have long understood. "The truth of an incident," as contemporary author Madeleine L'Engle puts it, "may lie artistically far from the facts of that incident."[5] Throughout her writing life, Wilder blurred historical fact with what she considered the greater truth found only in a good story; so did her daughter. In a letter to her mother in 1938, Lane wrote that, the truth "is a meaning underlying" fact and that changing, revising, or modifying events to make a stronger book "is not fact but it is perfectly true."[6]

Perhaps it is not surprising, then, that the persona Wilder assumed during her lifetime—which has since become legendary—is not exactly factual either, though it does make a good story: a Missouri farm woman in her mid-sixties with virtually no publication experience writes her first book. She is "a lovely, white haired fragile appearing woman," who draws on "her wealth of memories" to produce classic books for young Americans.[7] As she published book after book—eight during her lifetime—the legend flourished. Wilder herself, consciously or unconsciously, contributed to it. When a reporter asked her in 1949 what advice she would give young writers, she replied, "I hardly feel competent to do that, for all I did was write what happened to me." The fact that she wrote her early drafts on wide-lined school tablets added charm and credibility to her story.[8] So did her description of her writing process. "After I would write something," she told one reporter, "I would set it back for a month or so and let it cool. Then I would read it back and maybe change it a little before I sent it in."[9]

Yet, Wilder was not an unpublished, completely inexperienced writer when she sat down to write that first book. Nor was her writing process quite as simple as she let on. She did far more than change her stories "a little" after they had gone cold, and she did not write in isolation from her remote Ozark farm. Instead, Wilder worked in collaboration with a gifted, meticulous editor—Rose Wilder Lane—and her books evolved and deepened as her skills as a novelist matured. Furthermore, Wilder's success was not inevitable or even easy. Her writing ambitions dated from her adolescence in Dakota Territory, when she began writing poems and received praise for her student theme on ambition, which she kept and eventually inserted into *These Happy Golden Years*. She served a lengthy apprenticeship as a farm journalist and grappled with Lane's initial advice to write for adult markets, not children. Ultimately, Wilder persevered through the usual trials and tribulations that face most American novelists as they struggle to find their voices, their publishers, and their readers. Wilder grew creatively, learning from her daughter, her editors at Harpers & Brothers, her agent, and ultimately from herself. Her emergence as a novelist revealed her commitment and passion to the craft of writing fiction.[10]

And the fiction Wilder produced, while it was clearly autobiographical, demonstrated her emerging understanding of story: conflict, character, plot, dialogue, description, narrative, and theme—all bound up with her love of family, the prairies of the Middle Border, and the West. In that same speech she delivered in Detroit, Wilder told her audience: "I began to think what a wonderful childhood I had had. How I had seen the whole frontier, the woods, the Indian country of the great plains, the frontier towns, the building of railroads in wild, unsettled country, homesteading and farmers coming in to take possession. . . . Then I understood that in my own life I represented a whole period of American history."[11]

But the greater truth of fiction, the satisfying arc of a good story, ultimately interested Wilder far more than the precise details of her own past. The facts she embellished, changed, and eliminated from her family's history—and her own life—transformed the real Laura Elizabeth Ingalls, the girl born to Charles and Caroline Ingalls on 7 February 1867, into the fictional Laura Ingalls, an immortal character in American children's literature, born in 1932 when Harper & Brothers released *Little House in the Big Woods*.

1

Once upon a Time, Years and Years Ago

1860–1869

The initial inspiration for the Little House books sprang from Wilder's memories of her father, Charles P. Ingalls. "Pa was no business man," she explained to her daughter in 1937. "He was a hunter and trapper, a musician and poet."[1] Scribbled on the back of a letter from Marion Fiery of Alfred Knopf Publishing, the first editor interested in her fiction, Wilder wrote: "I would be especially glad to have Knopf publish those stories of my father's. They impressed me very much as a child and I still have great affection for them."[2] In fact, the death of Charles Ingalls in 1902 may have prompted Wilder to envision her childhood memories as material for a story—and a wider audience. Among the writing fragments she included in a file titled "Ideas for Work," which dates perhaps from 1903, is a memory from Wilder's early experiences on Silver Lake in Dakota Territory.[3]

Like many accomplished writers, Wilder let the idea simmer—for twenty-two years. When she took it up again in 1925, her mother, Caroline Quiner Ingalls, had died the year before. Writing her aging aunt Martha Carpenter, her mother's sister, Wilder asked for help with an article she had been invited to write for *The Ladies Home Journal* on "our grandmother's cooking." She began by asking for the recipe for vanity cakes but quickly expanded her request. She wanted stories from her mother's childhood. "Could you, I wonder, tell the story of those days and any special stories that you remember about things that happened then," Wilder asked. "Just tell it in your own words as you would tell about those times if only you could talk to me." She told Aunt Martha that she wanted the stories as a record for the family and possibly for Lane to use for publication. But Wilder's request was so precise that it is hard to imagine she wanted these stories only for her daughter:

> As you begin to tell it so many things will come back to you about the little everyday happenings and what you and mother and Aunt Eliza and Uncle Tom and Uncle Henry did as children and young folks, going to parties and sleigh rides and spelling schools and dancing school. . . . About your work and school too. Also about away back when Grandma was left a widow and the Indians used to share their game with her and the children, if I remember right.

Furthermore, Wilder made a suggestion that only a professional writer would make: she offered to pay a stenographer to transcribe these recollections.[4]

No stenographer was needed. Carpenter replied just a few months later. She sent recipes for cottage cheese pie and vanity cake, "just made out of egg and flour [and] a pinch of salt," and described at length how maple-sugar parties, quiltings, corn-husking parties, howling wolves, panthers in the woods, and hitching oxen to a large sled so "all that could piled on" for a "merry time."[5] Despite her aunt's help, Wilder never wrote that story for *The Ladies Home Journal*; instead, she put the letter away and let the idea continue to simmer. But clearly, Wilder was incorporating influences from both her parents. Although Pa emerges alongside Laura as the central characters in the Little House books, Caroline Ingalls's influence on Wilder's writing is just as important. Together the two literally made Wilder's fiction possible.

Charles Ingalls and Caroline Quiner met and eventually married in Jefferson County, Wisconsin, near the small town of Concord on 1 February 1860. Throughout the first years of their marriage, the American Civil War raged to the east and south. Only a few episodes relating to the family's war-time experiences touch the pages of the Little House books. Pa's brother George, for example, arrives at the dance at Grandpa's in *The Little House in the Big Woods*, wearing "his blue army coat with brass buttons." He plays his army bugle and walks with a swagger. Pa tells Laura, "George is wild, since he came back from the war." Much later in *The Little Town on the Prairie*, when Laura wears a hoop skirt for the first time, she scorns the old-fashioned hoops that had been in style during the Civil War era. "'I think it was silly, the way they dressed when Ma was a girl" she tells her sister Carrie.[6]

Somehow Charles Ingalls managed to escape service in the Union Army. Two more of his brothers—Hiram and Lansford James—enlisted late in the war and saw virtually no action, but Caroline's brother Joseph Quiner was killed during the Battle of Shiloh in April 1862. Wilder herself was born just two years after Robert E. Lee surrendered at Appomattox. Charles Ingalls was a musician and poet—not a soldier—and this fact may help explain why Wilder's books provide so little historical context for this period of her family's life.[7]

The Ingallses of Jefferson County were a closely-knit clan, and in 1862, when Charles's father, Lansford Ingalls, could not pay the mortgage on his property, the whole family, including his married sons and their wives, moved west to heavily forested Pepin County. The first child of Charles and Caroline Ingalls, Mary Amelia, came into the world there on 10 January 1865. Wilder was born two years later in the Wisconsin woods. Her parents named her Laura Elizabeth for Charles's mother, Laura Colby Ingalls. But before the year was out, Charles Ingalls sold his property in Wisconsin, made a down payment sight unseen on property in Missouri, and, along with Caroline's brother Henry Quiner and his wife Polly (Charles's sister), moved the family to Chariton County in north-central Missouri during the spring of 1868. Wilder was just over a year old.[8]

Her first experience as a citizen of Missouri did not last long. In 1869, the Ingalls family crossed the Missouri–Kansas border and settled about thirteen miles south of Independence, Kansas, on the Osage Indian Reserve. This location is where Wilder began her unpublished memoir, "Pioneer Girl": "Once upon a time years and years ago, Pa stopped the horses and the wagon they were hauling away out on the prairie in Indian Territory. 'Well Caroline,' he said, 'here's the place we've been looking for. Might as well camp.'" A paragraph later, Wilder placed herself in the scene: "I lay and looked through the opening in the wagon over at the campfire and Pa and Ma sitting there. It was lonesome and so still with the stars shining down on the great, flat land where no one lived." Even in this first recounting of her memories, the prairie took on the haunting persona that characterizes Wilder's accomplished fiction. From the beginning, the West was part of her family.[9]

The handwritten draft of "Pioneer Girl" was written in 1930, before Wilder envisioned her first novel. At the time, Wilder's objective was to publish the manuscript as nonfiction, as a one-volume memoir. But George Bye, the literary agent handling the manuscript as a favor to Rose Wilder Lane, did not warm to it. "It didn't seem to have enough high points or crescendo," he complained. "A fine old lady was sitting in a rocking chair and telling a story chronologically but with no benefit of perspective or theatre."[10] For Wilder scholars today, however, her autobiography offers a factual record of her childhood and charts her growth as a writer of fiction. It also illuminates the gaps between Wilder's fiction and the facts of her own life, illustrating how she supplemented the fragmented, impressionistic memories of childhood with stories she had heard from her parents and older sister Mary. It is important to point out that in "Pioneer Girl," Wilder does not mention her birth in Wisconsin or her family's short residency in Missouri. Even when setting out to write nonfiction, Wilder apparently did not believe it necessary to include all the facts from her childhood. From the beginning, she was more concerned with fitting her family's story into a larger pioneering experience. As she later explained in the speech delivered in Detroit during the book fair: "I realized that I had seen and lived it all—all the successive phases of the frontier, first the frontiersman then the pioneer, then the farmers and the towns."[11]

Still, "Pioneer Girl" presents a more complete picture of the Ingalls family history than Wilder's Little House novels. Once Wilder embarked on writing fiction, she knew her story needed a strong, clean, forward motion. In *Little House in the Big Woods* and *Farmer Boy,* she built those books around the calendar year, showing how families had lived their everyday lives sixty years earlier. Later, as the idea of a fictional series took shape, Wilder created a different story line; the forward motion that united her remaining books focused on moving west. From the opening pages of her third book, *Little House on the Prairie,* until Pa files his homestead claim in Dakota Territory in her fifth book, *By the Shores of Silver Lake,* the Ingalls family never retraces its steps. They always move ahead—from Wisconsin, to Indian Territory, to Minnesota, and on to Dakota Territory. And even then, Pa does not feel settled. In *These Happy Golden Years*, the last book in the series published during Wilder's lifetime, Pa confesses, "I would like to go West. . . . A fellow doesn't have room to breathe here any more." Ma, of course, reminds him that the Dakota prairies are vast; besides, she says, "I thought we were settled here." But the fictional Laura understands: she "knew how he felt for she saw the look in his blue eyes as he gazed over the rolling prairie westward from the open door where he stood."[12] This thematic emphasis—always looking west, never turning back—is the spine, the rigid, inflexible backbone of the entire series.

In reality, the Ingalls family backtracked more than once, and Wilder followed its meanderings with much more accuracy and precision in "Pioneer Girl." The story she tells in her autobiography is less about moving west and more about making ends meet.

2

From Indian Territory
to the Big Woods

1869–1874

Wilder's earliest childhood memories sprang, not from the Big Woods of Wisconsin, where her first novel takes place, but from what she called Indian Territory in Kansas. In fact, Wilder scribbled that phrase across the front of the "Fifty Fifty" newsprint-ruled tablet that contains the opening scenes in "Pioneer Girl." This first draft, written in Wilder's precise but flowing handwriting, became the foundation for at least two more versions of her memoirs and for her novels as well. Its opening pages include episodes readers of *The Little House on the Prairie*, Wilder's third book in the Little House series, would recognize.[1]

In "Pioneer Girl," Charles Ingalls, whom Wilder called Pa, built his family a log house from trees in a nearby creek bottom in Indian Territory. He brought "back a cook stove, a window to put in the window hole and some lumber to make a door" from a town forty miles away. In this first chapter, Wilder included perhaps one of her earliest memories: her father carrying her to the cabin window to see the wolves outside, howling in the night, where they are "all sitting in a ring around the house, with their noses pointed up at the big, bright moon, howling as loud and long as they could, while Jack [the brindle bulldog] paced before the door and growled." In this earliest draft, Wilder wrote about the Indians (who often came to the house), the fevers and chills that descended on the family, the Christmas when the creek was too high for Santa Claus to cross, the Indian babies Wilder longed for, and the family's departure from their little house on the prairie. These adventures cover just thirteen hand-written pages in the original manuscript of "Pioneer Girl";

Little House on the Prairie, which includes many of these episodes, spans over three hundred pages in its final published form.[2]

Despite its brevity, Wilder's depiction of the Ingalls family's experience in "Pioneer Girl" reveals significant differences from her fictional account of their life in Indian Territory. For example, her sister Caroline Celestia was born in Indian Territory on 3 August 1870; in Wilder's first novel, Carrie is a baby in the Big Woods of Wisconsin and goes west to Indian Territory with the rest of the family. A "Mr. Brown," not the beloved Mr. Edwards of the Little House series, was the neighbor who delivered Laura and Mary's presents from Santa Claus when the creek flooded. The fire in the chimney occurred not in the family's little house in Indian Territory (as it does in *Little House on the Prairie*), but in a "log house with a big fireplace" in Missouri, where the family stayed on their trek out of Kansas. And perhaps an even more unsettling discovery: Charles Ingalls not only traded his horses Pet and Patty for a larger pair, but he threw in Jack the bulldog as well—"because Jack wanted to stay with Pet and Patty as he always did."[3] In Wilder's fiction, Jack is the family's loyal canine companion through three books, and he dies peacefully of old age in her fifth novel, *By the Shores of Silver Lake*.

Not many writers would want their readers to see their first drafts. The initial tentative, foggy shape a story takes on paper rarely resembles the final polished work readers see in print, whether nonfiction or fiction. Writers are often finding their way through a first draft, experimenting, trying simply to capture the essence of the story on paper. In longer, book-length works, writers are often unsure if the story will sustain itself from the beginning on through the middle and end. In fact, many writers destroy their early drafts because they have so little in common with the version they send off to their editors. When Wilder wrote the opening pages for "Pioneer Girl," she had not considered transforming the facts of her life into a fictional series. The manuscript was her own personal story, a memoir, an unembellished attempt to set family stories and memories on paper, a rough draft.[4] Furthermore, she could not possibly have envisioned future generations of scholars who would dissect her life story for devoted readers around the world. Still, the rough draft of "Pioneer Girl" illuminates the facts underlying Wilder's earliest memories and illustrates that, before she became a novelist, she was a capable storyteller.

How reliable are the details Wilder presented in her memoir? After all, when "Pioneer Girl" opens, she was only two, going on three years old. How much could she actually remember from this period of her life? Readers, and even Wilder's first editor, posed similar questions about *Little House in the Big Woods*. "We seem to be a little in the dark as to the exact source of your material," wrote Harper & Brothers editor Virginia Kirkus in December 1931, before the book was published. "I had understood when your manuscript was given to me to read, that it was autobiographical. . . . Won't you send us an autobiographical sketch so that we can see just how this material fits into your own background?"[5]

Wilder scholars have meticulously checked and double-checked even the most obscure details from the various unpublished versions of "Pioneer Girl" and her published novels. They have found discrepancies in names, dates, and places. Her memory clearly was not perfect. In "Pioneer Girl," Wilder occasionally confused or misspelled the names of schoolteachers, shopkeepers, or family acquaintances; referred to neighbors who are not listed in official county or census records; or overestimated distances between farms, homesteads, and towns. Yet, a memoir, by its very definition, can never be entirely factual. It is an impressionistic remembrance of the past, a reconstruction of memory. For "Pioneer Girl," Wilder relied on family accounts to supplement those vivid fragments of memory from her earliest childhood. Though her memories became more expansive, detailed, and personal as "Pioneer Girl" tracked Wilder's growing maturity, they exhibit the same minor inconsistencies of those memories she patched together from earlier periods of her life. Her memoir is inaccurate—as anyone's would be. Yet, it relates the facts of her life more directly than her fiction.[6]

The truth is that the Ingalls family lived on the Osage Indian Reserve for roughly a year. The 1870 census shows that the C. P. Ingles family (the census taker misspelled Ingalls) lived about thirteen miles from the town of Independence, in Rutland Township, Montgomery County, Kansas, just west of Walnut Creek, on 13 August of that year. Charles and Caroline Ingalls, along with a handful of others, settled on the reserve illegally. The census taker, Asa Hairgrove, identified Charles as a carpenter, and estimated the value of the Ingallses' "personal estate" at two hundred dollars. He left the column blank that asked for the value of the family's real estate. He did so for everyone in Rutland Township, noting on the last page of the census that he provided no real estate values for anyone there because "the Lands belonged to the Osage Indians and Settlers had no title to Said Lands."[7]

Neither Wilder's fiction nor her drafts of "Pioneer Girl" explain why her parents settled illegally on the Osage reserve. Instead, her entire focus was on the family's experiences there, often with Indians. When two strode into their house while her father was away, she and Mary "cuddled close to Jack with our arms around his neck" as their mother cooked for the Indians. Later, when a large number of Indians camped at the nearby creek, the family was frightened by their nighttime "shouting and screaming," which "sounded much worse than the wolves." At one point, Wilder recalled that she remembered waking up in the middle of the night to see her father dressed and holding his gun.[8]

Wilder developed these episodes later into fully formed, dramatic scenes for *The Little House on the Prairie*, but her memoir was as silent as her novel about the family's motivation. In "Pioneer Girl," she jumped directly from the episode about Indian babies, which she wanted for their "bright, black eyes," to her family's departure from Indian Territory. She wrote only one cryptic line of explanation: "The soldiers were taking all the white people off the Indian's land."[9] In a later typed version of "Pioneer Girl," Lane struck out the word "taking" and inserted the word "driving."[10] In *Little House on the Prairie*, Wilder elaborated, but only slightly. When the fictional Pa learns that the federal government is sending the military to escort the settlers out of Indian Territory, he says, "If some blasted politicians in Washington hadn't sent out word it would be all right to settle here, I'd never have been three miles over the line into Indian Territory."[11]

We cannot know if Wilder invented Pa's motivation for the novel or if this version was how the family came to remember it. Wilder scholar John E. Miller described the complexities surrounding the settlement of the Osage reserve during this period, which involved the competing interests of railroad companies, local boosters, land speculators, and the Osage nation itself. But within the context of Wilder's fiction, Pa's claim that the government encouraged settlement in Indian Territory reinforces his strength of character and fuels the forward action of the unfolding series. Pa settles his family in Indian Territory, not as part of a greedy land grab, but to fulfill the government's vision—and his own—of westward expansion; although he leaves disillusioned, he does it on his own terms, not waiting to be forced out by the United States Army. Furthermore, within the framework of the novel, the Ingalls family is not defeated by this loss; they are ennobled by it, continuing to move west in true pioneer spirit.[12] "Everything was just as it used to be before they built the house," Wilder wrote in the last chapter of *Little House on the Prairie*. "Pa and Ma and Carrie were on the wagon-seat, Laura and Mary sat on the wagon tongue." Later, as the family camps for the night, they sing a song, accompanied by Pa's fiddle, "with a lilt and swing that almost lifted Laura right out of bed." As she falls asleep, Laura begins "to drift over endless waves of prairie grasses, and Pa's voice went with her, singing."[13]

In reality, however, the family did not move west. Instead, they returned to Wisconsin, to "the place we had left when we went west. The land was Pa's again, because the man who bought it from him had not paid for it."[14] Several scholars have speculated that this financial setback may be the real reason Charles Ingalls decided to leave Indian Territory. Gustaf Gustafson, the man who had bought the Wisconsin property from Ingalls in 1868, could not pay up. With nothing to show for their first venture into the West, it made financial sense for the Ingalls family to retrace their steps and reclaim their farm near Pepin, Wisconsin.[15] Wilder herself was just four years old when the family moved back east, and her description of this journey in the rough draft of "Pioneer Girl" lacks the characteristic joy she later evoked when the fictional Ingalls family moved west. She remembered that her family traveled "for days and days, sleeping in the wagon at night, until we were very tired." Arriving at their destination, they found "the house was larger than the one we left on the prairie. . . . There were lots of windows and the house was very comfortable and cozy set down among the hills in the Wisconsin woods."[16] It was the spring of 1871.

Gustaf Gustafson still occupied the place, so the Ingalls family temporarily moved in with Wilder's Uncle Henry and Aunt Polly. In "Pioneer Girl," Wilder explained how close the two families were: "Uncle Henry was Ma's brother; Aunt Polly was Pa's sister and we learned that the cousins [Louisa, Charley, Albert, and Lottie Quiner] were double cousins, almost like sisters and brothers." *Little House in the Big Woods*, on the other hand, only hints at the closeness between the extended Ingalls and Quiner families, bringing them together at Christmastime and for special occasions like the dance at Grandpa's, but the thematic focus always remains on Pa, Ma, Mary, Laura, and Carrie. They live in their own cabin in the Big Woods. In reality, however, it was several weeks before the Ingalls family reclaimed their house. In the meantime, Wilder recalled that she and her cousins "had great times playing together."[17]

The stories and memories Wilder gathered from this period of her life form the basis for her first novel, *Little House in the Big Woods*. Readers of her fiction would again recognize key episodes in her memoir when Charles Ingalls saved the family's bacon after a bear broke into the pig pen; when her father told her and Mary the story of Grandpa Ingalls and the panther; and when, on long Sunday afternoons after Christmas, Caroline Ingalls read the girls stories from Charles Ingalls's "big green book, 'The Polar and Tropical Worlds.'" Charles played his fiddle, the family went to the dance at Grandpa's house, and naughty cousin Charley was stung by swarming yellow jackets. Furthermore, the Laura of the memoir and the Laura of Wilder's fiction clearly share common characteristics. Both share the nickname Half-Pint and have the strength of a little French horse. Even in her first nonfiction draft of "Pioneer Girl," Wilder created strong, vivid scenes to illustrate how she came to be characterized that way. In the first instance, her father came home from checking his traps in the woods and called out, "'Where's my little half pint of cider half drank up?'" Wilder then explained, "That was me because I was so small." A few pages later, she described how her father "would put his fingers through his hair to make it stand on end" and then corner Mary and herself like a mad dog. When she dragged Mary over the woodbox in a desperate leap, Wilder's father remarked, "You may be only a half pint of cider half drank up, but by Jinks you're as strong as a little French horse!"[18]

Once again, however, this section of the memoir differs significantly from Wilder's fiction. Her little house, for example, was not even in the "Big Woods." In her first draft of "Pioneer Girl," Wilder explained that their house was "set down among the hills in the Wisconsin woods." A few pages later, she added, "It seemed the 'Big Woods' as Pa called them were just north of us a ways." Her grandfather and Uncle Peter, on the other hand, did live in the Big Woods. Black Susan, the cat, inhabited both Wilder's factual and fictional little houses in Wisconsin, but "Pioneer Girl" also introduced Wolf, their black-and-white spotted dog, who stayed behind with Black Susan when the family eventually moved west. A more important difference, however, occurs in how "Pioneer Girl" portrayed everyday life in that little house in the Wisconsin woods. The extended Quiner and Ingalls families played a large role in Wilder's early child-hood. So, too, did nearby neighbors. Right after the dance at her grandfather's, for example, Wilder described with even more detail a dance at the Huleatts, their prosper-ous neighbors. Thomas Huleatt was "an Irish gentleman," Wilder recorded, "and everyone was proud to be invited" to his place.[19] In *Little House in the Big Woods,* the only dance occurs at Grandpa's, without any mention of the Irish gen-tleman and his family.[20]

Nor does the novel mention Wilder's first experience at school. The Barry Corner School was "only a little way down the road," Wilder wrote in "Pioneer Girl," and Mary, who was six years old, started school there along with several Quiner and Ingalls cousins and the Huleatt children. Wilder was still too young to go to school, but she studied reading with her big sister after dinner, learning her words and letters so well that "to Ma's surprise, I could read as well as Mary." Eventually, she went to school to hear her sister "speak a piece." Wilder recalled walking to the schoolhouse as the two girls swung the dinner pail between them. When they arrived, the classroom was crowded with "lots of boys and girls I didn't know."[21] Clearly, the real Ingalls family did not live in the isolation that characterizes the fictional family's experience in *Little House in the Big Woods*, which opens with this description: "As far as a man could go to the north in a day, or a week, or a whole month, there was nothing but woods. There were no houses. There were no roads. There were no people."[22]

This difference is important. The fictional family's isolation sets them apart, makes them special, and gives their everyday lives an almost archetypal quality. In fact, the activities Wilder describes in the novel—salting and smoking venison, butchering hogs, making butter and cheese, harvesting maple syrup—are linked to the family's heroic survival in a harsh environment. Furthermore, she links this survival to the changing seasons: her first novel spans a year in the life of the Ingalls family. This organizational scheme deepens the archetypal pattern, making *Little House in the Big Woods* a memorable and important first novel.

Virtually none of this distinctiveness appears in the rough draft of "Pioneer Girl," where Wilder briefly described how her father made bullets and loaded his gun but otherwise offered only sketchy details about pioneer life. In the memoir, Wilder wrote closer to the facts of her experience; in her novels, she transformed these experiences into an almost mythic kind of truth. She deliberately heightened her family's social and physical isolation, a transformation that ultimately strengthened not just her first novel, but the remaining books in the series.

Some time in 1873, when Wilder was six, Charles and Caroline Ingalls decided to leave Wisconsin and move west. Again, "Pioneer Girl" provided no motivation for the move. Wilder simply wrote, "Then one day Ma put our things in boxes, Pa loaded them into the wagon, we all got in and Pa drove a long time through the woods."[23] Charles and Caroline Ingalls sold their farm in October 1873 for one thousand dollars. They spent the fall and early winter living in Wisconsin with Peter and Eliza Ingalls. The two families planned to travel west together early the next year, before Lake Pepin thawed. Peter Ingalls had decided to move his family to a farm in southeastern Minnesota; Charles and

Caroline would continue farther west.[24] Before the families could leave, however, the children of both contracted scarlet fever. Wilder explained, "This sickness worried the fathers and mothers for we must drive across the lake before the ice got soft and thin."[25]

Although Wilder herself had not completely recovered, the families set out to cross the lake in early February. Wilder "was carried all rolled up in blankets, even my head covered up so I would not take cold," she recalled. Although she could not see anything from her bundle of blankets, Wilder remembered hearing terrifying sounds as the family's wagon crossed Lake Pepin. She knew as a child that people were drowned in the lake by trying to cross it too late in the season, and when she heard "the horses' feet go 'splash,' 'splash,' in water," she was terrified. Her mother comforted her, and the next thing Wilder knew, she woke up in bed in a hotel. A paragraph later, Wilder remembered that her father woke her up again to present her with a "pretty little book of verse" for her birthday.[26]

In her fiction, Wilder eliminated or transformed much of this material. *Little House on the Prairie* opens with a chapter set in the Big Woods of Wisconsin titled "Going West." Pa has decided to pack up and move the family to Indian country. Wilder explains his motivation this way: "Wild animals would not stay in a country where there were so many people. Pa did not like to stay, either. He liked a country where the wild animals lived without being afraid." That place was the West. Pa quickly sold the house, the cow, and her calf. And before the family left their little house, wagons brought the rest of the family through the Big Woods to say goodbye. Pa, Ma, Mary, Laura, Carrie, and Jack set out to cross Lake Pepin and face the challenges of the frontier alone.[27]

In reality, of course, Wilder and her family did not travel west alone, and their destination was not Indian Territory. It was Plum Creek in southwestern Minnesota.

3

A Light-Colored, Fleecy Cloud

1874–1876

Once safely across the lake, the two Ingalls families took refuge in a house "so close to the creek that if we had fallen out of the back window we would have dropped into the water," Wilder remembered. The weather was too cold for travel, and she still suffered from the lingering effects of scarlet fever. "Sometimes my ears hurt me so much I couldn't play," she wrote. The families lingered in that house beside the creek through the spring thaw and beyond. One of Wilder's most vivid memories came during her stay there, and her description of it in "Pioneer Girl" foreshadowed the mastery and skill she would bring to her fiction: "One night Mary lay sleeping beside me but I lay awake looking through the bedroom door at the firelight flickering and the shadows moving in the room outside. Pa was sitting in the shadows where I couldn't see him but I could hear his fiddle singing. It was all so beautiful it made my throat ache."[1]

The two families moved on when the weather warmed up. Peter and Eliza Ingalls settled their family on a farm they had rented near the Zumbro River in southeastern Minnesota; Wilder's family continued west. Unlike their tiresome journey east from Indian Territory to Pepin, Wisconsin, this move was full of joy and wonder. Wilder's recollection in "Pioneer Girl" expressed the sheer delight she took in the journey: "The grass along the road was fresh and green in the springtime and it was a delight to camp at night in a little nook somewhere beside the way. . . . We'd see the sun go down, hear the birds twitter their sleepy good nights and sleep with David and Sampson (Sam for short) crunching their oats in their feed box at the back of the wagon, with just the thin wagon cover between their heads and ours. Sometimes Pa would sit awhile by the campfire and play his violin."[2] In the spring of 1874, this blissful journey west ended at what appeared to be a blissful spot: a farm along Plum Creek, just two and a half miles from Walnut Grove, Minnesota. In her memoir, Wilder called it a "pretty place by the very nicest creek we had seen."[3] The family moved into the dugout, which she described so vividly in her fourth novel.[4]

On the Banks of Plum Creek provides an abbreviated and fictional account of this period of the Ingalls family's pioneer experience in Minnesota. It balances the fictional family's joy in their new life—the formation of the Congregational church; their friendship with Reverend Edwin Alden; Laura, Mary, and Carrie's first Christmas tree—with the overall theme of pioneer courage in the face of adversity. After all, at the heart of the book is financial ruin brought on when a shimmering cloud of grasshoppers, as devastating as the plague in Genesis, descends on the family's farm. It is also in this book that Laura's fictional character begins to emerge more distinctly. She defies Ma to play in the flooded creek and is nearly drowned; she excels at school; and she squares off for the first time against her infamous rival Nellie Oleson. At one point, Mary says, "'I couldn't be as mean as that Nellie Oleson,'" to which Laura replies, "'I could. I could be meaner to her than she is to us, if Ma and Pa would let me.'"[5]

Wilder's real life experiences on the banks of Plum Creek, however, were far more complex, and her remembrance of them in "Pioneer Girl" is often more candid and less rosy than the similar episodes she fictionalized in her novel. Furthermore, she deleted whole chunks of her life during this period from her fiction. The family actually lived on their Plum Creek farm and in the little settlement of Walnut Grove, Minnesota, from 1874 until 1876, when they moved east—to Burr Oak, Iowa. They returned to Walnut Grove in

1878 and stayed there until the spring of 1879. In "Pioneer Girl," Wilder included vivid details about this period of her life, and they reveal that the Ingalls family struggled much harder to make ends meet than the fictional family. Not only did the real family battle a plague of grasshoppers, but they also suffered through multiple business failures, life-threatening illnesses, and the death of a child.

The grasshopper plague stands at the center of the Plum Creek experience in "Pioneer Girl," as it does in the novel. This experience defined the family's life there and ultimately sent them east into Iowa. And like the novel, "Pioneer Girl" initially presents an almost idyllic life along Plum Creek. The Ingalls bonded with the Nelsons, their Swedish neighbors (in the novel, Wilder identified them as Norwegian). Charles Ingalls worked for Eleck Nelson during much of 1874, and Wilder spent a great deal of time with Mrs. Nelson. Not only did she learn to milk a cow under the older woman's guidance, but, she wrote, "I was with her so much that Pa said I talked English like a Swede and I could easily understand when Mrs. Nelson talked her language with the other Swede neighbors."[6]

Charles Ingalls planted his first crop on Plum Creek and built the family a house in the spring of 1875, when they moved out of the dugout. By this time, the real family had joined the recently formed Congregational church in Walnut Grove, contributed to the collection for its church bell (an impressive $26.15, as opposed to the $3.00 contribution Pa makes in the novel), and Laura and Mary were attending school.[7] Then disaster struck:

> At dinner one day, Pa was telling us that the wheat in our field was so tall it would just stand under his arms, with long, beautiful heads and filling nicely. He said the grain was all soft and milky yet but was so well grown he felt sure we would have a wonderful crop.

Just then we heard someone call and Mrs. Nelson was in the doorway. . . .

"The grasshoppers are coming! The grasshoppers are coming!" she shrieked. . . .

We raised our faces and looked straight into the sun. It had been shining brightly but now there was a light colored fleecy cloud over its face. . . .

And then we saw that the cloud was grasshoppers, their wings a shining white making a screen between us and the sun. They were dropping to the ground like hail in a hailstorm, faster and faster.

As in *On the Banks of Plum Creek*, Charles Ingalls fought to save his beautiful crop, but lost. There were no green things in sight, Wilder remembered, "and the ground looked like a honeycomb it was so full of the little round holes where the grasshoppers had laid their eggs."[8]

In the novel, the Ingalls family goes to church the following Sunday; Pa works briefly for Mr. Nelson; and despite the family's grim financial future, Pa bravely says, "No pesky mess of grasshoppers can beat us! We'll do something! You'll see. We'll get along somehow."[9] In "Pioneer Girl," Wilder's recollection was bleaker: there were no crops and no money for food. One day, she remembered, "Pa told us goodbye, put on his hat and carrying his coat over his shoulder, started walking east to find work in the harvest fields." Wilder then added an important detail: Charles Ingalls walked to the eastern harvests because the family could not scrape together money for train fare.[10]

While Charles Ingalls was away, Caroline and her girls depended heavily on assistance from the Nelsons. Wilder recalled in her memoir that the Nelsons were good neighbors and described how Eleck Nelson singlehandedly saved the Ingallses' house from a raging prairie fire after the first grasshopper infestation. In *On the Banks of Plum Creek*, this incident occurs later, and Ma plays an active role in saving the house. By making such subtle changes to her fiction, Wilder emphasized her family's independence and allowed her characters to solve their problems more heroically.[11]

Charles Ingalls returned to the Plum Creek farm in the fall of 1875 and moved his family into Walnut Grove for the winter.[12] In "Pioneer Girl," Wilder described the town as "tiny," with a church, "two small stores, a blacksmith shop, a little school house and a few houses where people lived." The Ingallses' rental house in Walnut Grove was "behind the church, and not far from the schoolhouse," suggesting that they moved into town so the girls could get to school safely that winter. An even more compelling reason for the move may have been the fact that Caroline Ingalls was pregnant. Soon after they were settled, Wilder remembered: "Coming home from school one day, we found a strange woman getting supper, and a little brother beside Ma in the bed. We were very proud of him and always hurried home from school to see him."[13] The baby's name was Charles Frederick Ingalls, and he was born 1 November 1875. The family called him Freddy. *On the Banks of Plum Creek* mentions neither his birth nor the move into town.

In the spring of 1876, the family returned to their farmhouse on Plum Creek. Shortly thereafter, Caroline Ingalls became desperately ill. It was during what Wilder called the "spring freshet," a phrase that went on to become a chapter title in *On the Banks of Plum Creek*, but there the parallel ended. During the spring freshet in the memoir, flood waters of Plum Creek formed a barrier, cutting the family off from Walnut Grove and the doctor forty miles away. Charles Ingalls, unable to leave his wife's side, told Laura, who was nine at the time, to run to the Nelson house for help. When she reached the creek, Wilder recalled, "It terrified me, for the footbridge was standing away out in the middle of the stream, with yellow, foaming water running on both sides and just over the top of it." As she waded in, the water rushed over her knees. Nelson saw her there, told her to go back, and went for the doctor himself. When she got back to the house, Caroline was better, and Wilder's father asked her why she was wet. "When I told him," she wrote, "he said, 'By Jinks!'"[14]

The story as told in the memoir is significant not only because it illustrated Wilder's obedience and courage as a child, but also because it underscored the Ingalls family's deepening financial crisis. Caroline Ingalls recovered, but not before the doctor had made three house calls to Plum Creek. Wilder reported that her father then bought some seed and planted a small field of grain. She recalled that he decided "not [to] sow much because if the grasshoppers hatched they would eat it anyway." More likely, after Caroline's illness, Charles Ingalls could not afford to buy enough seed for more than a small field, regardless of grasshoppers.[15]

Although the threat of yet another grasshopper season hung over this part of her life, Wilder described at length how she and Mary played and fished in Plum Creek, their Sunday school experiences at the Congregational church, their adventures at school, and their playmates in town. Her closest friend was a girl named Nettie Kennedy, who had red hair that Wilder thought was "wonderfully pretty." Also among her schoolmates in Walnut Grove were Nellie and Willie Owens. Their father owned one of the two stores in Walnut Grove, which meant that the children had "wonderful toys, tops, and jumping jacks and beautiful picture books." They were not generous with them, and Wilder commented that she and Mary "would not have been allowed to be so rude and selfish" had they had such splendid toys. When Wilder began to write novels, she used her memories of Nellie Owens, along with those of two other girls she met later on, to create the fictional Nellie Oleson, a character most readers love to despise.[16]

The tone of "Pioneer Girl" darkened once more with the grasshoppers' return in the summer of 1876. The thousands of grasshopper eggs hatched into tiny insects that rose out of the holes in the ground and ate their way to adulthood. They ate Charles Ingalls's small field of grain, and he declared that he had had enough. He would not stay in such a "blasted country," his daughter recorded.[17] Never would the Pa of *On the Banks of Plum Creek* let a blasted country get the best of him. When the grasshoppers hatch in the novel, Pa again goes east for the harvest to earn money to see the family through another winter, and Mr. Nelson helps Ma save the Plum Creek house from the prairie fire. Pa returns after being caught in a terrific blizzard, and the book ends at Christmastime with the Ingalls family savoring an oyster stew in their little house on the banks of Plum Creek.[18]

Historian John E. Miller makes an important point in his extremely thorough biography of Wilder. In 1873, the year before the Ingalls moved to Walnut Grove, grasshoppers had significantly damaged the farmers' crops in the area. It is hard to imagine that Charles Ingalls would not have known this fact when he bought the Plum Creek property the following year.[19] "Pioneer Girl' is curiously silent on this point. The novel, on the other hand, clears Pa of any knowledge about the farm's recent history. "I can't make out why Hanson [from whom Pa buys the farm] sowed such a small field," he tells Ma, as he explains his hasty purchase of the farm in *On the Banks of Plum Creek*. "It must have been a dry season, or Hanson's no farmer, his wheat is so thin and light."[20] Whether he knew about the grasshopper infestation of 1873 or, like his fictional counterpart, was blissfully ignorant of it, Charles Ingalls clearly took a risk when he bought the property. Two years later, he let it go.

The family left Walnut Grove in the summer of 1876, shortly after Charles Ingalls sold the Plum Creek farm in July. Wilder reported that William and Mary Steadman, her parents' friends, probably from the church in Walnut Grove, had traded property for a hotel in Burr Oak, Iowa.[21] Mr. Steadman asked the Ingalls to be partners in the business, which would officially change hands in the fall. Charles and Caroline agreed, but they decided to leave Walnut Grove right away. They headed east for a visit with Peter and Eliza Ingalls on their farm along the Zumbro River. Perhaps because she was on her way to see her cousins, Wilder's account in "Pioneer Girl" of the first part of their journey east was lighthearted. She noted that on their first stop out of Walnut Grove, their mother insisted on combing everyone's hair. "Little Brother Freddy," Wilder remembered, "didn't have much hair to comb." She added, "It was nice to be in the big, fresh outdoors all the days and nights." When they arrived at Uncle Peter's, Wilder recorded that the cousins once again fell into an easy companionship—picking plums together, fetching the cows home at dark, and roasting wild crab apples over campfires when cold, rainy weather set in.[22]

This idyllic period ended abruptly. Freddy fell ill. When the doctor arrived, the young Wilder expected he would save the baby, just as the doctor at Plum Creek had saved her mother. "But little Brother got worse instead of better and one awful day he straightened out his little body and was dead." He died 27 August 1876. He was nine months old. The family buried Freddy in Minnesota and began the next phase of their journey east. "We felt so badly to go on and leave Freddy," Wilder remembered, "but in a little while we had to go on to Iowa to help keep the hotel. It was a cold miserable little journey."[23] They arrived in Burr Oak, Iowa, in the autumn of 1876; Wilder was almost ten years old. Over fifty years later, when she began to fictionalize her life, she used none of her family's experiences there in her Little House books.

4

A Story in Itself

1876–1879

In her memoir, Wilder remembered the Masters Hotel (named for its previous owners but also referred to as the Burr Oak House) as large and pretty, with a hall dividing the parlor from the barroom at street level, guest bedrooms upstairs, and the dining room, kitchen, and kitchen bedroom on a lower level. This place was home for the first few months the Ingalls spent in Burr Oak. Wilder was not, however, as impressed with the town: "Burr Oak was a small town, but it was not a new, clean little town like Walnut Grove. It was an old, old town and always seemed to me dark and dirty." Having that barroom—or saloon, as Wilder sometimes called it—so close to their living quarters in the hotel made the family uneasy. "Pa and Ma didn't like the saloon next door either and we were a little afraid of the men who were always hanging around its door," she wrote. One image of the saloon especially impressed Wilder: seven bullet holes left in the door between the dining room and kitchen; the son of the hotel's previous owner had tried to shoot his wife in a drunken brawl. Later this family would deeply influence the course of Wilder's young life.[1]

A certain grittiness, even seediness, characterized the episodes Wilder remembered from her life in Burr Oak. An unsavory group of young men in their early twenties bullied the school's callow young principal; the beau of the hotel's hired girl went on a drunken binge, lit a cigar, and died instantly when the whiskey fumes on his breath ignited; a storekeeper dragged his wife by her long hair, poured kerosene on the floor, and set their bedroom aflame. Wilder herself fell victim to the unsettling undercurrents in the town when she had to submit to voice lessons from Mr. B. L. Bisbee, "one of the richest men in Burr Oak and our best paying, steady boarder," because "he must be pleased if possible." And later one of the town's most prestigious families—Dr. and Mrs. Alfred Starr—approached Caroline Ingalls about adopting Wilder, who was then about ten years old. Eunice Starr, Wilder recalled, "wanted a little girl to help her around the house and keep her from being lonesome." Reading between the lines, the Starrs perhaps thought the Ingallses had one too many mouths to feed. "But Ma smiled at me and said she couldn't possibly spare me," Wilder recorded.[2]

The Ingalls family's first Christmas in Burr Oak, celebrated just a few months after Freddy's death in 1876, was sad and disappointing: "Ma was always tired; Pa was always busy." Not long afterwards, all three Ingalls girls came down with measles, a seemingly routine circumstance that would reap unfortunate consequences for the family. William and Mary Steadman and their children were also disagreeable. Wilder's memories of Mary Steadman and her three little boys, including the baby she and Mary cared for, were all negative. The unhappy relationship that developed between the two families probably influenced Charles and Caroline's decision to move out of the hotel in the autumn of 1877 and into a set of rooms above a grocery store "on the other side of the saloon." Wilder recorded that at about the same time they no longer helped in the hotel.[3] In a letter to her daughter Rose Wilder Lane from 1937, Wilder provided more perspective on the family's decision to abandon their partnership in the hotel: "Steadman handled the money and someway beat Pa out of his share. I don't suppose there was much."[4]

Yet, the family stayed on in Burr Oak. Charles Ingalls found a job at a feed mill, where he ground corn and wheat with the family's team of horses. Wilder's parents continued to worry that their new living quarters were still too close to the saloon, but their new home in those rooms over the grocery store were pleasant, sunny, and clean, Wilder recalled.

Still, when the hired girl's beau literally went up in smoke in the barroom next door, Charles Ingalls had once again had enough. He rented "a little red brick house out on the very edge of town" from Bisbee, Wilder's odious music teacher. The family's financial situation stabilized: not only were they living in a house again, but they could afford a cow. Wilder's baby sister, Grace Pearl Ingalls, was born in this little brick house on 23 May 1877. "Her hair was golden like Mary's and her eyes were blue and bright like Pa's," Wilder wrote in "Pioneer Girl."[5]

Although many critics and scholars speculate that Wilder's experiences in Burr Oak were either too sad or too seedy to be included in her fiction, it is important to point out that not all her memories of this period fit either of those descriptions. "Pioneer Girl" contains a humorous story about Bisbee trying to put out a saloon fire with a bottomless bucket; a sustained account of Wilder's achievement when she learned her multiplication tables and graduated to the upstairs class at the Burr Oak school; and rhapsodic passages about taking the cow to pasture and rambling through a magical old graveyard. "Even if it rained," she noted, "the wet was nice on my feet and the rain felt good on my face and on my body through my thin, summer clothes." She even included a touching story about a boy living near the graveyard in a small stone house. People, she said, called him "an idiot, whatever that might be." His grandmother greeted Wilder on her rambles and gave her roses and cookies. She summarized: "That was a delightful summer! Work and play were so mixed that I could not tell them apart."[6]

Why then did Wilder exclude Burr Oak from her fiction? Certainly, the real family's experiences there had a different feeling and character than the wholesome, independent pioneer situations Wilder created for her fictional family in *On the Banks of Plum Creek* and *By the Shores of Silver Lake*, the two novels in which, chronologically, she could have placed the Burr Oak material. And Freddy's death was an enormous loss, one which, even if fictionalized, might have undermined the fundamental optimism of Wilder's novels. "It is a story in itself," she explained to Rose Wilder Lane, "but does not belong in the picture I am making of the family."[7] Furthermore, the real family's detour into eastern Iowa would have undercut the overarching theme of moving west, which binds the Little House books together. The fictional Ingalls family always looks forward, not back.

Still another factor that Wilder may have considered as she measured her life story against the essential conventions of good fiction was what Burr Oak might have revealed about her father—his character and his ability to care for his family. Without a doubt, the Ingallses had a tough time making ends meet in Burr Oak. By late 1877, Wilder, who was then going on eleven, "knew we needed money." Charles Ingalls's job at the feed mill had dried up, Wilder confided to Lane: "I learned too that if all the debts were paid, dr. bills, grocery bills, and rent, . . . we wouldn't have enough money to pay our expenses."[8] In "Pioneer Girl," Wilder mediated this assessment by saying, "Pa did not like an old settled place like Burr Oak; a dead town" without a railroad. He began to play "lonesome, longing music" on his fiddle, including "There's a Happy Land Far Away." That longing to move west was clearly part of her father's character—the real Charles Ingalls as well as the fictional one. But what he did next in Burr Oak was something the fictional Charles Ingalls would never do: he packed up his family and skipped town in the middle of the night.[9]

Wilder recorded in her memoir that her father asked Bisbee, the family's landlord, "to wait for the rent, promising to send it to him in a little while." Bisbee refused and threatened to confiscate the family's team of horses and sell the animals to pay the Ingalls's debt. "Pa was very angry," Wilder recalled. "He said he always had paid all he owed and he would pay everyone else but he'd 'be darned if he'd ever pay that rich old skinflint Bisbee a cent.'" Her father sold the family's cow, perhaps to pay moving expenses, loaded up the wagon, and the family left in the dark. They did not stop until just before daylight when they were safely across the county line.[10] They spent the next few days traveling west—not toward the frontier, but back to Walnut Grove, Minnesota. They had escaped their landlord and saved a month's rent, but even more hard luck and sadness lay ahead.

During the winter of 1878, the Ingalls family lived with John and Luperlia Ensign in Walnut Grove. Although Wilder wrote that their hosts welcomed them home and insisted that they share their living quarters, it is possible that Charles and Caroline could not afford anything else. Charles Ingalls went to work in a store and split living expenses with the Ensigns. Eventually, he went to work for William Masters, who had opened a hotel in Walnut Grove and became one of the town's most prosperous citizens. Masters had moved to Walnut Grove from Burr Oak in the mid 1870s; he sold the Masters Hotel in Burr Oak to the Steadmans, and his son was the one responsible for those seven bullet holes that fascinated Wilder when she and her family lived there. By the spring of 1878, Pa bought a town lot on credit from Masters in the pasture near the Walnut Grove Hotel. He built the family a house, and Wilder became a "town girl," a term she used in *On the Banks of Plum Creek* to describe her rival Nellie Oleson. Wilder and her sister Mary enrolled in the school, Charles and Caroline rejoined the Congregational church, and her father was soon the town's justice of the peace. Other than planting a kitchen garden, he abandoned farming, another important difference between Wilder's fiction and her life.[11]

Much of her memoir describing this period focuses on her social life in the bustling, gossipy little town of Walnut Grove. Wilder, who turned eleven in 1878, entertained her first proposal of marriage there—from Howard Ensign, who was about the same age. He asked Wilder to marry him when they grew up, and she recalled that she considered it seriously. But when Howard started to cry as Wilder played with his rival, the preacher's son, Albert Moses, she turned him down. It was not manly to cry. "I was disgusted," she wrote.[12] Among Wilder's new acquaintances at school was Genieve Masters, one of the younger members of the Masters clan. She "sneered at the other girls in school because they were westerners"; she wore nicer clothes than her classmates; and she bragged about her New York connections. To faithful readers of Wilder's fiction, this description sounds like Nellie Oleson. But Nellie Owens, Wilder's first rival in the real Walnut Grove, was still around, and the two girls—Nellie and Genieve—struggled for domination over Wilder and her classmates. Wilder herself emerged as the victor "because Genieve and Nellie each being eager to win me to her side would play what I wanted to play and do as I said in order to please me."[13]

Nevertheless, Wilder's rivalry with Genieve continued, especially as all the girls their age took a new and more mature interest in boys. Wilder feigned having a crush on Silas Rude, a new and intriguing classmate, only because Genieve was interested in him. He was different from the familiar Walnut Grove boys with their "rough hair and freckled faces," and he also cultivated a wild-boy image. "Silas said he was 'Rude by name and rude by nature,'" Wilder remembered. Wilder's pseudo-crush convinced her parents, who finally intervened. Charles Ingalls told her, "Any boy who would fool around with the girls, instead of playing with the other boys like a man, was no good, a sissy." Wilder confessed that she had known the truth about Silas but did not want Genieve to win his attention.[14] Clearly, Genieve Masters was a second model for the fictional Nellie Oleson, but there was a third yet to come in Dakota Territory.

Wilder filled portions of the second and third Fifty Fifty tablets of her draft of "Pioneer Girl" with stories about the people she and her family knew in Walnut Grove during their second stay there. Wilder was more mature and quickly developing an interest in the adults around her. During the summer of 1878, for example, she went to work in the Masters Hotel, where she washed dishes, waited on tables, and took care of Mrs. Masters's grandchild. She witnessed an unfolding love triangle involving the family's pampered and deceitful daughter Matie Masters; Fanny Starr, an old acquaintance from Burr Oak (a daughter of the Starrs who had wanted to adopt Wilder just a few years before); and a licentious young Dr. R. W. Hoyt. Matie Masters apparently stole Dr. Hoyt from Fanny Starr by seducing him, and the Masters family organized a hasty wedding. When Matie was "taken sick" and later died, Caroline Ingalls said, "'Matie would better have let Fanny Starr have him than to have gotten him that way'"[15] Wilder also spun two other extended yarns in this section of her memoir—one about a grasping, greedy woman who cheated her sister out of a "beautiful old place" back east, and another about the sad fate of a neighbor. These stories reveal Wilder's interests and insights into the adult world, but they are also significant because her daughter later used them in her own fiction. Lane lifted the plots and characters directly from "Pioneer Girl" and put them into two short stories published during the early 1930s.[16]

Another disturbing adult story that Wilder told in this portion of her memoir does not appear in either her daughter's fiction nor her own. When Wilder was twelve in early 1879, and school was out of session, she moved out of her family's home to stay in rooms over the Masters store with Nannie Masters, wife of Will, the man who had shot up the Burr Oak Hotel all those years ago. Nannie suffered from fainting spells, and Wilder was hired to look after her. She recalled that the work was unpleasant, "for I never knew at what moment Nannie would fall without a word or a sign and lie as if dead." Wilder had to loosen Nan's clothes and revive her by sprinkling water on her face. Will Masters was clearly an alcoholic, supplied with whiskey by the unsavory

Dr. Hoyt. Wilder had not been long at the job when one night she woke to find Will Masters leaning over her. "I could smell the whiskey on his breath," she recalled. "I sat up quickly. 'Is Nannie sick?' I asked. 'No,' he answered, 'lie down and be still!' 'Go away quick!' I said, 'Or I will scream for Nannie.'" Will left, and the next day Wilder returned home.[17]

None of this new-found worldliness emerges in Wilder's fiction about her life in Walnut Grove. The fictional Laura remains a country girl throughout *On the Banks of Plum Creek* and into the next novel, *By the Shores of Silver Lake,* where Wilder's fictional self is surrounded by her immediate family. Though she is sometimes occupied with schoolgirl rivalries and activities in town, they are not part of her everyday experiences. Wilder saved those stories for a later book in the series—*The Little Town on the Prairie*—and used them to illustrate her main character's transition from a bright but sheltered girl into a vivacious, accomplished young woman. Once again, Wilder demonstrated her understanding that fiction must have shape and a clear forward motion. Just as the fictional Ingalls family always moves west until they reach Dakota Territory, the fictional Laura must continue to confront new experiences. She can blossom and mature into a town girl just once.

Wilder may also have chosen not to fictionalize her Walnut Grove experiences because she recognized that they would detract from the major conflict looming on the horizon in the remaining novels: Mary's blindness. This situation was so central and unique to the real family's experience that it could not be eliminated from the novels. "I can't take Mary along in the story as she should be," she wrote Lane, "if she were not blind. . . . A touch of tragedy makes the story truer to life and showing the way we all took it illustrates the spirit of the times and the frontier."[18] In "Pioneer Girl," Wilder perhaps unconsciously built to this revelation in the sections dealing with the family's return to Walnut Grove by focusing on the growing tension between herself and Mary before she went blind. As the leader of her crowd at school, Wilder was a tomboy, sometimes leading even prissy Nellie Owens and Genieve Masters into rough play with the boys—throwing snowballs, sledding, even playing baseball. Mary objected to these activities, and "once when she took both hands full of my loose, long hair and tried to hold me I stiffened my neck and dragged her to the door where she caught some of the snowballs herself before she let me go," Wilder confessed. Mary, of course, reported the event to their mother, who then told Wilder that she was too big to play like that anymore. She would soon be thirteen, and her mother admonished her to "be more of a lady."[19] Wilder would develop the tension between the two sisters much more fully in *Little House on the Prairie* and *On the Banks of Plum Creek*, until Mary's blindness binds the characters together for the remaining novels in the series.

During her last winter in Walnut Grove, Wilder twice moved out of the house to earn the family extra money by staying with different branches of the Masters family. The only job she attributed to Charles Ingalls during that winter was a one-day stint making brooms with her employer. "I knew things were not going well at home," she wrote, "because Pa could not get much work and we needed more money to live on." In the spring, Charles Ingalls's employment prospects brightened. He got a job mending a fence for Masters and picked up some carpentry work. But by then Mary, who had been unwell that winter, became desperately ill.[20]

It began, Wilder recorded, as a pain in the head, but quickly worsened. Mary became disoriented and so feverish that Caroline Ingalls cut off her daughter's long blond hair to keep her cool. Mary then suffered a stroke "with one side of her face drawn out of shape."[21] Surprisingly, her overall condition improved after the stroke, but as she slowly regained strength, her vision deteriorated. Despite the family's poverty, the Ingalls summoned two doctors to examine and care for her—Dr. Hoyt and Dr. Jacob Wellcome, who declared that "the nerves of her eyes had the worst of the stroke and were dying, that nothing could be done." In his opinion, Mary had not fully recovered from measles, which had struck the family in Burr Oak. The doctors determined that the lingering illness triggered the stroke. "The last thing Mary ever saw was the bright, blue of Grace's eyes," Wilder recorded.[22]

Shortly thereafter, Charles Ingalls's sister Docia Forbes stopped at the family's house and made him an offer he could not refuse. She and her husband, Hiram Forbes, had agreed to work as contractors in the Chicago & North Western Railroad camps. Crews were extending the track from Minnesota into Dakota Territory. Aunt Docia, as Wilder called her, offered her brother a position as "book-keeper, company-store keeper, and time-keeper"; most importantly, the job "would pay him a good salary."[23] Charles Ingalls sold the house the next day. The family's final move west into Dakota Territory was about to begin. So, too, were the experiences that Wilder would transform into her most vivid and compelling fiction.

5

The Great New Country: Dakota Territory

1879–1880

Charles Ingalls left immediately for Dakota Territory, and Wilder recalled that he had been gone a month when he sent back his first pay check. When Mary was strong enough, Caroline Ingalls arranged for the rest of the family to travel by train to Tracy, Minnesota, which was the end of the line. They left Walnut Grove in September. For the first time, the family moved west, not with a horse and wagon, but by steam engine, and Charles Ingalls was not part of the adventure. Although Wilder had her hands full on this journey, helping with the baby and luggage, she regretted that the trip was so short. They left in the morning and arrived in Tracy by noon. Perhaps the most important part of this experience, however, was Wilder's new role as Mary's "eyes," and even in the rough draft of her memoir, she linked this important responsibility to going west. Wilder remembered that she "told Mary about everything I saw for we were on our way again and going in the direction which always brought the happiest changes."[1]

Beginning with this trip, Wilder's autobiography included extended descriptions of the scenes around her. Whether this shift reflected Wilder's new responsibility to Mary, her joy in the unsettled west, or her own ability to remember this part of her life more vividly, the emphasis on description is pronounced and often eloquent. After relaying how the family arrived in Tracy, spent the night in a "quiet and gloomy" hotel, and started off toward Dakota Territory in a lumber wagon with their father, who had arrived from the railroad camp, Wilder wrote poetically about a prairie sundown: "The sun sank lower and lower until, looking like a ball of pulsing, liquid light it sank gloriously in clouds of crimson and silver. Cold purple shadows rose in the east; crept slowly around the horizon, then gathered above in depth on depth of darkness from which the stars swung low and bright."[2]

Did Wilder's adolescence, spent describing people, places, and scenes for Mary, contribute to her development as first a storyteller and later a writer? It certainly trained Wilder to observe the world around her closely, to develop an eye for detail, and to convey it all with clear but vivid vocabulary. These skills are essential for a writer. In a letter about an editor's interest in the manuscript that would eventually become *Little House in the Big Woods,* Rose Wilder Lane praised Wilder's unique descriptive powers. "You make such perfect pictures of everything," she told her mother.[3]

From Tracy, Charles Ingalls drove the family west to the railroad camp near the new town of Brookings (Wilder spelled it "Brookins"), where Uncle Hiram and Aunt Docia Forbes, along with their children Lena and Gene, were working.[4] Lena, who was a year older than Wilder, introduced her to the new freedom and excitement that living in a railroad camp on the wide, open Dakota prairie provided. Together they hitched Lena and Gene's black ponies to a wagon and drove into the country to bring home some washing. The ponies "ran most of the way, their long, black manes and tails blowing in the wind while we shouted and sang," Wilder recalled in her memoir. This joyful drive into the country brought Wilder sobering realizations, as well. She and her cousin discovered that the woman who had been hired to do the washing had not delivered it because she had been arranging a wedding for her daughter. "'She is only thirteen,'" the woman said proudly, "'but it is just as well to be married young.'" The young bride was roughly the same age as Wilder and her cousin. The two girls talked soberly about it on the trip back to camp and decided they were glad not to be in the young wife's place.[5]

Wilder included the episode in expanded scenes in *By the Shores of Silver Lake,* where she ends the chapter with Laura and Lena riding the two ponies bareback, reveling in their freedom as unencumbered, unmarried girls. Even though Laura falls off twice and "once the pony's head hit her nose and made it bleed," the fictional Laura finds the experience "wonderful."[6] In "Pioneer Girl," however, Wilder was not quite as daring as her fictional counterpart. She rode around a bit but admitted, "I was timid for I had never ridden a horse before."[7] As a novelist, Wilder gave her main character the courage and daring she herself lacked when challenged by free-spirited Lena and those equally free-spirited black ponies on the Dakota prairie.

The Ingalls family soon packed up their wagon and moved forty miles farther west to the railroad camp on Silver Lake in Dakota Territory. "Almost at once," Wilder wrote in her memoir, "we drove through the breaks along the river; crossed the [Big] Sioux river and were out on the broad prairie that looked like a big meadow as far as we could see in any direction." The prairie could be as menacing as it was beguiling, and a lone rider followed the family's wagon at a distance. Charles Ingalls kept looking behind them as a man on a white horse overtook the first rider and the two men came on together. Caroline Ingalls continued to be apprehensive, but her husband identified the second man as Big Jerry, who "was a half breed, Indian and French, a gambler, some said a horse thief, but a darned good fellow." This character reference could hardly have warmed Caroline Ingalls's heart, but for Wilder the episode clearly illustrated the turbulent, wild, ambivalent, and sometimes lawless atmosphere that she came to admire about Dakota Territory. In *By the Shores of Silver Lake,* Wilder titled the chapter where Big Jerry appears as "The West Begins." Although the fictional family consistently moves west from the *Little House on the Prairie* through *By the Shores of Silver Lake*, Wilder's chapter title implies that, for her, the real West, the true West, began in Dakota Territory. It was a "great, new country, clean and fresh around us," she asserted in her memoir.[8]

When the family arrived at the Silver Lake camp, Wilder learned that her Uncle Henry Quiner, Caroline's brother, was also working there, along with his children, Louisa and Charley. Even so, Wilder devoted little time in her memoir to her extended family. Years later, she explained in a letter to her daughter: "As I remember it there was no great excitement. We were not excitable, usually. Pa sometimes. . . . I don't think Ma ever was. She would not be—was not excited at finding Uncle Henry at the R.R. camp. It seems to me we were rather inclined to be fatalistic—to just take things as they came. I know we all hated a fuss, as I still do."[9]

In "Pioneer Girl," as well as in *By the Shores of Silver Lake,* Wilder focused on the lawlessness of the railroad camp and the coarseness of the men who lived there. But the real Ingalls family was less isolated in their railroad shanty than Wilder portrayed in her fiction.[10] For one thing, Charles Ingalls's assistant in the company store took his meals with the family. Often Big Jerry joined them. At one point in "Pioneer Girl," Wilder reported that as her father's assistant stood in their doorway watching a fight brewing between Big Jerry and "a big Irishman," the man exclaimed, "that damned fool Jerry will kill him!"[11] In *By the Shores of Silver Lake*, Pa warns the girls to stay away from the "rough men" of the camp and their "rough language," but in Wilder's memoir, the men and their language are part of the household.[12]

Furthermore, when company representatives from the Chicago & North Western Railway visited the camp, Caroline Ingalls and Wilder herself cooked and served them meals. This responsibility increased as the camp broke up in the late fall of 1879, and Wilder's extended family—the Quiner and Forbes clans, who had run the cook shanty—moved east. It fell to Wilder and her mother to feed the crew who remained behind, and it became an important turning point in Wilder's life. "We had no time for sewing," she recalled, "and alas my dresses wore out until I had no change. Mary had been wearing long dresses and was taller than I, but as she had an extra dress, I put it on. Then I pinned up my hair, because my long braids hanging got in my way and hindered the work. So there I was a young lady with long dresses and hair done up."[13] Wilder was twelve, going on thirteen.

Shortly thereafter, the last of the railroad crew left, and the family moved into the surveyors' house, a grand place by Wilder's standards in those days: "There was one large room, kitchen, dining room and living room in one. From one side of this opened the pantry. a bedroom and the stair door between. On the other side was a large leanto [sic] bedroom and storage room. The upstairs was all in one."[14] The surveyors' house, built by the railroad for its surveyors in 1879, is still standing, and the Laura Ingalls Wilder Memorial Society, Inc., in De Smet, South Dakota, now maintains it. The one large room that Wilder described measures just over twelve feet by fifteen feet, four inches.[15]

Wilder's fiction depicting this period again focuses on the tightly knit Ingalls family, their isolation and courage as they spend the winter of 1879–1880 alone on the prairie. "All the way between the Big Sioux and the Jim, there was nobody at all except them, there in the surveyors' house," Wilder wrote.[16] In reality, the family had a boarder that winter, Walter Ogden, a homesteader who did not want to spend the lonely winter on his own claim several miles east of the railroad camp. In the memoir, Wilder stated simply, "It seemed that it might be wise to have another man around." She added that the family had one other bachelor neighbor six miles away, but they did not see him that winter. The memoir also reveals that their family friend, Robert Boast, stayed with them before Christmas while Charles Ingalls filed on a homestead at the land office in Brookings. The claim was "a mile south of where the town of De Smet was laid out."[17]

In a letter to Lane in 1932, Wilder was even more specific: "the N.E. 1/4 of Section 3 Township 110—Range 56."[18] After Ingalls returned, Boast went to Iowa, promising to bring his wife back in time for Christmas.

Wilder's memory of this sequence of events—and its timing—were probably faulty. Although Boast returned with his wife and celebrated the Christmas of 1879 with the Ingalls and Walter Ogden in the surveyors' house, land records indicate that Charles Ingalls actually filed for the homestead in Brookings on 19 February 1880. The February filing is consistent with the novel's time line, when Pa files for the homestead just in the nick of time—before the "Spring Rush" or land boom of 1880—and with the help of the fictional Mr. Edwards. In writing the novel, Wilder corrected the chronology and elevated the importance of the incident to the Ingalls family saga by reintroducing the character of Mr. Edwards from *Little House on the Prairie*. She also deliberately staged the homestead filing scene in *By the Shores of Silver Lake* for more dramatic effect.[19] "As to the place where homesteads were filed," she wrote a De Smet acquaintance in 1939, "that chapter is fiction. Such things did happen in those days and I placed it there to emphasize the rush for land. You understand how those things are done in writing. . . . The book is not a history but a true story founded on historical fact."[20]

Both the memoir and the novel pinpoint the moment when the spring rush into eastern Dakota Territory began—in February 1880. Wilder and her family marked it "when along in February on another cold, snowy night we heard a shout outside the door." Pa opened it to find two men seeking refuge from the cold—their old friend, the Reverend Edwin Alden from Walnut Grove, and his companion, another missionary. The two "had been sent out into the west to plant churches along the line of the new railroad."[21] Chance brought the Ingalls family and the Reverend Alden together that night, but this coincidence was not as extraordinary as it might appear. Thousands of homesteaders from all walks of life poured into Dakota Territory between 1878 and 1887. As the Chicago & North Western Railway extended its railroad line into Dakota Territory, it platted townsites along the way every seven to ten miles so that farmers could drive into town and back home within a day. This strategy, combined with the Homestead Act of 1862, which allowed settlers to claim one hundred sixty acres as their own after living on it for five years, made Dakota Territory seem irresistible to men like Charles Ingalls, who believed that prosperity glimmered just beyond the setting sun.[22] As Pa says in *By the Shores of Silver Lake,* "'Well, girls, I've bet Uncle Sam fourteen dollars against a hundred and sixty acres of land, that we can make out to live on the claim for five years.'"[23]

Railroad companies advertised aggressively, both in the eastern United States and in Europe. "Best Wheat Lands, Best Farming Lands, Best Grazing Lands in the world," one advertising brochure proclaimed.[24] How quickly did the population grow? The 1870 census revealed that just under twelve thousand people, excluding American Indians, lived in what is now South Dakota; ten years later, the non-Indian population had grown to over eighty thousand. By 1885, almost a quarter million people resided in the area. Once the rail lines were extended west across Dakota Territory to the Missouri River, most homesteaders came by rail.[25] But in the spring of 1880, before the tracks were laid west of what is now Brookings, South Dakota, the first wave of setters during the Great Dakota Boom found more conventional means of transportation. "Slowly at first one a day, then later in crowds they came," Wilder wrote in "Pioneer Girl," "wagon loads, hack loads, buggy loads of men stopped on their way to the forts and towns further west."[26] Her fictional characters experience the boom, as well. "It looks like the whole country's trying to file on land," Pa observes in *By the Shores of Silver Lake.*[27]

Many land seekers sought shelter with the Ingalls family in the surveyors' house, where the family took them in because it was the only place "in a long days travel in either direction." As a result, "the house was always full of strange men," Wilder recorded, with as many as eighteen men sleeping "in the one bed in the lean-to and on the floor of the two rooms" downstairs. Running a temporary boardinghouse was exhausting work, as Wilder so vividly portrayed in *By the Shores of Silver Lake,* but in reality it was not a totally new experience for her, as it was for the fictional Laura. Wilder's jobs in Burr Oak and Walnut Grove, as well as the work she had done with her mother serving railroad officials in the railroad shanty, prepared her for all the cooking and cleanup she did during that spring rush. On a day when Caroline Ingalls had to stay in bed with a headache, for example, Wilder alone prepared breakfast and lunch for the crowd, and Mrs. Boast helped with supper. Wilder was certainly less sheltered and more experienced than the character she created for her novels.[28]

During the family's final days in the surveyors' house, the town of De Smet began to take shape. Named for a Jesuit missionary, Father Pierre De Smet, its first building was anything but spiritual. According to Wilder, the first business was a saloon, quickly followed by a grocery story and, "to our great relief, a hotel."[29] Charles Ingalls bought two town lots, and on 3 April 1880, the family moved out of the surveyors' house and into a building he had hastily constructed on Calumet Avenue (Main Street in Wilder's novels). In fact, it was not quite finished when they moved in and provided little shelter against a spring blizzard that caught the family by surprise. She wrote about this in *By the Shores of Silver Lake,* but its parallel episode in "Pioneer Girl" is striking because of its much more intimate glimpse into the Ingalls family's daily life. In both accounts, the first signal that something is wrong comes when Charles Ingalls sings the sunflower song, his favorite tune for hard times. In the novel, Laura hears the song from behind a curtain that Pa eventually draws aside to shovel snow off the girls' beds.[30] In the memoir, Wilder looked from under the covers to see everything covered with snow: "Pa was standing barefoot in it, pulling on his pants." Telling his daughter to lie still until he shoveled off the snow, he continued to sing "while he shook the snow off his socks and out of his shoes and put them on."[31] Obviously, the real family was not as concerned with privacy as the fictional one.

Later that month, the railroad crews finished laying tracks through De Smet, and by the end of the summer, the town had a depot, schoolhouse, bank, lumberyard, livery stable, drugstore, dry goods store, two grocery stores and hotels, and a furniture store. Church services were held in the depot. Later, in part because of Charles and Caroline Ingalls's involvement, Congregational church services were conducted in the new schoolhouse. The new Kingsbury County government was also taking shape, and Wilder recalled that her father was active in its formation. Eventually he became a school commissioner and justice of the peace.[32]

Charles Ingalls sold his first building and put up a second on his remaining lot. He also built a claim shanty on his homestead a mile south of town but the family remained in De Smet—until a nearby murder sent shock waves through the little town. A claim jumper killed a young man who had briefly camped behind the Ingalls's building while he built a claim shanty for his wife and two small children. In both the memoir and the novel, this event spurred the family to abandon town life and live "on the sweet prairie." Rose Wilder Lane later used this same story as the basis for an episode in her novel *Free Land*.[33]

Despite their high hopes for their new homestead, the family was again impoverished. In "Pioneer Girl," Wilder recalled that her father spent all summer finishing the building in town, putting up the claim shanty, planting a crop of turnips, digging a well, and making hay from the nearby slough grass. Although his carpentry skills could have landed him ample work during the construction flurry in town, he had little time for paying work as he built the farm. While no mention was made of their financial difficulties, Wilder recalled, "I knew our funds must be very low and when I noticed Pa leave the table after eating very little when I knew he must be hungry, I understood that he was leaving the food for the rest of us."[34] When the haying was done, Charles Ingalls earned some cash as a carpenter, but the fall of 1880 was short; winter came fast and hard. The family had little time to replenish their cash reserves or to brace themselves against the long winter ahead.

6

A Malignant Power of Destruction

1880–1881

October 1880 brought "dull, gray days,' as the Ingalls family lingered in their claim shanty. Charles Ingalls told Caroline that the ducks and geese were flying high over the sloughs instead of stopping to feed on the grasses on their way south. He "didn't like the looks of the weather," Wilder wrote in "Pioneer Girl," and he had reason to worry. Their claim shanty did not offer adequate protection against the elements. "It was raining harder when I went to sleep," Wilder recalled, "and there was a drip, drip, of rain on the bed covers over my shoulders where it came through a hole the wind had torn in the tar paper covering the roof. We never paid any attention to so slight a discomfort and so I slept soundly." Wilder awoke the next morning to hear her father singing his sunflower song again and a blizzard raging outside. It was the first of many in what Wilder called the "Hard Winter of 1880/81."[1]

Her novel about this period of the family's life ultimately took on a less forbidding title, *The Long Winter*, but she and Rose Wilder Lane initially protested this change. "My mother has written a book about the Hard Winter," Lane wrote their literary agent in 1940, "and I think an attempt to conceal that fact from the book's reader is worse than futile. . . . My god, if THE HARD WINTER as a title is too depressing, what is the book?"[2] From the beginning, first in "Pioneer Girl" and then in *The Long Winter*, Wilder stressed that the essential story from this period of her life hinged on hardship and survival. "We would lie in our beds those nights, listening to the wind howl and shriek while the house rocked with the force of it and snow sifted in around the windows and through the nail holes . . . for the houses were only shells at best," she remembered. Later she added, "It is times like this that test people."[3]

The Long Winter is Wilder's strongest, most powerful and cohesive novel, perhaps because the real Ingalls family's struggle was so inherently dramatic, even mythic. In fact, Lane had wanted to use this material herself and in 1932, eight years before her mother's book was published, sent her literary agent a synopsis proposing a novel titled "The Hard Winter." "There was a lot of fun through it all," Lane wrote. "Everybody starved but nobody died."[4] Her agent could not sell the idea, and eventually, Lane scaled back her vision for this book and used the hard winter as the basis for a single chapter in her novel *Free Land,* published in 1938, two years before *The Long Winter* came out. Yet, Lane's retelling of the story line lacks the immediacy, drama, and stark descriptive power Wilder brought to both her memoir and her fiction.[5] Wilder's memories of the hard winter were vivid and clear. "It has been rather trying, living it all over again as I did in the writing of it," she wrote just before publication of *The Long Winter*, "and I am glad it is finished."[6]

Many of the family's experiences during this winter went directly from Wilder's memoir into her novel virtually unchanged. Both the real and fictional families moved into the office building in town after that first blizzard; they twisted hay into sticks for fuel when the town ran out of coal and lumber; they ground seed wheat in a coffee mill to make flour for mush or biscuits; they measured out the last of their potatoes sparingly. "It seemed as though we had been grinding wheat and twisting hay for years," she commented in her memoir.[7] In a 1938 letter to her daughter, Wilder recalled, "We were shorter of food than any one" in town.[8] She estimated the population of De Smet that winter at about one hundred; real townspeople and events appear in the novel with slight variations. In both fact and fiction, an old Indian passing through town warned people to prepare for a terrible winter. Together Cap Garland and the "youngest Wilder boy" risked their lives between blizzards to buy wheat from a homesteader who lived twelve miles southeast of town, dividing it among hungry townsfolk. De Smet was, in fact, cut off from supplies when the Chicago & North Western Railway discontinued service there from November to January (when a passenger and mail train came through) and then again from January until May.[9]

Wilder also personified the winter of 1880–1881 as a relentless blizzard in both her memoir and her fiction. "It did its best to blot out the town, but *that* [emphasis added] it couldn't quite manage," she recalled in ' Pioneer Girl." Later in the manuscript, she described the series of blizzards as "a malignant power of destruction wreaking havoc as long as possible, then pausing for breath to go on with the work. Or as Pa forcably [*sic*] put it, 'The blizzard just let go to spit on its hands.'"[10] Yet, as closely as Wilder's memoir and fiction correspond in the retelling of this period of her life, she changed one significant fact: the family actually shared their home during all of the hard winter with young George and Maggie Masters of Walnut Grove. In fact, the couple's first child was born in the late fall in the Ingallses' upstairs room with the help of Caroline Ingalls and Cap Garland's mother. There was no doctor in the new town.[11]

The association between the families was not a pleasant one. Wilder remarked that the family liked Maggie but not George, "who was much like his father,' the family patriarch back in Walnut Grove, Minnesota. In fact, the elder Masters had apparently sent his son and wife packing because Maggie was having a baby "much too soon after the time she was married."[12] In a letter to Lane, Wilder explained how they came to stay: "We thought they were leaving [De Smet] but George put it off. Then winter set in and caught them. There was no where else they could stay. Every house was full and Pa couldn't put them in the street."[13] The Masters were broke and appeared to feel no obligation to help cope with the hardships the two families faced living under one roof. Charles Ingalls did the chores "while George sat by the fire" or "lay snug and warm in bed," Wilder recalled. George Masters was the first to sit down for a meal, gobbling up the scarce food and "not denying himself even for Maggie as we did because of her nursing the baby." In that cold and claustrophobic household, everyone huddled around the kitchen stove. "Mary had her rocking chair on one side, close up to the oven door," Wilder wrote in her autobiography, "and Maggie with her baby had a rocking chair in the other warm place on the other side of the stove, with the heat from the open oven door on her feet and knees." George Masters crowded next to his wife, while the rest of the family "did the best we could." Grace spent her time on Mary's lap, and Caroline, Laura, and Carrie bunched together in front of or behind the stove, always making room for Charles when he returned from doing chores.[14]

Wilder's decision to drop George and Maggie Masters from her fiction had nothing to do with their shotgun wedding or any concerns over what is now called family values. She dropped them because their presence in a novel about the hard winter would detract from her vision of keeping the Ingalls family and their struggles at the heart of her book and the entire series. As the novel was being written, Lane suggested that Wilder add a set of characters to live with the fictional family that winter—if not George and Maggie Masters, then Robert and Ella Boast from *By the Shores of Silver Lake*. "We can't have anyone living with us," Wilder snapped back, adding that it "would spoil the story." She also understood that if the fictional Boasts spent the winter with her fictional family, then their hardships would "mostly vanish." Boast had a team of horses and, in keeping with his character, "would help haul hay and he would help twist it. He would help grind wheat. Mrs. Boast would leave the baby in a chair by the fire and help." Wilder concluded, "The point of the situation would be blunted" and the family "must be alone."[15]

Yet, the fictional family does receive assistance from two relatively new characters in the series, the Wilder boys. In the novel, they share "hot, syrupy pancakes" and "a brown slice of ham" with Pa when he ventures out into the town one night between blizzards. More importantly, the brothers charge Pa just "a quarter" as he helps himself to their secret stash of seed wheat when his family faces starvation. Almanzo, the younger brother, says, "'What's a little wheat between neighbors? You're welcome to it, Mr. Ingalls.'"[16] For the first time in her novels about the Ingalls family, Wilder switched point of view. She shifted the action away from Laura's perspective and placed it squarely in Almanzo's. Again, Wilder made this decision deliberately and while it might appear to contradict her vision of the heroic Ingalls family struggling alone against the elements, it served the larger, deeper purposes of her story. Almanzo Wilder was Laura's future husband; he had to be appropriately heroic to be worthy of her—and even of Pa. The real Almanzo had gone for the wheat to feed the town. "He got it before anyone went hungry," Wilder wrote in a letter explaining her vision of the novel to Lane. She added that his kindness was essential to the book, far more important than the secondary characters (the Boasts or the Masters) that Lane had championed.[17]

Wilder had introduced the character of Almanzo (along with his big brother Royal) in her second novel, *Farmer Boy*. That book centers on Almanzo's childhood in Malone, New York, and, like *Little House in the Big Woods*, follows a year of family life. It focuses on what Wilder called the "little everyday happenings": going to school, making popcorn on cold winter nights, cutting ice from the nearby pond, trading with the tin peddler, harvesting crops, shearing sheep, breaking calves.[18] *Farmer Boy* is a companion book to *Little House in the Big Woods,* and it opens when Almanzo was "not quite nine years old."[19]

The real Almanzo Wilder was born 13 February 1857, making him ten years older than Laura Ingalls, the young woman who caught his fancy over twenty years later. His family was far more affluent than hers. Although Wilder fictionalized her husband's childhood in *Farmer Boy* (Almanzo has three siblings in the book, for example, not the five he had in real life), she did not make significant changes to the family's financial circumstances. For example, in Chapter 8 we read: "Almanzo was proud of Mother in her fine Sunday clothes. The girls were very fine, too." Almanzo's father was even more impressive, for "his horses were the best horses in New York State, or maybe in the whole world."[20] Because of his family's relative wealth and stability, the real Almanzo received more formal education than Wilder did. He and his siblings attended the Franklin Academy in Malone, where they received the equivalent of a high-school education. In the 1870s, the Wilder family moved to southeastern Minnesota, and in 1879, when Almanzo was twenty-two, he and his older siblings, Royal and Eliza, struck out for Dakota Territory. The three of them filed adjoining claims in Kingsbury County on 21 August 1879. Almanzo's homestead was a mile north of the De Smet townsite.[21]

In "Pioneer Girl," Almanzo made his first appearance as a friend of Charles Ingalls. During the hard winter of 1880–1881, Wilder remembered that her father "was quite a favorite among the other men and used to spend some time where they gathered with the Wilder boys who were batching a little way down the street." Throughout this section of her memoir, Wilder did not give Almanzo a first name. He was usually part of a duo—"the Wilder boys"—or simply identified as "the youngest Wilder boy." That is what Wilder called him even when he and Cap Garland braved the elements searching for seed wheat. Perhaps Wilder hoped to create suspense around the younger Wilder boy or to deepen the surprise for her imagined readers when he eventually became her beau later in the memoir. Whatever her motivation for withholding Almanzo's name in this section of "Pioneer Girl," Wilder clearly credited him with playing an important role in her family's survival during the hard winter, a role she deepened and dramatized when she wrote her fictional account.[22]

By May of 1881, winter finally loosened its grip. The prairie turned green, and the hard winter came to an end. George and Maggie Masters went west that month, and the Ingalls family moved back to their claim shanty. "Town was just a place to spend the winter," Wilder noted. She filled the next nine pages of her original draft of "Pioneer Girl" with vivid, sometimes ecstatic descriptions of the prairie and the family's homestead. She wrote about the "little reddish brown and black striped gophers" and the harmless garter snakes that "slithered across" her path. She described the masses of wild prairie roses, which she considered "the sweetest roses that ever bloomed," and in a rare parenthetical statement, she addressed her daughter directly, "(You are their namesake, my dear)." At this point in her life, Wilder was fourteen years old, and although her father spent much of the summer of 1881 in De Smet working as a carpenter during the town's continued building boom, she preferred solitude: "I didn't care much for all these people. I loved the prairie and the wild things that lived on it, much better."[23]

Her preference was about to change—in part because of that Wilder boy; in part, because of all the other eligible young men who were charmed by the young and blooming Laura Ingalls.

7

Bessie and Manly

Wilder attracted many more young men than her fictional counterpart, whose only beau in the novels is Almanzo Wilder. The first gentleman caller interested in the real Laura Ingalls was Alfred Thomas, a young lawyer who stopped by the Ingalls house unexpectedly before one of the town's many social events. He lingered and lingered and lingered, then inexplicably left. Charles Ingalls, however, guessed the young man's intentions: Thomas had hoped to escort Laura to the event. "I was indignant," Wilder remembered. "If he wanted to take me why couldn't he say, 'Come go with me!' and not be such a coward."[1] Wilder was perhaps fourteen, no more than fifteen.

Thomas never asked her out, but she had other offers and accepted them. Ernest Perry, who had helped her father break sod that spring, invited her to a party. She liked Perry, she wrote, but she "didn't like the kissing games" and always managed to let the kisses land on her ear. She accepted a second invitation from the young man, but this time, he went too far. On the way home, "Ernest pulled the robes higher around me and forgot to take his arm away. I was too shy and embarrassed to do anything about it but I made up my mind not to go again." Perry, however, was persistent and surprised Wilder with a party at the Ingalls house. Although her autobiography is silent about her method, Wilder disentangled herself from Perry and his friends. In a parenthetical note, she added that Perry had emigrated to Oregon, where he long remained a bachelor "for the sweet sake of his ideal of me."[2]

Similarly, Wilder also continued to correspond with

"Clarance Huealett," who was a red-haired Irish boy that she had known in Wisconsin. She also confided in her memoir that she found the Wilder boys' hired man—Oscar Rhuel—"quite handsome" and something of a "romantic figure." And she was more than a little interested in Oscar Edmund ("Cap") Garland, something that perceptive readers of *Little Town on the Prairie* have long suspected. In fact, Wilder confessed that on the night when Almanzo Wilder walked her home from a revival meeting for the first time in 1882, she had been "noticing Cap" both before and after the church service. The real Laura Ingalls was certainly much more attracted to the opposite sex than the fictional character she created.[3]

Almanzo Wilder's courtship of Wilder was complicated, not only by her interest in other young men, but by her decision, shortly after their first walk together, to teach school. When she was not yet sixteen, Wilder accepted a job at the Bouchie School, twelve miles south of De Smet, and boarded with the Louis Bouchie family. In her novels *Little Town on the Prairie* and *These Happy Golden Years,* Wilder changed the name of the school to the Brewster School, perhaps to protect the identity of the dysfunctional Bouchie family. But nothing could change the misery of Wilder's first teaching post, and her fiction mirrored her real experience. Indeed, the unhappy Mrs. Bouchie wielded "a knife in the dark," as Mrs. Brewster does in *These Happy Golden Years*, threatening to kill herself or her husband as a way out of Dakota Territory.[4] Wilder recalled that she watched from between the curtains as Mr. Bouchie "lay on his back on the bed, with one foot out from under the covers. He seemed to be lying quietly but I could see that every muscle was tensed." His wife was standing beside the bed and holding a large kitchen knife. "This was the picture for just an instant," Wilder recalled, "then she turned and took the butcher knife to the kitchen, muttering a jumble of words as she went." Wilder found sleeping almost impossible after the incident. Almanzo Wilder spared her the anguish of long weekends trapped inside a tiny claim shanty with the Bouchies. He braved blizzards and extreme cold to drive Wilder home in his snug two-person cutter. The temperature, she remembered, dropped to twenty to thirty below zero on most of those rides.[5]

While Wilder clearly appreciated Almanzo's kindness, she did not welcome his affections. "I was only going with him for the sake of being home over Sunday," she revealed, "and fully intended to stop as soon as my school was out." She continued to identify him only as "the youngest Wilder boy" throughout this section of "Pioneer Girl." He still did not merit a real name. Only after he accepted an indirect challenge from Cap Garland ("God hates a coward"), braved extreme cold (thermometers in De Smet froze at forty-five degrees below zero), and managed to bring Wilder home from the Bouchie School without injury did Wilder give her persistent hero a name in her autobiography—and then it was the formal "Mr. Wilder."[6] He had not yet won her heart.

When she came home from the term at Bouchie School, Wilder confessed in "Pioneer Girl" that she "had rather hoped to . . . go with Cap," but he was interested in Wilder's friend Mary Power. She let another suitor, Arthur Johnson, take her home from church one night and later somewhat reluctantly rejected the attentions of Fred Gilbert, who, while nice, "was a green country boy and I didn't like his style." Still, something *had* shifted. Wilder could not deny the growing attachment she felt between herself and Mr. Wilder. They "had been through blizzards, near-murder and danger of death together," she admitted. Wilder was also honest about her own sex appeal. On those long, bitterly cold sleigh rides between Bouchie School and De Smet, she had not been a "beautiful thing" to look at, with a thick hood over her hair and ears and a veil over her face.[7]

Almanzo Wilder, on the other hand, was not only a persistent suitor, he was also a savvy one. After she finished her work at the Bouchie School, Almanzo let Laura Ingalls stew in her own juices. One bright Sunday afternoon in 1883, she watched Mary Power and Cap Garland, Frank Harthorn and May Bird, Alfred Ely and Laura Remington, Fred Gilbert and Minnie Johnson, and Arthur Johnson and Hattie Dorchester flash by her window in cutters built for two, their laughter floating on the wind. Finally, when she could bear it no longer, a familiar driver pulled up in a familiar cutter and asked if she would care to go for a ride. Wilder dashed for coat and hat, not veil and hood, and snuggled in beside him, forgetting how she had vowed to dump him. When Wilder remembered, she "laughed aloud with pure enjoyment of the joke even though it was on myself."[8]

She also decided it was time to call him something other than the youngest Wilder boy or Mr. Wilder. He told her that his parents called him "Manzo," Wilder recalled, and his brother Roy called him "Mannie." Wilder thought Manzo was ugly and told him, "I'll call you Manly like Roy does." When he pointed out that she had mistaken the nickname, she decided to call him Manly anyway, for "Mannie was silly." The newly named Manly was equally opinionated about Wilder's given name. He told her that he had a sister named Laura and never liked the name, Wilder remembered. He then asked for her middle name, and she responded with an old nursery rhyme: "Elizabeth, Elispeth, Betsy and Bess went over the river to seek a birds nest. They found one with three eggs in. They each took one and left two in." Manly settled on Bessie.[9] Bessie and Manly. They had become a couple, and people had to take them seriously.

During the summer of 1881, the Ingalls family began to talk about sending Mary to the "Iowa College for the Blind at Vinton, Iowa." After haying time that November, Charles and Caroline escorted Mary over four hundred miles east by train to the college, known then as the Iowa School for the Blind. The decision to send Mary to college did not signal a change in the family's financial fortunes; they remained strapped for money. Charles Ingalls was doing carpentry work in town that summer, and Wilder had taken a job in a dry goods store, making shirts for homesteaders. She earned twenty-five cents a day, slept in the attic over the store, and ate with the shopkeeper's family (she did not go home with her father after every work day as Laura does in *Little Town on the Prairie*). It was not a pleasant experience, but Wilder used her earnings to help fund Mary's college expenses. Of course, the family needed much more than Wilder's earnings—or even her father's—to finance her sister's education. Certainly, the family made sacrifices during the seven years Mary Ingalls was in school, a reflection of their consistent commitment to education, but, in fact, they also received government assistance, something that Wilder mentioned in neither her autobiography nor her fiction. Dakota Territory actually paid for Mary's tuition; the family paid for her room and board, books and supplies, and clothing.[10]

Although Mary's departure for college marked a significant change in the family, Wilder devoted little space to it in the original draft of "Pioneer Girl." The family took comfort in the fact that the oldest daughter was in a safe place in which she could pursue her studies. "She had always loved to study, had been the bright one always, while I had been slow and stupid at my books," Wilder commented.[11] By the time "Pioneer Girl" was typed in 1930 and Rose Wilder Lane had edited the manuscript, this passage had changed significantly. Mary's opportunity was linked to an entirely new observation: "And I, who wanted a college education so much myself, was so very happy in thinking that Mary was getting one."[12] This change clearly related to the regret Wilder often expressed about not graduating from high school, but she did not fail to graduate because she was slow or stupid. As she pointed out in a later passage in the original draft of "Pioneer Girl," she was actually the best scholar in De Smet and had clearly mastered the essential concepts required for teaching in December 1882, when she received her first teaching certificate at age fifteen. Wilder was intelligent and hardworking. She taught school to help pay for Mary's college expenses but also to fulfill her own ambitions.[13]

Between 1882 and 1885, Wilder taught at the Bouchie School; the Perry School, a mile south of the Ingalls homestead; and the Wilkins School, just over three miles northwest of De Smet. She even substituted briefly for the regular teacher in De Smet's "downstairs" classroom for the younger children during the fall of 1884. Wilder was a conscientious teacher, genuinely concerned about her students and their progress. She devoted several pages in "Pioneer Girl" to describing the most challenging students she faced at each school. Furthermore, throughout her teaching career and during her courtship, Wilder continued to attend school herself. When her favorite schoolmaster, Van Owen, discovered she had skipped school one day to skate at De Smet's new roller-skating rink, Wilder was mortified—not because she had been caught, but because "I had not set a good example" to fellow students.[14]

Education was so important to Wilder that she emphasized its life-changing role in her fiction as well as her autobiography. In both, she went to great lengths to explain her own failure to graduate. She dropped out of high school in De Smet only after Owen told her there would be no graduation exercises that spring because Wilder was the only student qualified to graduate. She would have to wait another year, an impossibility for her. She had already agreed to marry Manly in the fall and needed extra money for their new household. So Wilder promptly signed a contract with the Wilkins School, which forced her to leave high school before the spring term ended. Later, when Owen fully understood the impact of his decision, he begged her to finish the term and promised to graduate her by herself. Wilder declined because she feared the Wilkins School Board would not be able to find another teacher before its term began.[15]

During this period, Wilder also had her first brush with a professional writer and received her first praise for her own writing. The latter came from Owen, who praised Wilder's first composition—"Ambition." It was such an important moment in her life that she wrote about it in "Pioneer Girl" and in *These Happy Golden Years,* where fact and fiction again converged. She wrote the whole composition based on the dictionary definition of ambition and closed with a quotation from Shakespeare, she noted in her autobiography. In *These Happy Golden Years*, she reproduced the piece in its entirety.[16] Yet, "Ambition" is neither imaginative nor original. Countless students over the years have built their essays and compositions around dictionary definitions and Shakespearean quotations.

Why did this incident have such meaning for Wilder? Perhaps it was the recognition she received from her teacher, who validated the value of her writing and its potential. Perhaps, on a deeper level, this praise reinforced a more personal and private dream: to write her own book someday. In her fiction, Wilder created a scene between Laura and Mary that hinted at just such an ambition:

> "I am planning to write a book some day," [Mary] confided. Then she laughed. "But I planned to teach school, and you are doing that for me, so maybe you will write the book."
>
> "I, write a book?" Laura hooted. She said blithely, "I'm going to be an old maid schoolteacher, like Miss Wilder. Write your own book!"[17]

The irony Wilder packs into this scene works on many levels, but perhaps its real strength is the insight it provides into the dreams that fueled her drive to become a writer.

Good writing begins with passionate reading. Even in Walnut Grove, Wilder read voraciously and lost herself in the stories she read. While babysitting for Nan Masters, for example, she would snatch the opportunity to read stories in the *New York Ledger*. "Great stories they were of beautiful ladies and brave, handsome men, of dwarfs and villians [*sic*], of jewels and secret caverns," she remembered. She would lose herself in the pages and emerge with a start if the baby cried or her employer reminded her to set the table for meals."[18] Shortly after the Ingalls family arrived in De Smet, Wilder took the next step in her writing journey and began writing poetry. Most of it is not especially memorable, but one, entitled "The Difference," reveals that even as an adolescent, Wilder was sensitive to the subtleties of vocabulary and what they can reveal about character:

> My neighbor and I
> Can never agree
> Kind reader be judge
> Between her and me.
>
> I go to the school
> Which she attends
> In which I have "chums"
> And she has "friends."
> She works "difficult problems"
> While I do "hard sums"
> She says it "continues"
> While I say it "runs. . . . "[19]

Furthermore, as early as 1902, Wilder was making notes about story ideas. In 1911, she began writing for a newspaper, the *Missouri Ruralist*; and in 1919, she published an article in *McCall's* and wrote her first children's stories.[20]

Given Wilder's persistent interest in reading and writing, it is entirely plausible that the fictional scene she created for Laura and Mary in *These Happy Golden Years* reflected a private ambition that the first composition she wrote for Owen in De Smet had sparked. Wilder's initial experience with a working writer, however, did not merit any attention in her fiction. Mrs. Brown, the stepmother of Wilder's good friend Ida Brown, was "literary." She wrote for church publications, Wilder reported in "Pioneer Girl," but in the process, she neglected "her personal appearance and her house which was always in a dirty disorder." Years later when she was writing columns for the *Missouri Ruralist*, Wilder frequently provided her readers with tips on improving their personal appearance and running a cleaner, more efficient household.[21]

As Wilder matured, her attention increasingly turned to these themes. Lengthy passages in *These Happy Golden Years* are devoted to descriptions of the fictional Laura's clothes—everything from her hoop skirts and starched petticoats to the "beautiful brown poplin" and her sage-green poke-bonnet lined with blue silk.[22] Wilder's autobiography followed this pattern, as well. She included descriptions of her clothes, her hats, and even her appearance: "My hair was worn, these days, combed smoothly back and braid[ed] in a thick braid that was wound around and around at the back of my head covering the whole back and pinned snugly in place. My bangs had grown out." In contrast, however, to her fictional counterpart, Wilder revealed in "Pioneer Girl" that she "liked to sew." In the early 1880s, she frequently worked as a seamstress, earning as much as fifty cents a day.[23]

During the summer of 1884, Wilder worked for De Smet dressmaker and milliner Florence Bell, who further encouraged Wilder's fashion sense. Wilder maintained an active interest in fashion for the rest of her life and passed it on to her daughter. The two of them corresponded frequently on the subject. In 1937, Wilder wrote, "Don't you love the styles this spring?" She had gotten a catalogue from Bellas Hess of Kansas City and declared the clothes to be "the prettiest for years and years."[24] Back in 1884, however, a part of Wilder had remained true to her tomboy self. In her autobiography, she wrote that she began wearing corsets during the family's first spring in De Smet, but she would not wear them except when dressed up. She would never wear them "as tight as the other girls did or as Ma thought I ought to if I were to have a pretty waist."[25] Readers of the Little House series know that, when Charles Ingalls married Caroline Quiner, he could "span her waist with his hands."[26] But Wilder told her mother that she did not want anyone to span hers.[27]

Wilder may not have wanted anyone's hands around her waist in 1884, but clearly her courtship with Manly had grown more serious and more intimate. During an especially wild buggy ride, the wind whipped the ostrich feather tips from Wilder's hat, and she barely saved them. Manly, struggling to control the horses, responded as only a man in love would. "Put them in my pocket," he said. Despite the plunging horses, he knew instinctively what was important to Wilder, as frivolous as it might seem to anyone else, and she tucked them into his coat pocket. This small but important act of kindness held little significance to Wilder at the time. Instead, she was angry with Florence Bell for not sewing the feathers on her hat more securely. But the signals Wilder missed in her youth, or chose not to see, were obvious to other people. "'A man of his age does not fool around with a girl so long for nothing,'" one of Wilder's acquaintances told her, and throughout the courtship scenes in "Pioneer Girl," Wilder conveyed her own reluctance to believe this despite Manly's gentle persistence. But after a separation of three months, Wilder finally acknowledged, "I hadn't known that I missed him, but it was good to see him again, gave me a homelike feeling."[28]

Perhaps unconsciously—or consciously—Manly played Wilder off against a winsome neighbor, Stella Gilbert, who became yet another model for the fictional Nellie Oleson. In her memoir, Wilder noted that Manly felt sorry for Gilbert because she had to work so hard. He thought she needed to have a good time now and then, and she sometimes joined them on their Sunday afternoon buggy rides. Wilder, who knew Gilbert better than Manly did, made no objection, but she spent the shared buggy rides thinking of how Gilbert pretended to be sick to get out of work and would then recover at night to go dancing. "If she had worked on his

[Manly's] sympathy, what did I care," Wilder concluded.[29] Obviously, Wilder did care—cared enough to transform this episode from her courtship into the memorable scene in *These Happy Golden Years* when Laura forces Almanzo to choose between herself and Nellie Oleson.[30]

"Pioneer Girl" and *These Happy Golden Years* also paint a parallel portrait of the frontier magic that bound the young lovers to each other: a love of horses, a fearlessness in managing them, and an appreciation for the boundless Dakota prairie. They would drive forty, fifty, and sometimes even sixty miles on a Sunday afternoon, gathering wildflowers. They once drove out to visit the Boasts and waited there until the moon rose at 2 A.M. When much later Manly dropped Wilder off at home, a light was still on in the sitting room. Her mother called out, "'What time is it, Laura?'" Wilder breezily replied, "'Oh! I didn't look at the clock.'" On another summer evening, after an ice-cream social at the church, the young couple again rode in companionable silence under the stars. Wilder asked Manly what he was thinking, and he replied that he was wondering if she might want an engagement ring. In her autobiography, Wilder wrote: "I gave a startled gasp. 'That would depend,' I said, 'on who offered it to me?' 'Would you take it from me?' he asked and I said 'Yes!'" They kissed for the first time, and Wilder went into the house, "not quite sure if I were engaged to Manly or to the starlight and the prairie."[31] The fictional Laura plays harder to get. After a similar sequence in the novel, Laura says, "Then it would depend on the ring." She does not let the fictional Almanzo kiss her until he places the pearl and garnet ring on her finger the following Sunday.[32] Wilder thus heightened her fictional character's independence and resistance to love, marriage, and conformity.

Bessie and Manly were married on the morning of 25 August 1885 by the Reverend Edward Brown in his home at about eleven o'clock in the morning. Ida Brown and her fiancé, Elmer McConnell, witnessed the marriage. Wilder wore the black cashmere dress she described in *These Happy Golden Years* and refused to pledge that she would be an obedient wife, just as she did in the novel. Wilder ended her autobiography in much the same way she ended *These Happy Golden Years*, reveling in her "new estate" and the security of having her own home on the prairie.[33] But neither "Pioneer Girl" nor *These Happy Golden Years* hinted at the struggle, loss, and hardships that Bessie and Manly suffered during the first and perhaps most painful years of their enduring and successful marriage.

8

A Faint Air
of Disillusion
1885–1894

When readers came to the end of Wilder's novel *These Happy Golden Years* and wrote her asking, "What happened next?," she sidestepped the question with a short, uncomplicated response: "After our marriage Almanzo and I lived for a little while in the little gray house on the tree claim."[1] And though she ends "Pioneer Girl" as she does *These Happy Golden Years*—with a detailed description of that little gray house— Wilder added in her autobiography that she learned after their marriage that they owed five hundred dollars on the house. They would not be able to pay that until the farm was sold. "But that was nobodys [*sic*] fault," she added, "and is another story anyway."[2] What Wilder did not tell her readers was that a relentless series of financial losses and personal tragedies tested her resilience during the first nine years of her marriage. Years of drought across eastern Dakota Territory and a deepening financial crisis provided the foundation for what must have seemed like a nineteenth-century variation on the Biblical story of Job.

Like most homesteaders in eastern Dakota Territory, Manly went deeply into debt, believing unfailingly in next year's crops to be harvested from the rich prairie sod. In addition to the five-hundred-dollar mortgage he took out on the house, Manly invested heavily in equipment for the farm—a sulky breaking plow, binder, mowing machine, hay rake, weeder, seeder, and new wagon. His decisions to take out loans to finance his farm and tree claim were not unusual; homesteaders across Dakota Territory did the same thing, considering it was the only way to build a profitable, working farm. Furthermore, Manly was an experienced farmer, unlike many who staked out claims in the West, and it had always been his ambition to own his own place.[3] In *Farmer Boy*, Wilder gave the father character a speech that almost certainly reflected Manly's philosophy about farming. "A farmer depends on himself, and the land and the weather," James Wilder says to the young Almanzo. "If you're a farmer, you raise what you eat, you raise what you wear, and you keep warm with wood out of your own timber. You work hard, but you work as you please, and no man can tell you to go or come. You'll be free and independent, son, on a farm."[4]

Yet, because of their indebtedness and the whims of weather and fate, the Wilders were far from independent. They lost an entire wheat crop to an August hailstorm roughly a month before their first wedding anniversary in 1886. Wilder was pregnant, expecting their first child that December. With their wheat lost, a baby on the way, and winter looming ahead, the couple decided they needed more cash. If they moved back to Manly's original homestead, which he owned free and clear, they could rent out their comfortable home on the tree claim and mortgage the homestead for eight hundred dollars. With the ready cash, they could buy seed for the following year, make improvements to the primitive claim shanty on the homestead, and get through the winter. The additional mortgage kept alive their dream of turning a profit on farming.[5]

In late August, Wilder and Manly moved back to his homestead, and there on 5 December 1886, their daughter Rose was born. Dr. Ruggles A. Cushman delivered the baby; Caroline Ingalls and Elizabeth Power, the mother of Wilder's friend Mary, helped with the birth.[6] In *The First Four Years*, a novel that Wilder herself chose not to revise for publication, the fictional Laura observes, "Rose was such a good baby, so strong and healthy that Ma stayed only a few days." All the same, she added, "A hundred precious dollars had gone for doctor bills and medicine and help; . . . but after all, a Rose in December was much rarer than a rose in June, and must be paid for accordingly."[7] The couple had only a brief respite to enjoy their new baby before the cycle of disaster resumed. In July 1887, the Wilders' barn burned to the ground.[8]

The following year brought a more serious and lasting crisis: first Wilder and then Manly developed diphtheria. "Laura's attack had been dangerous," Wilder wrote in *The First Four Years*, "while Manly's was light." Rose went to live with her Ingalls grandparents; Wilder and Manly remained on their homestead, nursed by his brother Royal, who temporarily moved in with them.[9] Although Lane was not quite two years old at the time, her memories of this period were especially vivid and haunting: "For a long time I had been living with Grandpa and Grandma and the aunts in De Smet because nobody knew what would become of my father and mother. Only God knew. They had diff-theer-eeah; a hard word and dreadful. I did not know what it was exactly, only that it was big and black and it meant that I might never see my father and mother again."[10] Both Wilders recovered, but driven by worries about his livestock and the fate of his farm, Manly defied doctor's orders and went back to work too soon. In *The First Four Years,* Wilder described the stark result: "one cold morning he nearly fell as he got out of bed, because he could not use his legs properly."[11] Manly had suffered a stroke; he was only thirty-one years old.

Other than the spare, unadorned prose of *The First Four Years,* Wilder left no intimate, personal record of her feelings about Manly's illness. In this posthumously published novel, she wrote with restraint, even emotional detachment, about Laura's reaction to what had to be a deep and heart-wrenching blow. The Almanzo of her novel *These Happy Golden Years* and of her autobiography—strong and capable—was forever gone; yet, the Laura of *The First Four Years* wastes no time wallowing in the past. She focuses on the present with a fierce determination to persevere, to accept the man her husband has become: "From that day on there was a struggle to keep Manly's legs so that he could use them. Some days they were better and again they were worse, but gradually they improved until he could go about his usual business if he was careful."[12] Lane's memories confirmed her parents' apparent determination to accept fate and move on: "[W]hen I saw my father again he was walking slowly. He limped through the rest of his ninety years and was never as strong as he had been."[13] Before Wilder married Manly, she had written a poem titled "So Far and Yet So Near" about their separation during the autumn of 1884, when he and his brother Royal made a loop into Nebraska, Iowa, and Minnesota with "a stock of notions to sell on the road."[14] In one line of the poem, Wilder spoke of hearing his "manly tread." For the rest of her life, that manly tread would be the sound of a man determined not to be an invalid.[15]

Despite Manly's resolve to return to work on the farm, he and Wilder looked squarely at the realities of his handicap and recognized their new limitations. They sold the homestead. The buyer agreed to assume the eight-hundred-dollar mortgage and pay them an additional two hundred dollars. Wilder and Manly then moved back to the tree claim. At about the same time, they went into partnership with her cousin Peter Ingalls. Together they bought one hundred Shropshire sheep, gambling, correctly, that livestock could keep the farm afloat as the drought deepened on the Dakota plains. At roughly this same time, Charles and Caroline Ingalls permanently moved into De Smet. In 1887, he had built the family a small but snug home on Third Street. Over the years, he added rooms to the house and made a living primarily as a carpenter. He continued to play an active role in civic affairs, serving in capacities as varied as deputy sheriff and justice of the peace to town clerk and street commissioner. Mary, who graduated from college in 1889, Carrie, and Grace continued to live at home.[16]

A year after Wilder and Manly battled diphtheria—1889— South Dakota became a state, and drought conditions worsened. Wilder was pregnant again and, in August, gave birth to a son, who, in *The First Four Years,* arrives "before the doctor could get there." No records exist to indicate that Wilder and Manly named their little boy, but within a month, he was dead. In the novel, the baby "was taken with spasms, and he died so quickly that the doctor was [again] too late."[17] Grace Ingalls, who was twelve years old at the time, recorded in her diary on 27 August 1889, "Laura's little baby boy only a month old died a little while ago, he looked just like Manly."[18]

But misfortune was not finished with the Wilders that summer. Just days after their baby's death, they also lost their house. Grace wrote at length about it in her diary:

> Last friday Manly's house caught fire and burned to the ground. The furniture in the front room and in the bed room and pantry was saved but nothing in the kitchen where the fire stared. Laura had just built a fire in their stove went into the other room and shut the door so she could sweep when the noise of the fire startled her and on opening the door she saw the roof and side of the kitchen was on fire . . . help came soon but they could not save the house and only some of their old clothing was saved.[19]

Years later, Rose Wilder Lane, then an established essayist and short story writer, provided a different account. "And later it was I, alone in the kitchen and helpfully trying to put more wood in the stove, who set fire to the house," she wrote in a national magazine in 1926. "My mother was still ill in bed [recovering, perhaps, from childbirth]. She saved herself and me, but nothing else."[20]

So what really happened? On the one hand, Lane had a tendency from the beginning of her career to write copy that would sell, that would tug on her readers' heartstrings. Even when writing nonfiction, she rearranged the facts to suit her story better. On the other, Lane explained in the same 1926 article, "The best—and the worst—that can be done for a child is to shelter him from the facts." Perhaps Wilder's portrayal of the fire in *The First Four Years*—and even Grace's in her diary—were attempts to relieve young Rose of any responsibility. If so, they did not succeed. "I quite well remember," Lane concluded, "watching the house burn, with everything we owned in the world, and knowing that I had done it."[21]

Although Manly and Peter Ingalls, who was living with the Wilders at the time, built a two-room shanty on the tree claim for the family to winter in, they decided that the only way to break their cycle of misfortune was to leave De Smet. In a journal entry dated 18 May 1890, Grace Ingalls recorded that Laura, Manly, and Rose, along with Peter, were moving to Minnesota in a covered wagon and were driving the stock, except for the sheep, which they had sold "to the butchers for five hundred dollars." Grace rejoiced that her sister would "have her pretty poney [*sic*] for the journey to ride on part of the time."[22]

The Wilders traveled to Spring Valley, Minnesota, and stayed with Manly's parents, James and Angeline Wilder, for over a year. Peter Ingalls kept moving, and in October 1890, he, along with Manly's little brother Perley and Joe Carpenter, one of Wilder's cousins, decided to make their fortunes in Florida. Perley and Carpenter returned to Minnesota; Peter stayed. By early 1891, perhaps prompted as much by the toll the harsh Minnesota winter exacted on Manly's health as by Peter's enthusiasm for the South, Wilder and Manly decided to move as well. Their destination was Westville in southern Florida, along the Choctawhatchee River. They left Minnesota on the train in October 1891. Wilder was not happy in Westville and reportedly took to carrying a revolver.[23] "We went to live in the piney woods of Florida," she wrote years later, "where the trees always murmur, where the butterflies are enormous, where plants that eat insects grow in moist places, and alligators inhabit the slowly moving waters of the rivers. But at that time and in that place, a Yankee woman was more of a curiosity than any of these."[24]

In August 1892, the Wilders returned to De Smet, where things were no better. They had been married seven years and still had not found their place in the world. Fate seemed to have conspired against them. "There had been too little rain," Lane wrote of the time and place. "The prairies were dust. . . . Crop after crop failed. Again and again the barren land must be mortgaged, for taxes and food and next year's seed. The agony of hope ended when there was no harvest and no credit, no money to pay interest and taxes; the banker took the land." The Wilders lost their final parcel of land in Dakota Territory.[25] It was time to move on again.

The temptation when writing about Wilder's early married life is to rely heavily on *The First Four Years*, her last novel, published in 1971, fourteen years after her death. Because Wilder left no diaries or letters behind from these years, the book appears as an irresistible source for insights into her personality and emotional responses to the relentless tragedies that marred her life as a newlywed and young mother. While Wilder undeniably drew on her own experiences for this novel, it is dangerous to assume that her main characters are literal projections of her younger self and her husband. By the time Wilder wrote the draft for *The First Four Years* (originally titled "The First Three Years and a Year of Grace"), her understanding of character development, plot, and theme had deepened. She also understood that the literal facts of her life did not always serve the larger purposes of story. She had been "stretching a point," in her fiction over five novels by the time she first suggested the idea of an adult book, a "grown-up story about Laura and Almanzo," to her editor at Harper's in 1937.[26] Like the other books in the series, *The First Four Years* is fiction not autobiography. The feelings Wilder ascribed to her characters are not necessarily her own.

Furthermore, the fictional Laura Ingalls who weds Almanzo Wilder in *These Happy Golden Years* is not the same fictional Laura of *The First Four Years*, who reluctantly agrees to marry Manly, as he is called in this final book. One Laura is optimistic, joyful, and accepting; the other is critical, shrewd, and calculating. Laura in Wilder's grown-up story wants nothing to do with farming, and she throws Manly's dreams back in his face the minute he proposes: "'I don't want to marry a farmer. I have always said I never would. I do wish you would do something else.'"[27] Nowhere in *These Happy Golden Years* did Wilder hint at a conflict between Laura and Almanzo about his ambition to farm. In fact, from the moment the fictional Almanzo appears in *Farmer Boy* through the final pages of *These Happy Golden Years*, his success as a fearless, shrewd, and successful homesteader gains first Pa's respect and than Laura's. Indeed, throughout the entire Little House series, Laura enthusiastically embraces farming—milking cows, helping Pa make hay, sometimes even working in the fields. But in *The First Four Years,* the new, adult Laura objects to farming "'because a farm is such a hard place for a woman. . . . Besides a farmer never has any money.'" Clearly, this Laura is a different type of woman, one who aspires to something more than being a farm wife, who resents hard work, and who agrees to marry only after Manly promises, "'If you'll try it for three years and I haven't made a success in farming by that time, I'll quit and do anything you want me to do.'"[28]

Which of these Lauras, if either, corresponds to the "real" Laura Ingalls Wilder? While it is impossible to know entirely, Wilder's autobiography does provide insight into the real Wilder's response to Manly's marriage proposal. In "Pioneer Girl," she accepted him the moment he popped the question. And nowhere in the autobiography did Wilder even hint that she disapproved of farming on general principle or of Manly's dedication to working the land.[29] Still, as many readers and most Wilder scholars have noted, not only does Laura's character shift dramatically from *These Happy Golden Years* to *The First Four Years*, but the entire voice and tone of the novel shifts as well. Indeed, the change in voice is so pronounced that it may explain why publication of *The First Four Years* took so long.

In a letter to a prominent children's librarian dated 8 April 1969, Harper's editor Ursula Nordstrom wrote:

> The young man [Roger Lea MacBride] who inherited all the assets of Laura Ingalls' Wilder's daughter, Rose Wilder Lane, came in a few days ago and dropped the casual remark that there is a NINTH WILDER MANU-SCRIPT, written after *These Happy Golden Years*. I asked why in mercy's name we had never been given it and he explained that it covers the first year of married life for Laura and Almanzo and that there is a faint air of slight disillusion in it, which Laura's daughter thought not suited for the feeling of the 8 published books.[30]

That "faint air of slight disillusion" weighed heavily on Nordstrom and her associates at Harper's just a few months later when they read the manuscript. Yet, to her credit, Nordstrom refused to alter Wilder's voice or her characterizations in editing *The First Four Years*. In a letter dated 18 November 1969, she wrote: "You ask how much leeway do we have [in editing or changing Wilder's ninth manuscript]. Well, I think Rose Wilder Lane's grandson . . . would let us do some judicious editing, but I think we just better not. . . . I would hate like hell to tamper with this."[31]

Since then, a variety of scholars have created a variety of interpretations to explain why the last Wilder novel sounds so radically different from the preceding eight, including perhaps the most controversial: that the manuscript of *The First Four Years* illustrates that Wilder was an inferior writer whose success with the previous books depended entirely on the heavy editing and ghostwriting skills of her daughter.[32] From the correspondence trail between Wilder and Lane, it certainly appears as if *The First Four Years* was the only manuscript that Lane did not see in her mother's lifetime. Wilder kept it from her, perhaps because Lane's response to the idea for the book was lukewarm. "As to your doing a[n adult] novel, there is no reason why you shouldn't if you want to," Lane wrote, "but unless by wild chance you did a best-seller, there is much more money in juveniles."[33]

Although Wilder's editor had responded enthusiastically to this same idea, Wilder seemed more concerned about Lane's tepid support. In an undated letter to her daughter from probably the same period, Wilder defended her idea: "I thought it might wangle a little more advertising for the L.H. books if I said I might write the grownup one. It was not a promise and if I didn't it wouldn't matter." Still, Wilder was serious enough about the project to make sure that Lane, who was working on her adult novel *Free Land* and borrowing heavily from her mother's manuscript of "Pioneer Girl," had no objections. In the same letter, Wilder asked Lane if she "ever expected to use the framework of 'The First Three Years'" in her own work. Wilder did not want to intrude on her daughter's career or use material—even if it was her own—that Lane had plans for. In that spirit, Wilder added, "I could write the rough work. You could polish it and put your name to it if that would be better than mine."[34] Wilder had already done something similar for Lane, because much of the material her daughter used in *Let the Hurricane Roar* and *Free Land* came directly from "Pioneer Girl." Perhaps Lane's less than enthusiastic response to her mother's projected grown-up story reflected a deeply held worry that her mother's book would eclipse her own. Indeed, after both their deaths, *The First Four Years* did just that. Few people read Lane's novels today, and if they do, it is usually because their interest in Wilder led them to Lane.

The question of Wilder's shift in tone for the grown-up book remains unanswered: why is the final novel so different from the other Little House books? Again, the answer probably lies in Wilder's perception that a novel for adults should appeal to a mature, perhaps even jaded, audience; the book's characterizations, plot, and theme had to reflect adult readers' more careworn vision of reality. Wilder essentially abandoned her Little House style and modeled the manuscript for *The First Four Years* on the work of a writer she admired: Rose Wilder Lane. In a column she wrote in the 1920s, Wilder identified Lane as a distinguished Missourian, whose books and short stories had been "published in the United States and England" and "translated into foreign languages."[35] Lane was the best writer Wilder knew—and Lane wrote for adults.

A close examination of *The First Four Years* and Lane's *Let the Hurricane Roar,* published in 1933, reveals that the two novels have a similar voice, a similar theme. Both deal with newlyweds struggling against the harsh realities of frontier life: Charles and Caroline in *Let the Hurricane Roar* and Laura and Manly in *The First Four Years.* These characters, identified only by their first names in both books, are almost archetypal. They are symbols of perseverance and determination, character types that are lost to the modern world. In both novels, the writing is lean, spare, and restrained. Here, for example, is how Lane portrays Caroline's feelings right after her wedding to Charles in *Let the Hurricane Roar:*

> At first Caroline was sad because she was leaving her family forever. She ached for the busy life with her mother and sisters in the log cabin, for her father's coming home from work or hunting, even for the oak tree by the door and the path to the spring. But these memories soon ceased to hurt her, in her happiness with Charles.[36]

Wilder's depiction in *The First Four Years* of Laura's departure with Manly on their wedding day has a similar feeling and tone:

> As Laura looked back, Ma, Pa, and Carrie and Grace were grouped among the young trees. They threw kisses and waved their hands. Bright green leaves of the cottonwoods waved too in the stronger wind of afternoon and

there was a little choke in Laura's throat for they seemed to be saying good-by, and she saw her Ma brush her hand quickly across her eyes.

Manly understood, for he covered Laura's hand with one of his and pressed it strongly.[37]

Wilder's passage contains more warmth and intimacy than her daughter's, but both exhibit a similar detachment. The characters are more like actors on a stage than real living, breathing people who steal their readers' hearts.

Even the way Wilder and Lane depict childbirth in the two novels is similar. Although Caroline is alone with Charles when their baby is born, and Laura is attended by Ma, Mrs. Power, and a doctor, these scenes unfold in a remarkably consistent way. In *Let the Hurricane Roar*, Caroline struggles "to make no outcry," to face childbirth with courage:

> Then everything became confused Daylight and darkness were mixed. She heard shrieks and knew they were hers; she could not stop them. Even Charles was gone. There was nothing anywhere but unbearable agony. She herself was ebbing, going—a last little atom fighting, failing—
>
> The baby was born in the morning of the second day.[38]

In *The First Four Years*, Laura does not worry about screaming but resists going to bed. Like Caroline, she gives in to the inevitable: "But soon she made no objections and only vaguely knew when Manly drove away again to fetch a friend of her Ma's." Then Laura is "borne away on a wave of pain," and she is only vaguely aware when the doctor arrives: "When Laura opened her eyes, the lamp was still shining brightly over the room, and Ma was bending over her with the doctor standing beside her. And in the bed by her side was a little warm bundle."[39]

Even the central conflict in the two books is similar. In *Let the Hurricane Roar*, Caroline struggles against the hardships of pioneer life imposed upon her by her husband's decision to go west; in *The First Four Years*, Laura struggles against the hardships of being a farmer's wife, of living her husband's dream. Ultimately, both characters come to accept their husband's ambitions as their own. At the end of *Let the Hurricane Roar,* Caroline looks into her baby's face and sees a light there shining from the future, a future in which her dreams of a big white house, rich wheat fields, and fast driving teams are realized.[40] Laura decides, in the final pages of *The First Four Years:* "It would be a fight to win out in this business of farming, but strangely she felt her spirit rising for the struggle." As Manly comes from the barn, she feels hopeful: "The incurable optimism of the farmer . . . seemed inextricably to blend with the creed of her pioneer forefathers that 'it is better farther on'—only instead of farther on in space, it was farther on in time, over the horizon of the years ahead instead of the far horizon of the west."[41] In many respects, *The First Four Years* is a kind of sequel to *Let the Hurricane Roar*, the story of the next generation on the Dakota prairies. Read together, these books clearly indicate Lane's influence as a writer of adult fiction on her mother's first and only attempt to write in this genre.

One question still remains: why did Wilder not seek publication of the manuscript during her lifetime? In 1937, Wilder was writing *By the Shores of Silver Lake*, and in her letter to Lane about her idea for a grown-up story, she added, "Anyway the other two [books in the series] come first and then we can see."[42] At the time, Wilder projected only two books to close out her series, one about the hard winter and the other about Laura's courtship and marriage. She would actually need three books to finish the series: *The Long Winter, Little Town on the Prairie,* and *These Happy Golden Years*. Furthermore, Lane's novel *Free Land* was published in 1938. Marketed as the companion piece to *Let the Hurricane Roar,* it was presented as a semibiographical account of her father's experiences as a homesteader. The jacket copy for the book, "A Word about Herself" from Rose Wilder Lane, read: "In the Dakotas men said that the government put up a quarter-section against $15 and five years' hard work, on a bet that a man couldn't make a living on the land. My father won the bet. It took seven successive complete crop failures, with work, weather and sickness that wrecked his health permanently, and interest at 36% on money borrowed to buy food, to dislodge us from that land."[43]

The book was successful—a bestseller. Wilder may have decided that *Free Land* had preempted her own grown-up story. Perhaps she simultaneously recognized her own strengths as a novelist, that her most engaging and unique gifts were as a writer of children's books. Novelist Eloise McGraw came to a similar conclusion about herself:

> I'm often asked how I started writing for children. I don't know—possibly from the totally mistaken idea that it might be easier, though I doubt that. I was never much interested in "easy." More likely it was because the books that filled my childhood had meant more to me than anything I'd read since. Whatever the subconscious reason, it was a lucky move—juvenile, book-length fiction is my niche. . . . I did write one adult novel. . . . It sold out a decent-sized U.S. edition and two foreign reprints, and I went back to juveniles without regret."[44]

Wilder, of course, had been interested in writing stories for children since her father's death in 1902. Perhaps she simply recognized her niche as a writer and put her adult story aside without regret, in the same way that the fictional Laura accepted her fate and moved on.

"'We'll always be farmers,'" Laura says at the end of *The First Four Years*, 'for what is bred in the bone *will* come out in the flesh.'"[45] But when Wilder and Manly returned to De Smet from Florida in 1892, they did not farm. Severe drought conditions, Manly's handicap, and a deepening national financial crisis that cost them their remaining land conspired against them. Instead, the family rented a house in De Smet, and Manly picked up day jobs in town, while Wilder "sewed at the dressmaker's from six o'clock to six o'clock every day but Sunday."[46] But bone *will* come out in the flesh. Wilder and Manly were saving money to buy a farm—not on the Dakota plains, but in what Wilder called "Land of the Big Red Apple," which was also how Wright County in southwestern Missouri billed itself.[47] After acquaintances in De Smet came back from there with glowing reports of abundant orchards and bountiful farms, Wilder and Manly decided that was where they could be farmers once again. With a one-hundred-dollar bill as a down payment to buy the farm of their dreams hidden in Wilder's portable writing desk, the family set out for Missouri in a two-seated hack on 17 July 1894.[48] Finally, fate began to smile on Wilder and her family.

9

The Sky Seems
Lower Here
1894–1911

When the Wilders set out for Missouri, they had few material possessions with which to banish misfortune. Wilder
once told a reporter, "We brought all our belongings—one
bed spring, a feather mattress, piece-work quilts, pots and
pans, a skillet, coffee pot and a little homemade cupboard."[1]
They also traveled with a hencoop full of Wilder's fluttering,
squawking hens. But Wilder also managed to pack away
two luxuries in the black hack that took her young family
to their new home: her portable writing desk, a shiny box of
polished wood that Manly had made for her, and her pearl-
handled pen. She kept these luxuries close and used them
almost every day when she wrote in the diary she kept during
this life-changing journey. Writing in a four-inch by six-and-
a-half-inch memorandum notebook from a New York life
insurance company, Wilder recorded her impressions of the
family's trek through South Dakota, Nebraska, Kansas, and
Missouri. The diary was published posthumously in 1962
as *On the Way Home*, with an introduction and afterword by
Rose Wilder Lane, who was seven years old when the family
moved to Missouri.[2]

Wilder began this journal with an entry on 17 July 1894,
that read, "Started at 8:40. Three miles out, Russian this-
tles." She reported that the wheat harvest was poor, grain in
Miner County south of De Smet was only eight inches high,
and a hot wind was blowing. She did not reveal how she said
goodbye to her parents and her sisters, nor did she record
any feelings of sadness or regret. Wilder was completely
unsentimental. Her journal was about the present—and
her family's future.[3] Lane recalled that family parting more

completely, although still without emotional overtones: "In the dawn next morning we said goodbye to Grandpa and Grandma, to the aunts Mary and Carrie and Grace, who all stood around to watch us go. . . . The mares were hitched to the hack; their colts, Little Pet and Prince, would follow them. . . . My mother sat beside me; beside her my father tightened the lines; everyone said, 'Goodbye goodbye!' 'Don't forget to write. I won't, I will, you be sure to. Goodbye!' and we drove away."[4]

The Wilders traveled with another area family, Frank and Emma Cooley and their sons Paul and George, who had also decided to start over in the Missouri Ozarks. Lane remembered that the two boys were older and that the families "had always known each other." They were close—close enough that the Cooleys knew about the one-hundred-dollar bill hidden in Wilder's writing desk.[5] As the families traveled south, they camped along rivers or springs, near farms, or on the outskirts of small farming communities. It was dusty and dry. At ten o'clock on the morning of 23 July, Wilder wrote, "It is 101° in the shade in the wagon, and hardly a breath of air." Along the way, she noted crops, soil, livestock, and farming operations. "Oats are running 30 to 60 bushels to the acre, wheat from 10 to 30," she recorded as the family passed through Fort Scott, Kansas. "All the wood you want can be had for the hauling and coal is delivered at the house for $1.25 a ton. Land is worth from $10. an acre up, unimproved, and $15. to $25. when well improved."[6] This appreciation for the business of farming combined with her ability to write about it with precision would serve her well years later as a columnist for the *Missouri Ruralist.*

Wilder was equally fascinated with the people she met along the way—Russian farmers north of Yankton, South Dakota; an elderly Canadian couple who owned property in Nebraska and the West Indies; "a great many colored people in and around" Topeka, Kansas. But mostly, the Wilders and Cooleys were interested in what their fellow emigrants along the road had to say. An entire population seemed to be on the move that summer—from north to south, from south to north: "An emigrant team is behind us and every minute I expect to hear the usual, Where did you come from? Where are you going? How are the crops up your way? This never—hardly ever—fails." Wilder and Manly, however, were most attentive when they met emigrant families headed north out of Missouri. On 26 July, they met a family from Moody County, Dakota Territory, who had traveled to Taney County, Missouri, in May. They had stayed only ten days and "would not live in Missouri if you gave them the whole of it. 'Why, hardly any of the houses have windows in them, just holes, and lots of the women have never seen a railroad train nor an organ,' and the land is awful stony." The next month, the Wilders met another family who had given up on southwestern Missouri after two months. "'Right there is the place to go if a man wants to bury himself from the world and live on hoecake and clabber,'" the man said.[7]

These accounts function as miniature scenes, complete with vivid details, colorful dialogue, and memorable characterizations. Although Wilder had no intention of publishing this journal as she was writing it in 1894, she was certainly in command of her material, and she intuitively employed essential principles of what today we call creative nonfiction, a genre grounded in fact that reads like fiction. Within the journal, Wilder also shared her perceived limitations as a writer: "We crossed the James River and in 20 minutes we reached the top of the bluffs on the other side. We all stopped and looked back at the scene and I wished for an artist's hand or a poet's brain or even to be able to tell in good plain prose how beautiful it was. If I had been the Indians I would have scalped more white folks before I ever would have left it."[8]

Wilder's voice—her style, humor, and personality—also emerged in these pages. "We crossed 11 creeks today, or one creek 11 times, I don't know which," she wrote on 3 August.

Earlier she had remarked that she and Emma Cooley had gone to buy milk at a house that they found "swarming with children and pigs; they looked a good deal alike."[9] The journal also included brief, insightful glimpses into the Wilders' marriage. On 31 July, the families camped in a willow grove outside of Schuyler, Nebraska, on the Platte River. While the Cooleys were in town, Wilder and Manly seized a rare moment alone together. They "left Rose to watch the camp" and went to the river so that Wilder could wade in the clear, warm water. "The sand was soft and warm but shifting," Wilder wrote in her diary. "It ran away right under my feet while I waded, or if I stood still it drifted over them. For fun I stood still until my feet were covered. As Manly said, we 'hit the dust' going, but we 'packed sand' coming back."[10]

As Wilder and her family reached the Ozarks, her descriptions became more vivid and lyrical. On 25 August 1894, she wrote: "We passed along the foot of some hills and could look up their sides. The trees and rocks are lovely. Manly says we could almost live on the looks of them." Three days later, they arrived in Springfield, Missouri, the largest city in the area. Home to almost twenty-two thousand people, Springfield contained "fine houses and four business blocks stand[ing] around a town square. . . . It is simply grand." They stopped to shop, buying shoes for Rose, shoes and a calico dress for Wilder, and a hat for Manly. Throughout the rest of their lives, all three members of the family would return to Springfield often, not just for clothes, but for farm equipment and machinery, furniture, and routine medical care. Leaving that afternoon, the family traveled a road that went "up hill and down, and it is rutted and dusty and stony but every turn of the wheels changes our view of the woods and hills. The sky seems lower here, and it is the softest blue. The distances and the valleys are blue whenever you can see them. It is a drowsy country that makes you feel wide awake and alive but somehow contented."[11]

They arrived in Mansfield on 30 August 1894 at 11:30 in

the morning "in a long line of 10 emigrant wagons." Her first impression of the town of three- to four-hundred inhabitants was positive. "There is everything here already that one could want," she wrote, although she was disappointed that there was no Congregational church. Manly immediately started scouting for property, looking at one place that "was not exactly suited." Wilder's journal ended there.[12] As her earliest sustained piece of writing, the diary demonstrated the unique skills she would later bring to her work as a columnist and, eventually, as a novelist. It displayed her eye for detail, vivid descriptions, memorable dialogue, realistic characterizations, and seemingly effortless prose. Clearly, Wilder knew how to write, even when she was writing for an audience of one.

Within a few days, Manly found a place that seemed promising, and the couple left Rose behind with Emma Cooley to take a look at it. When they returned, Lane remembered that her mother had "never talked so fast." The place was exactly what they wanted. It contained a spring of good water that ran all year long, a log house, woods, and it was close enough for Rose to walk to school. Best of all, it had an orchard of apple trees, over four hundred already planted. Manly and Wilder were so taken with the property, their daughter recalled, that they planned to slip that hundred-dollar bill from its hiding place in the writing desk and use it as a down payment that afternoon. In her afterword to *On the Way Home,* Lane described her mother in her excitement—"beautiful hair, roan-brown"; wearing her "black cloth wedding dress" that had come with them from Dakota; the "fold of ribbon, robin's-egg blue" pinned to her collar; and her "black sailor hat" with blue ribbon trim that tilted forward over her thick mass of pinned-up braids. Wilder was twenty-seven. "She looked lovely; she was beautiful," Lane recalled. "You could see my father think so, when she came out and he looked at her."[13]

From there, Lane's account turned sour: the hundred-dollar bill was not in the writing desk. "Everything changed," Lane said. "In the tight strangeness my father and mother were not like them; I did not feel like me." Her parents questioned her about the missing money, wondering if she had told someone about it. Her mother then asked if she had played with and lost it herself, pushing Lane for an answer. "I felt scalded," Lane remembered. "Don't cry," Wilder responded automatically, but Lane was angry and insulted. Everyone grew quiet, and Lane "sank slowly into nothing but terror, pure terror without cause or object, a nightmare terror," Lane recalled.[14] Her retelling of this incident focused almost entirely on Wilder and her fury; in this scene, she was at once beautiful and terrible, not the warm, loving mother most Wilder fans might expect.

Throughout her life and writings, both public and private, Lane characterized her mother as either the ideal of motherhood or its antithesis. In letters to Wilder, Lane addressed her as "Mama Bess" or "Dearest Mama Bess" and often filled them with messages of affection and concern.[15] "I love you lots, mother dearest—be good to my only mother and don't let her work too hard, won't you? Make her go hunting bird's nests just as soon as the snow melts, and violets. . . . Lovingly, Rose."[16] In one of her first autobiographical articles, Lane wrote, "My mother loves courage and beauty and books; my father loves nature, birds and trees and curious stones, and both of them love the land, . . . They gave me something of all these loves, and whenever I do something that I really can't help sitting down and admiring, I always come plump up against the fact that I never would have done it if I hadn't been wise enough to pick these particular parents."[17]

Privately, in her journals and letters to close friends, on the other hand, Lane expressed resentment and rage at the burden she felt in being Wilder's daughter—long before her mother became a legendary children's book writer. "My mother can not learn to have any reliance upon my financial judgment or promises," Lane wrote her close friend, writer Guy Moyston, in 1925. "It's partly, I suppose, because she still thinks of me as a child. She ever hesitates to let me have the responsibility of bringing up the butter from the spring, for fear I won't do it quite right!" In the same letter, she added that she knew that Moyston shared the same feeling about his own mother but that it was not so bad for him since he was not an only child. "And besides," she concluded, "you're a son, and I a daughter. Men aren't expected to stay at home."[18] This tug of war, as Lane envisioned it, was exclusively a mother-daughter battle. Her father stood on the sidelines.

Wilder herself was silent about the missing money. Her public recollection of the family's first days in Mansfield lacked Lane's melodrama. The Wilders bought a small acreage in "these beautiful hills and peaceful valleys, but only five acres were cleared," she revealed in an interview toward the end of her life. A one-room log cabin on the property "had no window, but light filtered in between the logs where the chinking had fallen out. So did the wind and the rain."[19] The money reappeared; it had been in the writing desk all along, lodged in a crack. The Wilders bought forty acres of Wright County land on 21 September 1894, and not long thereafter, Wilder named it Rocky Ridge Farm.[20] Writing for the *Missouri Ruralist* years later, she explained: "To appreciate fully the reason why we named our place Rocky Ridge Farm, it should have been seen at the time of the christening. . . . It was, and is, uncompromisingly ridge land, on the very tip-top of the ridge at that, within a very few miles of the highest point in the Ozarks. And rocky—it certainly was rocky when it was named."[21] On this farm, the Wilders "worked hard, but it was interesting and didn't hurt us any," she told a reporter in 1949.[22] They spent the first year clearing the land and making what improvements to the property they could afford. Initially, they lived on income from Wilder's hens and by selling off timber as they and a hired man cleared Rocky Ridge. In the spring of 1895, they planted more apple trees. That same year, the house at Rocky Ridge began to take shape, starting as a one-room addition to the original log cabin.[23]

In 1898, the Wilders moved into Mansfield and managed their farm from a house they rented in town. Their friend Frank Cooley had died, and Manly bought his hauling business; Wilder took in boarders.[24] Lane later wrote extensively about the poverty of those years—how as a little girl she picked and sold wild huckleberries and blackberries at ten cents a gallon to help supplement the family's income; how she "chased a rabbit into a hollow log and barricaded it there" so the Wilders could have stew for supper; and how she helped her mother churn butter to sell in town for ten cents a pound.[25] Yet, the Wilders' financial plight was probably no better or no worse than most of the residents in Wright County. Well into the early twentieth century, most Ozark counties were "cash poor." Rural families who had lived in the Ozarks since before the Civil War and those like the Wilders, who arrived in the late nineteenth century, were subsistence farmers, "families of modest means who could live off the land," according to historians Lynn Morrow and Linda Myers-Phinney. The Wilders "represented the general demographic trend."[26]

As for Wilder and Manly, they were persistent, determined, and innovative farmers. He raised corn and potatoes and gardened between the rows of the orchard "until the trees were eight years old." He then "seeded that land down to timothy [grass] and clover," the *Missouri Ruralist* reported. This approach gave the Wilders "a good hay crop out of the orchard, making two good crops from the land."[27] Meanwhile Wilder herself learned more about taking care of hens and getting them to lay.[28] She was especially fond of Leghorn hens, which she had first seen in De Smet when she and Manly were just beginning their courtship. "They were small and brown, looked like birds, and laid very, very small eggs," she reported in her autobiography.[29] The Wilders also received help from Manly's father, who visited Mansfield in 1898 and gave them four hundred fifty dollars, enough to buy their rental house.[30] Gradually their farm began to prosper, until it "supplied everything necessary for a good living," Wilder wrote in the *Ruralist*, and had "given us good interest on all the money invested every year since the first two. No year has it fallen below 10 percent, and one extra good year it paid 100 percent." In addition, Rocky Ridge Farm had more than doubled in value since the Wilders bought it.[31]

Beyond housekeeping, making a living, and nurturing Rocky Ridge with Manly, little is known of the fabric of Wilder's everyday life during her first decade in Missouri. The Wilders joined the Mansfield Methodist church, where they worshiped for the rest of their lives. Photographs from the period show the Wilders outside, basking in the natural beauty of the Ozarks: Wilder and Manly with friends on an excursion to a nearby cave; Manly and his brother Perley riding mules across Rocky Ridge Farm; Wilder standing beside the farm's spring or perched on a grapevine swing in the woods. The countryside was important to Wilder. "There is no other country like the Ozarks in the world," she said.[32] But in 1902, the prairies of South Dakota called Wilder home— not for a happy reunion with those she loved, but for a final vigil with her father. She was at his bedside when he died on 8 June 1902; she would inherit his fiddle. Manly's father had died shortly before and left Manly an inheritance of five hundred dollars. The Wilders invested the money in Rocky Ridge Farm, which eventually sprawled across two hundred acres.[33]

Other than an occasional photograph of Rose looking dour and well dressed (even when posing with her donkey Spookendyke), Wilder left no memories or impressions behind about her daughter's childhood. Lane, on the other hand, left many impressions in letters, diaries, and numerous autobiographical pieces. Consequently, the portrait that emerges from those years is overwhelmingly one-sided.

Lane wrote bitterly, passionately, and sometimes hysterically about her unhappy childhood in Mansfield. "I lived through a childhood that was a nightmare," she wrote in 1926. "No sensitive child who has gone to school from a poverty-beseiged home, in patched clothes, with second-hand books, fails to learn that human beings are barbarous." Yet the Wilders' struggle to make a living in the Ozarks was not atypical. The key, perhaps, to Lane's unhappiness was her marked sensitivity, a circumstance she herself admitted. "In a few years we were not so poor," she recalled. The quality of her clothes and belongings improved, but the other children's attitude toward her "still persisted, and I was too shy, too sensitive, to break it down. I was not invited to parties; I was 'left out.' I was hurt and lonely."[34] By her own admission, Lane was also willful, stubborn, and obstinate—almost from the moment she could talk. And she was impatient with people or situations that struck her as stupid—also from an early age. In a caption under a picture of herself at age two, Lane remembered that the photographer "kept putting my right hand on top of the left, and I kept changing them back because I wanted my carnelian ring to show. And in the end I won out."[35]

Lane was a good student and a voracious reader, perhaps inspired by the books Wilder often read aloud to the family.[36] Lane's intelligence and academic ambitions may also have isolated her from her Mansfield contemporaries, but more than likely, something more fundamental separated her from her peers. In an agricultural community, Lane exhibited complete apathy toward farming, which she associated with the pioneer experience. By her own account, Lane grew up on Wilder's stories about the frontier, and, what was worse, her mother considered the struggle to conquer Rocky Ridge Farm as much a part of the pioneer experience as her own parents' struggle against the elements had been a generation earlier. As an adult, Lane felt at once trapped and distinguished by this heritage. In trying to summarize her background in a letter to another writer, Lane wrote: "Pioneer, and pioneer-farming. . . . Pioneer American, maybe? That is all right; but I don't care about it. Don't dislike it, and I readily admit all the admirable qualities; I'm simply not interested. I was brought up on pioneer stories, and never a spark from me."[37] While Lane would eventually mine those experiences for her fiction, she longed for something more worldly. She was a city girl, trapped among graceless farmers—the ones that sprang from her mother's stories as well as the real, living, breathing Ozark families around her, whom she described as a sad lot—"men in overalls or ten-dollar Sears and Roebuck Sunday suits that are as uncomfortable on the wearers as the wearers are in them, thin-faced, straggle-haired women with babies in their arms and assorted children hanging to their dragged skirts, young girls in bright pink lawn waists and green-brown plaid skirts."[38]

By 1903, Wilder may have realized that Mansfield was not the right place for her daughter, and when Manly's sister Eliza Jane—or E. J., as she called herself—visited that year, the family decided to send Rose back with her to Crowley, Louisiana, where she could finish high school. Rose was sixteen. It was, in some ways, an odd twist of fate. Wilder would later portray Eliza Jane as an incompetent, heartless school teacher in her autobiography and in *Little Town on the Prairie*.[39] Yet, she entrusted her daughter's education—and her future—to "lazy, lousy, Lizy Jane."[40] The implication is clear: Wilder was ready to let her daughter cut those proverbial apron strings. When Rose graduated from high school in 1904, she returned to Mansfield only briefly, then headed for the big city, which in this case was Kansas City, where she launched a varied and unpredictable career path. "I have been office clerk, telegrapher, newspaper reporter, feature writer, advertising writer, farmland salesman," she wrote in 1935. "I have seen all the United States and something of Canada and the Caribbean; all of Europe except Spain; Turkey, Egypt; Palestine, Syria, Iraq as far east as Bagdad, Georgia, Armenia, Azerbaijan. California, the Ozarks, and the Balkans are my home towns."[41] Although Rose Wilder Lane returned to Rocky Ridge Farm periodically throughout her adult life, she resented every moment she spent there. One short entry from her journal, written in 1929, summed up a lifetime of frustration at the Ozark farm: *"I want to get away from here!"*[42]

Once Lane left the nest in 1904, Wilder experienced a burst of creativity, one that would define her life. At long last, she and Manly could build their dream house at Rocky Ridge, and the success they had made of their farm would launch her writing career.

10

The Result
of Evolution

Wilder and Manly began work on what would become the Rocky Ridge farmhouse in 1894, when they added "a box room with doors and windows" to the property's original log house. They moved this new room to the site of the current farmhouse and added a second room in 1896. "We were very proud of our two-roomed box house," Wilder wrote, though she regretted leaving the fireplace behind in the cabin. Already Wilder had dreams of something grander.[1] In a vivid scene from her afterword to *On the Way Home*, Rose Wilder Lane captured her mother's first vision of the Rocky Ridge farmhouse:

> It would be a white house, she said, all built from our farm. Everything we needed to build it was on the land: good oak beams and boards, stones for the foundation and the fireplace. The house would have large windows looking west across the brook, over the gentle little valley and up the wooded hills that hid the town, to the sunset colors in the sky. There would be a nice big porch to the north, cool on hot summer afternoons. The kitchen would be big enough to hold a wood stove for winter and one of the new kerosene stoves that wouldn't heat up the place worse in summer. . . . And in the parlor there would be a bookcase, no, *two* bookcases, big bookcases full of books, and a hanging lamp to read them by, on winter evenings by the fireplace.[2]

Despite the clear word picture, which she apparently painted for Lane around the time they moved to Mansfield, Wilder had to wait over a decade for her dream to come true.

In her own words, the house was "the result of evolution"—not merely cutting and pasting remnants of several structures together, but the evolution of the farm itself. Before work could begin on the house, the mortgage had to be paid, the farm fenced, and the barn enlarged.[3]

After Lane graduated from high school and moved to Kansas City, the Wilders sold their place in town, purchased building materials, and began construction on their dream home. As Wilder had told Lane all those years before, the house would almost literally spring from the land itself. "I have a fancy," Wilder explained in 1920, "that the farm home should seem to be a product of the soil where it is reared. . . . Such a house, well built, will last for generations."[4] The house at Rocky Ridge certainly reflected this fancy. It became an expression of the farm itself, the shared dream Wilder and Manly had nurtured through decades of misfortune, financial uncertainty, and hard work. "So far as possible, everything used in the building was to be a product of the farm, both for the sake of economy and because of the sentimental idea that we wanted the house actually to be a part of the farm." When the couple began talking about building in earnest, Manly apparently argued to keep adding on—one box room at a time with stairs and a loft. That was not what Wilder wanted: "There was material on the farm to build any kind of a house, I argued, so why not build a real house instead of an addition that would make it look like a town house in the poorer suburbs? That kind didn't belong on a farm, I insisted. It wouldn't look right among the trees, with the everlasting hills around it."[5]

Wilder's idea for the farmhouse was exceptional, especially given the time and place. In remote Wright County, Missouri, most farmhouses were exactly what Manly advocated for—a room added on here and there without a master plan. With her vision of how the house would seem organically to spring from its surroundings, Wilder brought originality and creativity to the project, much in the tradition of the nineteenth-century British Arts and Crafts Movement, which valued local materials, traditional craftsmanship, and a natural aesthetic. As artist and designer William Morris advised, "Have nothing in your houses that you do not know to be useful, or believe to be beautiful."[6] The finished farmhouse at Rocky Ridge is, in many ways, a work of art, as original in its own way as Wilder's fiction. From its massive beamed ceilings and open stairway in the living room, to the three massive rock slabs that form the fireplace, to the built-in cabinets and bookcases in the dining room and library, the entire house creates a storybook atmosphere. Yet, its story could only unfold and have meaning in the Ozarks. Manly and Wilder even found a "backwoods carpenter" with traditional training to smooth the oak boards and fit them together seamlessly.[7]

The entire house was physically scaled to fit the Wilders. Visitors today find the kitchen and dining rooms tiny, the main bedroom cramped, Wilder's study smaller than most contemporary walk-in closets. Manly was probably five feet, four inches tall; Wilder, just four feet, eleven. The kitchen countertop where she stood to knead bread stands a mere twenty-nine and a half inches off the floor.[8] The house suited them perfectly, something Lane never quite understood when, years later, she decided to build her parents a new house. The Rocky Ridge farmhouse cost the couple twenty-two hundred dollars and took "two years from the time we sawed the trees down to make the lumber." They completed it late in 1913, and Wilder, surveying her living room, was satisfied. "The effect is particularly good in summer when all the doors are open, making all the different parts of the house a harmonious whole," she wrote.[9] The house, indeed the whole of Rocky Ridge Farm, was an "expression of the mind and soul of the builder."[10]

Even before the house was finished, however, Wilder was exploring new outlets for her creative energies. Shortly after her father's death, she had written a scrap of a story about her family's experience in Dakota Territory; she had also recorded a humorous piece about a hillbilly family's reaction to the first automobile in the Ozarks. "They knew it was some kind of a varmit but had never heard one like it," Wilder wrote. The father tried to kill the automated creature, which appeared to have a man in its clutches. When the mother asked what happened, he said, "'I made it turn that man loose. Thar he is in the road!'" Not an auspicious beginning perhaps, but the dialogue was crisp and the punch line well delivered. Yet, her first published work had nothing to do with humor or her family in Dakota and everything to do with life on Rocky Ridge Farm.[11]

As Mrs. A. J. Wilder, she contributed a poultry column to the *St. Louis Star Farmer* based on her expertise in raising Leghorn hens. As insignificant as this publication experience may seem to us today, it was an unusual accomplishment for a farm woman living in Wright County, Missouri, in 1910.[12] Saint Louis, a major metropolitan area, was over two hundred and forty miles northeast of Mansfield. Thousands of women kept chickens throughout Missouri; Wilder was one of only a handful who wrote about them. "'She gets eggs in the winter when none of her neighbors gets any,'" an admiring friend told an editor.[13] Clearly, Wilder was an expert.

On 18 February 1911, her lucid prose and insight into the business of raising poultry led to the publication of her first article in the *Missouri Ruralist,* a weekly farm newspaper headquartered in Kansas City, Missouri. The newspaper had a modest circulation then—just fifteen thousand—and its stories focused on livestock and grain production, poultry, dairy, and the home. Established in 1902, the *Missouri Ruralist* had from the beginning viewed women as an important readership, and the year before Wilder began contributing to the paper, it endorsed women's suffrage. In December 1910, the *Missouri Ruralist* changed hands, and its editorial staff was looking for new contributors.[14] Wilder was in the right place at the right time. She proved to be such a popular writer for the publication that editor John F. Case profiled her in February 1918. "She has taken strong hold upon the esteem and affections of our great family. . . . She knows farm folks and their problems as few women who write know them," he observed. "And having sympathy with the folks whom she serves she writes well."[15]

Like many professional women writers, Wilder sometimes published her work under an androgynous pseudonym, using "A. J. Wilder," to give her work more credibility, especially when she wanted to extend her reach beyond the *Missouri Ruralist's* women readers and appeal to their husbands. In the early part of the twentieth century, it was perfectly acceptable for a woman to write an advice column to other women on "The Home Beauty Parlor," a Wilder piece dating from 1914; it was quite another matter for her to write about innovative farming techniques or the business of farming, stories that would appeal to male as well as female readers. Consequently, such major feature articles as "Rocky Ridge Farm" in 1911 and "My Apple Orchard" in 1912 appeared under the byline of "A. J. Wilder," her husband's initials, though both were undoubtedly written by Wilder herself.[16]

Wilder's work for the *Missouri Ruralist* was accomplished. She knew how to write for her audience, how to use concrete details that paint a vivid mental picture for her readers. "When I look around the farm now and see the smooth, green, rolling meadows and pastures, the good fields of corn and wheat and oats, when I see the orchard and strawberry field like huge bouquets in the spring or full of fruit later in the season, when I see the grapevines hanging full of luscious grapes, I can hardly bring back to my mind the rough, rocky, brushy, ugly place that we first called Rocky Ridge Farm," she wrote in July 1911.[17] She also used dialogue effectively, whether quoting neighbors or her own husband, lovingly referred to as "the Man of the Place" in column after column. "'Those durn hens are eating their heads off!'" the

Man of the Place exclaimed in one piece.[18] In another, after comparing his work on Rocky Ridge Farm to his parents' life in upstate New York, he conceded: "'I guess we're not having such a hard time after all. It depends a good deal on how you look at it.'"[19]

Wilder understood the conventions of her genre—the column or news feature—and structured her stories well, with interesting leads that engaged her readers right from the beginning. "How long has it been since you have seen an old maid?" she asked her readers in a 1918 column.[20] Her closing lines were also compelling. "Perhaps someday we will all have kitchens like the club kitchen lately installed in New York where everything from peeling potatoes to cooking the dinner and washing the dishes is done by electricity, but the birds' songs will never be any sweeter nor the beauties of field and forest, of cloud and stream, be any more full of delight, and these are already ours," she concluded in 1913.[21]

Many critics and even some fans dismiss Wilder's work for the *Missouri Ruralist* as amateurish or second-rate. Yet, agricultural journalism has a long and rich tradition in the United States, and the *Ruralist* was "the major state farm paper in Missouri" during the early twentieth century. In 1918, the year Wilder was profiled in its pages, the *Missouri Ruralist* had a circulation of 88,640.[22] The newspaper is still published today in both a print and an online version. The same cannot be said of many of the national consumer magazines Wilder aspired to write for in the 1920s—the *Saturday Evening Post, Century, Country Gentleman*. It is also worth noting that, although Rose Wilder Lane broke into the national press before her mother did, Wilder had found a regular home for her work long before her daughter did.

From 1911 until 1915, Wilder's byline appeared sporadically in the pages of the *Ruralist*. Critics and biographers assume she was struggling to learn the craft of writing or scrambling to find something to write about. While Wilder was indeed growing as a writer during this period, her creative energies were not entirely devoted to writing. She and Manly were planning and building the farmhouse at Rocky Ridge. She also became a club woman and was organizing clubs among farm women throughout southwestern Missouri.[23] As she explained to John F. Case at the *Missouri Ruralist*, "'I always have been a busy person, . . . doing my own housework, helping the Man of the Place'" about the farm.[24] Moreover, Case himself, who admired Wilder's work, did not arrive at the newspaper until 1913. Under his direction, the *Ruralist* developed "a more friendly, interesting, and personable style—a style that was fast-moving and easy to read, and easily understood by the farm audience." Wilder's writing was compatible with Case's new editorial direction.[25] Her bylines in the *Missouri Ruralist* appeared with more frequency after 1915, when she found both more time to write and an editor who appreciated her work.

As Wilder launched her writing career, Lane made changes in her life, as well. She had moved to San Francisco and, in 1909, married Claire Gillette Lane, a reporter for the *San Francisco Call*. Known as Gillette, he had also been a traveling salesman and perhaps even a flimflam man, selling vague promotional schemes in small midwestern towns. Shortly after their marriage, the Lanes left San Francisco and moved to Kansas City. Their only child—a son—died at or shortly after his birth. In 1910, Lane launched her own writing career—as a reporter for the *Kansas City Post*, but her tenure there did not last long. By the end of the year, the couple had moved to New York City, where Lane sold advertising space, presumably for a newspaper; a year later, she and Gillette returned to San Francisco. Strapped for money Lane drew upon her husband's contacts as well as her friendship with Bessie Beatty, a reporter for the *San Francisco Bulletin*, to reinvent herself as a freelance writer.[26] She was as new to the writing business as her mother, but that did not stop Lane from offering Wilder professional tips and advice. Perhaps the most useful was, "Why don't you go to Springfield and look for a good Underwood [typewriter], rebuilt?" Lane advised her mother to give the typewriter a one-month trial, then pay no more than fifty dollars for it in five-dollar installments.[27] Wilder took Lane's advice and began typing her stories for the *Missouri Ruralist.*

Although Lane herself was just starting out as a writer and was struggling to make ends meet after a series of bad business decisions, Wilder listened to her daughter and valued her opinions. It is clear from the remaining correspondence from this period that Wilder even shared with Lane the embryonic idea she had of writing her life story. Lane advised, "You must write just exactly what you think of Mansfield in your 'life story' when you come to it—just think you are writing a diary that no one anywhere will ever see, and put down all the things that you think, regardless." Lane also suggested that a letter Wilder had written to her mother about getting started in writing could be used verbatim. "I bet it's better than you could do trying to write it for the story," Lane concluded.[28]

If Wilder wrote an early draft of her life story at this period, it does not survive, nor does the letter that Lane referred to here. This correspondence, however, established a pattern between Wilder and Lane that would continue throughout their lifetimes—Lane confidently, sometimes stridently, providing advice and opinions about her mother's writing career; Wilder listening, responding, and, as her talents deepened, eventually questioning her daughter's counsel. Although Wilder and Lane became published newspaper writers almost simultaneously, Wilder apparently never ventured any constructive criticism or advice on her daughter's work. The early correspondence also produced another outcome—the idea that Wilder should visit San Francisco to learn about writing from Lane. In a letter addressed to "Muver dear," Lane wrote: "I'm awfully lonesome for you—I wish you were out here in this little apartment with me, writing for the papers out here. You would make such a good feature writer, and we would have heaps of fun."[29]

Before this visit materialized, however, Lane's professional life changed dramatically. Again through Bessie Beatty, Lane landed a job as her editorial assistant on the new women's page at the *San Francisco Bulletin* in early 1915. Lane wrote a regular column, which drew on her own experiences and observations about life, much as her mother's work for the *Missouri Ruralist* did. This new position placed Lane more securely into the writing life of San Francisco and exposed her to a community of well-known and successful working writers. She used this exposure to deepen and further her own writing career and her mother's. This career move took place just before the Panama-Pacific International Exposition of 1915, hosted by the city of San Francisco. Lane insisted that her mother come for a visit to write about the exposition for the *Missouri Ruralist,* to learn writing fundamentals from Lane herself, and ultimately to broaden Wilder's writing career. Manly would have to stay behind to run Rocky Ridge Farm. Initially, Wilder worried about leaving her husband behind but finally agreed to Lane's request. She left Mansfield on 21 August 1915, and when the train stopped in Springfield, not sixty miles away, she posted her first letter to Manly.[30]

When Wilder arrived in San Francisco almost a week later, the Lanes welcomed her warmly. Over the next two months, they escorted her to the exposition, to the Santa Clara Valley orchards, and to a poultry operation in Mill Valley. She rode electric streetcars, ate Chinese food, cruised at sunset beneath the Golden Gate Bridge. Rose Wilder Lane hosted a tea party with the women writers at the *Bulletin* in Wilder's honor. San Francisco—Lane's world—was an exhilarating experience for Wilder. "Please save my letters," she wrote Manly a few weeks after her arrival, "I might want to use some of the descriptions later."[31]

Wilder's gift for description had not diminished since

she had painted word pictures for Mary in Dakota Territory all those years before, though she sometimes felt unequal to the scenes she observed in California. "At Land's End I had my first view of the Pacific Ocean," she wrote. "To say it is beautiful does not half express it. It is simply beyond words. The water is such a deep wonderful blue and the sound of the waves breaking on the beach and their whisper as they flow back is something to dream about."[32] She grew more impatient with herself after visiting the exposition. "I am disgusted with this letter," she wrote Manly. "I have not done halfway justice to anything I have described."[33] And in another letter, she criticized herself for overusing the word beautiful until it lost its meaning, "but what other word can I use?"[34] Still, her brief description of Alcatraz was flawless: "The foghorn on Alcatraz is the most lonesome sound I ever heard and I don't see how the prisoners on the island stand it."[35] These letters revealed, as her journal twenty-two years before had not, a self-conscious working writer; Wilder knew that her letters to Manly might have a life beyond his private reading of them.

The letters also contain multiple references to the work Wilder was doing with Lane. They had made plans to work on stories the week of 13 September, and she was observing and describing the exposition in a book of notes a few days later.[36] She described the goals she and Lane had set for her as a writer:

> Rose and I are blocking out a story of the Ozarks for me to finish when I get home. If I can only make it sell, it ought to help a lot and besides, I am learning so that I can write others for the magazines. If I can only get started at that, it will sell for a good deal more than farm stuff. We are slow about it, for Rose has to do the work that draws her pay. I do the housework so that she will have time to help me with my learning to write and to go with me to see the things that I must see before I go away.[37]

Working with Lane was not only slow, sometimes it was tedious. Toward the end of her visit, Wilder admitted: "The more I see of how Rose works the better satisfied I am to raise chickens. I intend to try to do some writing that will count, but I would not be driven by the work as she is for anything and I do not see how she can stand it."[38]

Wilder's letters were also filled with concerns about Manly and their dog, and she sent him information on new farm machinery, techniques, and prices. Wilder was equally interested in her daughter's marriage, Gillette's perennial unemployment, and the Lanes' precarious financial situation, which was bound up with the Wilders'. She and Manly had loaned the Lanes two hundred fifty dollars several years before, increasing their mortgage on Rocky Ridge Farm to do so.[39] During Wilder's visit, Lane lobbied intensively for her parents to move to California and buy a small acreage, seemingly blind to her mother's fierce loyalty to the Ozarks and Rocky Ridge Farm. Wilder thought San Francisco beautiful, "but I would not give one Ozark hill for all the rest of the state that I have seen," she told Manly.[40] Over the next ten years, Lane would continue to try to impose her values on her parents, and the pressure would be a source of conflict and pain for them all, especially Wilder.

In October, Wilder landed a major assignment from the *Missouri Ruralist*. In her last letter from San Francisco, dated 22 October 1915, she told Manly that the newspaper had sent "orders for copy and recommendations that give me passes into the Fair and throws the whole Missouri part of it wide open to me. It is a shame they could not have sent it sooner." This new assignment, welcome as it was, delayed her return to Rocky Ridge but allowed her to do additional research and map out stories to finish in Mansfield.[41] By late fall, she was home again. Her story on the Panama-Pacific International Exposition made the front page of the *Missouri Ruralist* on 5 December 1915.

Over the next nine years, Wilder's byline appeared in

almost every issue of the newspaper. The *Ruralist* identified her as one of the publication's most inspiring writers. "Reading Mrs. Wilder's contributions most folks doubtless have decided that she is a college graduate," editor John Case wrote, adding that Wilder set the record straight. "'I never graduated from anything and only attended high school two terms,'" she said. Case got the last word: "Folks who know Mrs. Wilder, tho, know that she is a cultured, well-educated gentlewoman."[42] By 1919, Wilder's columns were appearing under a regular title, "The Farm Home," which changed in 1921 to "As a Farm Woman Thinks." She earned between five and ten dollars per column.[43]

While in San Francisco, Wilder had published her first work for children, short poems that appeared in a *San Francisco Bulletin* column called "The Tuck'em In Corner," for which Rose Wilder Lane was responsible. Appearing under the byline of Laura Ingalls Wilder, the first time Wilder used the name in print, the poems had such titles as "Naughty Four o' Clocks" and "Where Sunshine Fairies Go." If Wilder had published nothing but these poems during her lifetime, she would not be remembered as an important writer. Although she dabbled with poetry throughout her life, it was not her genre. The poems are, at best, mediocre. One begins: "The sunshine fairies cannot rest,/When evening bells are rung;/Nor can they sleep in flowers,/When bedtime songs are sung."[44] We read Wilder's poetry today only because of her prose—and because they were her first published works for children.

Despite Wilder's success with the *Missouri Ruralist*, Lane continued to urge her mother to do more, to move beyond farm journalism and write for prominent regional and national magazines. Lane herself was doing just that. Her work with the San Francisco paper led to assignments for such major consumer magazines as *McCall's* and *Sunset*. Her publishing credentials were so successful that, just five years after she launched her career with the *Bulletin*, she secured literary agents Carl and Zelma Brandt to represent her work to magazine editors and publishers.[45] Lane was soon advocating a career shift like her own for her mother. "There is no reason under heaven why you should not be making four or five thousand dollars a year," she encouraged.[46] In 1919, Lane used her influence with the editor at *McCall's* to secure an assignment for Wilder, her first with a national magazine, and aggressively began to coach her mother in the basics of creative writing. Wilder struggled to achieve her daughter's expectations for her, but was it what she really wanted?

Caroline Quiner Ingalls and Charles Ingalls, parents of Laura Ingalls Wilder, were the inspiration for Pa and Ma in the Little House books. South Dakota State Historical Society, Pierre

The Ingalls family posed for this photograph in 1894.
From left: Caroline, Carrie, Laura, Charles, Grace, and Mary.
South Dakota State Historical Society, Pierre

Laura and Almanzo Wilder returned to South Dakota
in the 1930s, when they toured the Badlands.
Laura Ingalls Wilder Home Association, Mansfield, Mo.

The Ingalls family lived in the surveyor's house in De Smet, Dakota Territory, during the winter of 1879. The house is still standing today.
Laura Ingalls Wilder Memorial Society, De Smet, S.Dak.

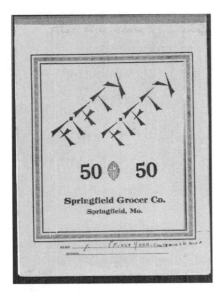

Laura Ingalls Wilder wrote her manuscripts by hand in Fifty Fifty school tablets.
Herbert Hoover Presidential Library, West Branch, Iowa

Helen Sewell and Mildred Boyle illustrated the first editions of the Little House books, which were released in the 1930s and 1940s.

By the Author of LITTLE HOUSE IN THE BIG WOODS

LITTLE TOWN
ON THE PRAIRIE

LAURA INGALLS WILDER

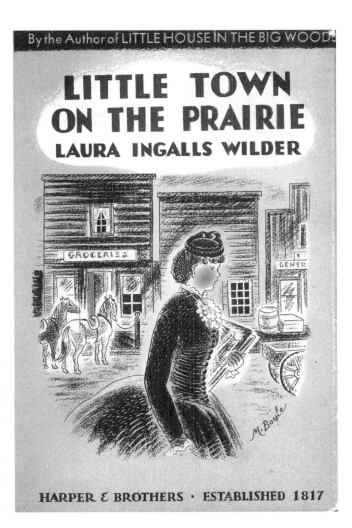

HARPER & BROTHERS · ESTABLISHED 1817

Rose Wilder Lane, daughter of Laura and Almanzo Wilder, worked with Laura on her books and was a successful writer in her own right.
Herbert Hoover Presidential Library, West Branch, Iowa

Laura Ingalls Wilder wrote many of her Little House books while living at the farmhouse on Rocky Ridge Farm in Mansfield, Mo.
South Dakota State Historical Society, Pierre

11

No Opportunity in Children's Stories
1919–1928

Wilder's piece for *McCall's* was called "Whom Will You Marry?" and appeared in June 1919 under the byline of Laura Ingalls Wilder, the first time this name appeared in print for national audiences. Written in first person—from Wilder's perspective as a farm wife—it focused on the dilemma of a fictional character who, perhaps coincidentally, was named Elizabeth, Wilder's middle name. The article opens as Elizabeth's childhood sweetheart is about to come home after a tour of duty during World War I. He wants to marry Elizabeth and settle down on a farm. Elizabeth, seeking Wilder's advice, asks, "'Would—would you be a farmer's wife if you had the chance to live your life over again?'"[1] Wilder's answer was, of course, yes, but the affirmation came only at the end of the article, after a long internal monologue with herself. And from the beginning, the piece took readers into unexpected territory. It did not focus on romance. Instead, the article explored, in an unsentimental way, Wilder's belief in the fundamental partnership of marriage, particularly for farm women.

"While the discussion for and against women in business has been raging over the country," Wilder wrote, "farm women have always been businesswomen, and no one has protested against it. No one has even noticed it." Wilder passionately argued that not only do farm women enjoy full and equal partnership with their husbands but that the work they do is important and deeply fulfilling: "There is a joy of spirit and a pride of power that come to a farm woman who is fully alive to her opportunities, meeting and solving problems, confronting and overcoming difficulties, refusing to become petty though attending to numberless details, or to be discouraged before threatened disasters." Although the article never revealed Elizabeth's decision, her path was clear. What woman could refuse such a life?[2]

Before sending the article off to *McCall's*, however, Wilder sent it to Lane, who was living in New York at the time. She edited the piece and then forwarded it to the magazine. Wilder was dismayed by the extent of the revisions, but Lane responded: "Don't be absurd about my doing the work on your article. I didn't re-write it a bit more than I rewrite Mary Heaton Vorse's articles, or Inez Haynes Irwin's stories."[3] But Wilder was not used to this kind of heavy-handed editing at the *Missouri Ruralist*, a fact she must have told Lane several times. "It is extraordinarily good [your] Ruralist stuff; always did stand out in the paper like a skyscraper on a plain," Lane praised. "But it won't go in Country Gentleman [another prominent national magazine of the period]," she added. "At least, it won't go and bring back any sizeable checks. It isn't Country Gentleman stuff; it's Ruralist stuff."[4] Lane made a good point: writers have to shift format, style, and tone when writing for different publications and different audiences. As Lane knew, successful writers must grasp this fundamental concept, but her advice ignored what troubled Wilder most—Lane's aggressive editing style implied that Wilder's manuscripts were second-rate.

To be fair, Lane's professional writing experience came out of a publishing environment—the daily newspaper business—where heavy-handed editing was the norm. The same practice exists at most newspapers today. Editors rewrite leads and opening paragraphs, shift paragraphs around, add details the reporter failed to put in, and cut out whole chunks of the story. Reporters often see these changes for the first time when their stories appear in print. Depending on a publication's editorial policy, this same process often happens in magazine publishing as well, and it was standard practice in the early twentieth century. Was Wilder's work inferior? Would *McCall's* have published "Whom Will You Marry?" without Lane's editorial skill? It is impossible to know, but Lane apparently considered her mother's work superior to other writers she edited, "for at least your copy was all the meat of the article," she told Wilder.[5]

In addition to the aggressive editing tradition in which Lane worked, her own rapid rise as a successful writer contributed to the way she reviewed and edited Wilder's early work. Based on her experience, Lane was extremely self-confident. In a later letter, filled with detailed editorial advice, she told her mother: "What I am trying to do is to give you the benefit of these ten years of work and study. I'm trying to train you as a writer for the big market."[6] Indeed, Lane's rise to the top of the publishing world from 1915 and into the 1920s was extraordinary. "Between 1915 and 1923," a reporter for the *Kansas City Star* noted in 1925, "this astonishingly energetic person found time, in spite of other activities and the writing of many short stories and articles," to publish seven books: *Henry Ford's Own Story* (1917), *Diverging Roads* (1919), *White Shadows in the South Seas* (with Frederick J. O'Brien, 1919), *The Making of Herbert Hoover* (1920), *The Peaks of Shala* (1923), a translation of *The Dancer of Shamakha* (1922), and *He Was a Man* (1925). The last book, about novelist Jack London, had gone "into three printings the first four weeks after it was published," the reporter added.[7] Such magazines as *Harper's* and *Country Gentleman* were paying Lane up to six hundred dollars for her short fiction. She had every right to be self-confident.[8] Buried deep in the same *Kansas City Star* article was a brief reference to Wilder, "the mother of Rose Wilder Lane, who is a writer, too."[9] Lane was famous; Wilder, though an acknowledged writer in the 1920s, was not.

As she struggled with her daughter's admonitions to write for the big market, Wilder's columns for the *Missouri Ruralist* increasingly became more personal, sometimes drawing on childhood memories. Although she continued to write about current events from 1915 onward (World War I, women's suffrage, presidential elections, and contemporary farm issues), Wilder also began to mine her own past. Her column entitled "The Hard Winter," published in 1917, focused on her memories of grinding wheat from "an ordinary coffee mill" and the lessons it taught her about self-reliance and survival.[10] "The Friday Night Literary," which appeared in the *Missouri Ruralist* in 1919, was also based on Wilder's memories of Dakota Territory and briefly recreated that time and place: "At early candle light, parents and pupils from all over the district gathered at the schoolhouse, bringing lanterns and candles and sometimes a glass lamp to give an added touch of dignity to the teacher's desk."[11]

Wilder stopped writing for the *Ruralist* in 1924, perhaps under continued pressure from Lane to write for more prestigious publications.[12] Even before "Whom Will You Marry?" was published in *McCall's*, Wilder drafted a second piece about modern girls and sent the manuscript off to her daughter for review. Lane was not impressed. "I don't think you have quite done it yet," she wrote in April 1919. "I don't think it 'hopeless' by a million miles, but as you say, I think you can do better with it." The letter also revealed that the idea for the new article originated with Lane, who "thought the subject would be an interesting one to you, that when you really began to think about it lots of new aspects of the question would occur to you, and that it would be fun to turn them around in your mind and work them out." Lane was not only nudging Wilder to write for such publications as *McCall's* and critiquing her work for them, she was also feeding her ideas. In this case, Lane began to suspect that modern girls was not an idea close to her mother's heart, because she added, "There's no use making onesself [*sic*] miserable for the sake of an article."[13]

Even so, for the next three-and-a-half single-spaced pages, Lane told Wilder how to improve the manuscript. Her advice was solid but basic, the kind of constructive criticism contemporary creative writing students get from their instructors every day. Lane told her to use concrete details when describing a character's physical appearance and to avoid abstract vocabulary: "[D]on't say 'conversing.' Say 'talking to.' Right out, like that." She also suggested a more conversational style, and in an extended passage, she explained the concept of "show don't tell": "[D]on't *say* those things were so, *show* that they were so. Your log cabin in the Great Woods, that is now farming land—your trip through Kansas, across the sites of cities today—the building of the railroad through the Dakotas, now the wheat fields that feed the world during the war—Make it all real, because you saw it with your own eyes. Make the reader see it with his eyes."[14]

Although the manuscript that Lane examined so closely does not survive, her letter makes it clear that Wilder was once again drawing on autobiographical material from her childhood. Ultimately, however, Wilder abandoned the manuscript. Though it is impossible to know why she did not complete it, Lane herself provided a clue. After encouraging her mother to rewrite the piece and send it off to *McCall's* before losing "the advertising value of the first one," Lane noted that she had found time to look at the children's stories that her mother had sent. A quick reading showed them to be good, "but they are not so important as the articles, for there is no opportunity to make a name with children's stories," Lane concluded.[15] Obviously, Wilder eventually proved her wrong, and perhaps even in 1919, Wilder inherently knew—as her daughter did not—that magazine work was not her true calling, that it did not interest her creatively.

Like her second *McCall's* manuscript, Wilder's first children's stories do not survive, but Wilder was taking some of Lane's advice to heart, writing short autobiographical sketches that included concrete details, conversational language, and the principle of "show don't tell." Many of these pieces focused on childhood or adolescent memories and served essentially as writing exercises for Wilder's more ambitious work in "Pioneer Girl" and eventually her Little House books. Here, for example, is the opening paragraph from one of her last "As a Farm Woman Thinks" columns for the *Missouri Ruralist* in December 1924:

> The snow was scudding low over the drifts of the white world outside the little claim shanty. It was blowing thru the cracks in its walls and forming little piles and miniature drifts on the floor and even on the desks before which several children sat, trying to study, for this abandoned claim shanty that had served as the summer home of a homesteader on the Dakota prairies was being used as a schoolhouse during the winter.[16]

An early character sketch of her father is just as vivid:

> My first memory is of his eyes, so clear and sharp and blue. Those eyes that could look unerringly along a rifle barrel in the face of a bear or a pack of wolves and yet were so tender as they rested on his Caroline (my mother) or me when I was sick. . . . His hair was thick and fine and he wore a tawny beard. He was the swiftest skater in the neighborhood, a strong swimmer and could travel miles on his snow shoes or tramp all day through the woods without fatigue. His arms were so strong he could break down a door with one blow of his naked fist and his strong arms carried me many a night when I was sick and restless.[17]

When Wilder's mother, Caroline Quiner Ingalls, died on 20 April 1924, Wilder's reaction to the telegram from South Dakota was more lyrical, less specific. "Darkness overshadowed the spring sunshine; a sadness crept into the bird's songs," Wilder wrote.[18] Just over a year after her mother's death, though, Wilder wrote to her Aunt Martha asking for old family stories and recipes.[19] Although Lane continued to pester Wilder to focus on magazine nonfiction, her deeper creative interests appeared to center on autobiographical writing about her childhood and adolescence. Wilder was looking for her niche.

Still, she dutifully followed Lane's advice and painstakingly worked on magazine assignments that her daughter negotiated for her. In a letter dated 12 November, probably from 1924, Lane announced that her literary agent, Carl Brandt, had accepted an offer from *Country Gentleman* of one hundred fifty dollars for Wilder's "kitchen article." Lane had once again edited Wilder's manuscript before it went to the magazine. She challenged Wilder to review the revised manuscript closely: "Study the structure of the sentences, and of the paragraphs. Note how the first two sentences plunge right into the subject, at the same time arousing interest." Lane admitted that her editorial changes may have contradicted earlier instructions to Wilder, but "methods differ with subject." She closed with an admonition: "Now, dearest Mama Bess, don't get excited and rattled about this. On the other hand, think about it, and don't overlook anything. If you'll just calmly do as I tell you, you will see that my predictions come out, in the end, however fantastic they sound to you."[20]

Judging from Lane's next letter to her mother—also dated that November—Wilder was dismayed that the kitchen piece was no longer her own:

> I'm sorry that—as you say—knowing it was my work that sold takes some of the joy out of it. It wasn't really *my* work. Please, don't run off with that idea. Dearest Mama Bess, in some ways you're like a frolicsome dog that won't stand still to listen; you are always grabbing and jumping and in a hurry. Listen. Please please, *listen.* All I did on your story was an ordinary re-write job. Don't go saying that you're glad I liked your other one, that it gives you courage. The thing that should give you courage is that this one sold.

Frankly, nothing is more humiliating to writers than to see their work come back edited or rewritten—no matter how ordinary the rewrite job. Wilder's reaction was ordinary in itself, something Lane should have recognized. She was clearly a gifted editor, but her editorial style must have been difficult to bear. She told her mother in the same letter, "You don't know how to write stuff for Country Gentleman. You never will know, until you stop and listen to what I tell you."[21] Lane's advice may have been sound, her editorial instincts solid, but she lacked another important talent that the best editors share: the ability to nurture writers and help them find a unique voice. As children's book editor Margery Cuyler points out, "The editor has a responsibility to articulate the strengths of a book [or article] as well as the sore points and to help the author revise without taking over and becoming the author."[22]

Whatever her intentions, Lane seemed more interested in forcing her mother's writing career into a mold much like her own, rather than teasing out Wilder's unique talent and deeper creative interests. Furthermore, Lane's tone toward her mother was patronizing—Wilder was a frolicsome dog that was simply untrainable. The subtext in Lane's letters from this period was often about power and control. She saw no reason why her mother should not have been earning thousands of dollars a year for the last five years, except that she did not take her daughter's advice. "You'd rather do the washing," Lane complained. "It isn't fair, now is it, really? Just because I was once three years old, you honestly oughtn't to think that I'm never going to know anything more than a three-year-old. Sometime you ought to let me grow up."[23] Ultimately, Wilder acquiesced to Lane's revisions, and "My Ozark Kitchen" was published in *Country Gentleman* on 17 January 1925; a second article, "The Farm Dining Room" was published later that year. Wilder, however, gave up on the magazine writing career her daughter envisioned for her and kept her creative ambitions to herself, focusing her attention elsewhere.

During the late 1920s, Wilder helped form the Athenian and Justamere Clubs, all-women groups devoted to intellectual inquiry and current events. From 1917 until 1927, she worked as secretary-treasurer of Mansfield's National Farm Loan Association, which granted farm improvement and development loans to small family farms. This position held authority and fiscal responsibility; her understanding of the business of farming explained her long tenure with the organization. *Missouri Ruralist* editor John F. Case praised Wilder's work for the association, remarking that her fiscal reports were perfect. In 1925, Wilder used her experience with the Farm Loan Association as a platform to run for the position of collector for the Pleasant Valley Township in Wright County. The only woman in a three-way race and running as an independent, she lost to a Republican in a Republican county. Wilder's activities during the late 1920s underscored not only her involvement with her community, but her business savvy and natural curiosity about national and international events. As a woman in her fifties, she was not an isolated, rural farm woman, nostalgic for the past. She was active and engaged with her world.[24]

Lane spent much of the 1920s living, working, and traveling abroad. She had divorced Gillette Lane in 1918, traveled across Europe with the Red Cross at the end of World War I, and explored the postwar Muslim world from Albania to Iraq. In between, she visited Rocky Ridge Farm. In fact, she lived at Rocky Ridge with Wilder and Manly from 1924 through 1926. During this period, a *Kansas City Star* reporter even identified the farmhouse as belonging to Lane, saying, "It's the kind of a house a writer who dreams dreams should have."[25] By the late 1920s, however, despite her impressive accomplishments as a writer, significant questions had emerged about Lane's artistic integrity and originality. Almost from the beginning of her writing career, she had focused on nonfiction, writing profiles about ordinary people for the *San Francisco Bulletin,* then branching out to *Sunset* magazine with pieces on such celebrities as Charlie Chaplin and Jack London. In 1920, *Sunset* magazine published her biography on Herbert Hoover in installments. Yet, Lane did not always stick to the facts. She fictionalized these biographies, making what her own biographer termed an "easy ethical slide," not just between fact and fiction, but between the truth and what would sell—and by extension, what would advance her career. By 1925, as her biographies came under closer critical scrutiny, Lane had edged more openly toward fiction, revising her serialized biography of Jack London into a novel, entitled *He Was a Man.*[26]

Complicating her image even further was the work Lane had done as a ghost writer on Frederick O'Brien's memoir, *White Shadows on the South Sea*, which became a bestseller during the 1920s. How much was pure invention and how much was fact? Furthermore, who wrote what? Where did O'Brien's work end and Lane's begin? She maintained that much of the work was hers, and she eventually took O'Brien to court. She won a modest settlement of twelve hundred dollars, which tapped into his earnings on the book.[27] Yet, Lane still saw the need to answer a public perception of dishonesty. "The important fact," she wrote to one of her accusers, "is that WHITE SHADOWS was not an attempt to cheat the public by selling lies as facts. So far as I know, there was no misrepresentation in the book."[28] In another letter to yet another critic, she added, "I rewrote it [*White Shadows*] but did not add or alter a fundamental fact."[29] These letters foreshadowed the questions readers and critics would have about the literal truth of Wilder's Little House novels and the role Lane played in creating them.

By the end of the decade, Lane was unsure about her career path. She was certainly drawn toward fiction, and she had successfully published short stories and bestselling novels. Nevertheless, she struggled with the idea that her work lacked artistry, that she wrote what sold rather than what would endure.[30] In a letter to fellow writer Clarence Day, she confided her insecurities. "There is no reason why I shouldn't settle down to short stories, except that my mind naturally runs to longer things," she said. "I don't know why, for heaven knows that everything there is to know about a novel coincides precisely with what I don't know about it. It isn't only a question of technique; I don't know the *feel* of a novel. . . . I don't know what a novel is when I meet it."[31]

Despite her professional insecurities, Lane continued her effort to exert control over her parents' lives. Starting in 1924, she sent five hundred dollars a year to Rocky Ridge Farm, certainly a generous gesture, though she continued to borrow from her parents, especially when she traveled abroad. In 1925, she bought her parents a 1923 blue Buick sedan, which they christened "Isabelle," then set out to teach them how to drive. Such generosity was not always easy to sustain. The freelancer's life was one of feast or famine. A lean year could be followed by fat; *Country Gentleman*, for example, paid Lane ten thousand dollars to serialize her novel *Cindy*. Wilder recognized the financial whims Lane endured as a freelance writer and worried about the sacrifices she imposed on herself to support her parents.[32] "We thank you a lot for sending us checks if you can spare them," Wilder wrote in the 1930s. "But we neither of us want you to work so hard because you feel you must help us. You are a dear, sweet thing to us all the time. You and your comfort and well being are more to us than anything else."[33] The wild swings in their daughter's income, however, did not shake Wilder and Manly's confidence in Lane's financial counsel; during the 1920s, they entrusted their investments to her. She placed virtually everything they had, along with her own money, into the investment firm of Palmer & Company in New York.[34]

In 1928, after intermittent years of travel and unsure

about the future of her own writing career, Lane decided to return to Rocky Ridge Farm. She was determined to build her own dream house there, just as her parents had done fifteen years earlier, but she would build her dream house for them—and she would move into their farmhouse. Once again, Lane planned to impose her will on theirs.

What happened next surprised them all.

12

Like her mother before her, Rose Wilder Lane had a clear
vision of what the ideal house at Rocky Ridge should be, but
hers was vastly different from Wilder's. She envisioned "a
darling cottage, sort of modified English cottage architec-
ture, done in field stone and Johns Manville Colorblende
shingles, with brick window-sills and a tiny bit of a brick ter-
race."[1] And unlike the farmhouse at Rocky Ridge, which ful-
filled Wilder's personal view of a house as the product of the
land around it, Lane's Rock House would draw on talent and
resources well beyond Wright County, Missouri. The basic
floor plan, essentially a five-room bungalow, was modified
from a generic mail-order design.[2] Lane hired a Springfield
architect, Eugene F. Johnson, to help her revise the plan and
bring a little piece of England to Rocky Ridge. "Do not worry
about placing an English house on a hillside," he wrote Lane.
"I have done this before with good results."[3] The contractor
came from Springfield, too; as did the lumber and the furniture, which came from two of Springfield's most prestigious
establishments.[4] Clearly, Lane built the Rock House to suit
her own tastes. As it took shape over the summer of 1928,
she and her companion, Helen Boylston, who joined Lane at
Rocky Ridge in June, drove to Springfield frequently to meet
with the architect, choose and inspect materials, and select
furnishings. At the same time, Lane planned and financed
extensive electrical, plumbing, and heating updates to the
farmhouse.[5]

Wilder and Manly were not involved in any of these decisions, except the biggest: for some inexplicable reason, they
agreed to move into Lane's dream house and give her theirs.

In a letter to her former editor at the *San Francisco Bulletin*, Lane explained that her mother "wanted a new house, but didn't want to bother with it in the building stages" and that she would not even see the house until it was finished.[6] Did Wilder really want a new house? Or was it simply easier to give in to Lane's plans? Did it occur to anyone that summer that the best solution would be for Lane and Boylston to move into the Rock House and leave Wilder and Manly in their own comfortable farmhouse? Yet, Lane seemed bent on presenting her parents with an English cottage, one that reflected her own and, by extension, superior tastes. Her one concession to Wilder: the exterior of the cottage was field-stone, a building material that Wilder had praised a decade earlier in the *Missouri Ruralist*.[7] As the Rock House slowly neared completion, Lane's tension rose. "The architect says, this is the period in the building of a house when the only thing to do is take plenty of aspirin, set the teeth, and hang on," Lane confided to a friend.[8] The architect himself, in a diplomatic note to Lane, hit on what was perhaps the major source of tension. He expressed his hope that Lane's parents would find enjoyment in the new house. "I know it will be a dramatic moment when your mother views the new home for the first time," he wrote.[9]

Wilder herself left no record of the dramatic moment, when, at Christmastime 1928, she stepped into the Rock House for the first time. "I am happy your mother was pleased with the house," the architect wrote to Lane shortly after the unveiling. "With that news I feel more than paid."[10] Obviously, Lane had told Johnson that her parents admired the house, but in a more candid moment, she wrote a close friend that an "unexpected turn of events," which she refused to describe, had robbed her of the thrill she had anticipated when Wilder saw the house for the first time.[11] Perhaps the Rock House never felt like home to Wilder. She would write "Pioneer Girl" and the first four novels of the Little House series in the Rock House, but as soon as Lane moved out of the farmhouse in 1935, Wilder and Manly moved back in and lived there the rest of their lives. Ultimately, she rejected Lane's dream house and the vision her daughter had imposed on her.

For Lane the gift was more extravagant than she expected. She had planned to spend four thousand dollars on it; instead, she spent eleven thousand, which probably explained why she did not continue to work with Johnson and embark on the next phase of her plans for Rocky Ridge—the building of a large, English-style lodge.[12] It was just as well she did not, for the lives of everyone living on Rocky Ridge Farm changed dramatically after October 1929, when the American stock market crashed.

"I am not yet actually broke " Lane wrote her literary agent in 1932, "but I contemplate that horrid future. . . . Just keep this in mind, would you? I mean, think of me as available if you see anywhere an opening suited to my talents."[13] From 1930 until well into 1932, money was tight for both households on Rocky Ridge Farm. The stock market crash wiped out the Wilders' investments in the Palmer Company. Lane felt a deep sense of responsibility for her parents' losses because she had recommended that they invest their money along with hers. As the Great Depression deepened and the family's financial losses mounted, Lane considered her parents to be financial "dependents." Rocky Ridge Farm offered the Wilders, Lane, and Helen Boylston, who was still living there, subsistence—but little else. Although magazine and book publishers across the country had slashed their budgets and were buying fewer and fewer new manuscripts, Lane continued to correspond with her literary agent in New York, hoping her reputation as a leading writer in the 1920s would carry her through the crisis.[14]

For Wilder herself, the crash apparently brought her a new sense of creative freedom. No longer interested in writing for the "big markets" as Lane had urged her to do, Wilder chose instead to follow her heart. In 1930, she began to work steadily on her autobiography, "Pioneer Girl." Wilder left nothing behind to explain why she chose this particular moment to write her life story, but perhaps it was triggered by a personal loss, not a financial one. On 17 October 1928, Mary Ingalls died. Just days before her death, Carrie Ingalls Swanzey wrote Wilder from her home in Keystone, South Dakota, where she was caring for Mary: "She has lost her speech and Laura I doubt if she rallies. The trained nurse was up from Rapid [City] on a baby case, and came to see her, she said nothing could be done and the Dr came and said so too. . . . She is not suffering just sleeping, real quiet." Mary was sixty-three.[15]

Charles Ingalls's death in 1902 had prompted Wilder to write a short sketch about her life on Silver Lake; a year after Caroline Ingalls's death in 1924, Wilder had written to her Aunt Martha Carpenter for stories about her mother's childhood. Losing her sister and perhaps aware for the first time of the certainty of her own mortality, Wilder may have decided she could no longer delay this project, which had been simmering for twenty-eight years. She wrote her first draft quickly, including occasional personal asides to Lane. In a section labeled "private," Wilder noted that shortly after Freddy's birth, "we caught the itch at school and couldn't touch the baby. Gosh how it did itch and Ma rubbed us with sulpher [sic] and grease and turned us before the fire to heat it in. We had an awful time."[16]

As this passage revealed, Wilder was writing "Pioneer Girl" for both a private and a public audience. She intended the manuscript for national publication and assumed that Lane would read and review it before sending it on to the Brandt agency. In the process, Lane suggested or simply made significant revisions to the manuscript. Here, for example, is how the typewritten Brandt version of "Pioneer Girl" begins: "Pa stopped the horses. 'Well, Caroline,' he said, 'Here's the place we've been looking for. Might as well camp.'"[17] Wilder's handwritten version opened with "Once upon a time."[18]

Other variations in the two manuscripts were more extensive. The Brandt manuscript painted fuller, more complete scenes, and it often provided perspective on the unfolding story, contrasting frontier experiences with the twentieth century or connecting Wilder's memories to her childhood self. In her original draft of "Pioneer Girl," for example, Wilder included a brief but vivid memory about an incident during a blizzard at Plum Creek in which two balls of fire came down the stovepipe in a storm. "We were frightened thinking the house would burn, but the balls though they looked like fire didn't burn anything. They would follow Ma's knitting needle around the floor and soon seemed to melt away and disappeared. Pa said they were electricity."[19] Here is that same scene in the Brandt version:

> At first we were frightened, thinking the house would burn, but though the balls looked like fire they did not even scorch anything. They rolled here and there on the floor, and when Ma drew her steel knitting needle along before them they followed it and seemed to be playing like kittens. Then they melted away and disappeared. Pa said they were electricity.
>
> Mary and I had never heard of electricity before. But Pa told us that it was everywhere—like God, I thought; that it was the lightning and that it was the crackling in a cat's fur when you stroked it.[20]

Because Wilder and Lane lived less than a mile apart, usually walking back and forth almost daily over a path connecting the two houses across the top of Rocky Ridge, they did not leave behind any correspondence that documents exactly how this collaboration worked.[21] There is no way to know conclusively if Wilder discussed the changes her daughter suggested before Lane typed the Brandt version, or if, as a seasoned newspaper editor might do, Lane simply took out a blue pencil and revised the manuscript on her own—without her mother's blessings.

It is hard to imagine, however, that Wilder would passively accept her daughter's editorial changes on a project that was so precious to her. She had always taken a great deal of pride in her writing and a sense of ownership about anything that appeared under her byline. During the 1920s, she had worried that Lane's changes to her manuscripts for *McCall's* and the *Country Gentleman* were so extensive that the articles were no longer her own. And later, in correspondence from the late 1930s after the Little House series was well underway, Wilder was passionately engaged in the editorial process. She argued with Lane about plot, characterization, and structure. In fact, Wilder often considered Lane's suggestions flat-out wrong. "I have given you a true picture of the times and the place and the people," she wrote Lane in 1938. "Please don't blur it."[22] To suggest, as some Wilder and Lane experts have, that Wilder was not engaged in the editorial process is to deny both her previous work as a writer and the later trail of correspondence between the two women.[23] Furthermore, in 1930, when Wilder wrote "Pioneer Girl," she envisioned the book as her life work, her legacy as a writer. A series of books, let alone a *fictional* series of books, had not yet flickered across Wilder's mind. Lane herself records in her diary that her mother hoped for prestige with her autobiography, not money.[24] Wilder cared deeply about "Pioneer Girl."

In May 1930, Lane sent the typewritten version of her mother's autobiography, a 160-page manuscript, off to Brandt and Brandt, who tried to market it, not as a book, but as a serial to national magazines. Rejections began to filter in almost immediately—from many of the magazines in which Lane herself had successfully published serials, including the *Saturday Evening Post*. These initial rejections do not necessarily reflect the literary merit of "Pioneer Girl."

Times were tough, even for well-established writers, and Lane herself sold only two manuscripts that year. Business was so bad that, despite the desperate state of her finances, Lane went to New York that fall and did what writers normally do in this situation: she fired her literary agent and hired a new one—George T. Bye.[25]

While in New York, however, Lane continued to promote "Pioneer Girl" and, despite more rejections, heard positive comments from editors about it. The *Ladies Home Journal* turned it down in November, but Lane met with Grahaeme Lorimer of the *Saturday Evening Post,* who told her it was "a grand piece of work, fascinating material and 'most intelligent writing,'" Lane wrote to Wilder, "and that they would undoubtedly have taken it, only they have in their safe some material which, broadly speaking, covers the same field." Lane then added: "They said if the same material were used as a basis for a fiction serial they'd take it like a shot. But I know you don't want to work it over into fiction."[26] The following year, the *Country Home* magazine rejected "Pioneer Girl" for the same reason. Wilder's autobiography, the editors wrote, "contains some very interesting pioneer reminiscences," but the magazine had "no place for non-fiction serials."[27] The market in 1930 and 1931 was ripe for fiction. Lane took note of this fact for her mother and eventually for herself.

13

Not a Great
Deal of Money
1931–1932

Despite the steady stream of rejections for "Pioneer Girl," Wilder refused to give up on it. George Bye, Lane's new literary agent, did not admire the manuscript, but he dutifully continued to market it to magazines, book publishers, and even as an entry to the *Atlantic Monthly*-Little Brown writing contest in 1933.[1] Unfortunately, "Pioneer Girl" never found a home, but Wilder and her daughter were already working on another project—a picture book for children, called "When Grandma Was a Little Girl." The twenty-two-page manuscript opened in this way: "When Grandma was a little girl, she lived in a little gray house made of logs. The house was in the Big Woods, in Michigan." The word "Michigan" is crossed out and replaced by "Wisconsin" in Wilder's handwriting.[2]

Lane had pieced this manuscript together from episodes in "Pioneer Girl," possibly without Wilder's knowledge. Wilder may have learned for the first time about the manuscript in a letter from Lane, who was still in New York in early 1931. "It is your father's stories, taken out of the long PIONEER GIRL manuscript," Lane explained, "and strung together as you will see." What motivated Lane to create a picture book text from her mother's autobiography is not clear, but she obviously recognized that sections from "Pioneer Girl" were better suited to young readers than to adults. This adaptation may have been the most significant professional favor Lane bestowed on her mother, for ultimately it launched Wilder's career as a children's book writer. It moved her pioneer material away from adult editors, who saw it primarily as reminiscences about the good old days, and into the hands of children's book editors, who immediately recognized its unique literary qualities. Although Lane had strung the manuscript together for "When Grandma Was a Little Girl," she clearly viewed the work as Wilder's. "You make such perfect pictures of everything," she wrote her mother, and "the characters are absolutely *real*. . . . It is really your own work, practically word for word."[3]

Lane sent the "Grandma" manuscript to her friend, children's book author and illustrator Berta Hader, who, in turn, shared it with Marion Fiery of the Children's Book Department at the publishing house of Alfred A. Knopf. Fiery was interested in the manuscript right away and wrote Wilder an enthusiastic letter about it. "I like the material you have used," Fiery commented, "it covers a period in American history about which very little has been written, and almost nothing for boys and girls." Aspiring writers of children's books always dream of getting a letter like this one, but, and there is always a *but* when editors communicate with writers, Fiery wanted revisions before issuing Wilder a contract on the book, a standard request in children's book publishing then and now. "Would you be willing to make some editorial changes on the manuscript?" Fiery queried.[4]

In this initial letter, Fiery asked Wilder to lengthen the manuscript and to add more details "about the everyday life of the pioneers, such as the making of the bullets, what they eat and wear, etc."[5] This point was critically important because, if Wilder agreed, it would shift the entire focus of the story. Fiery hoped that "When Grandma Was a Little Girl" would become, not a memoir, but a fictional story that captured the essence of life as a pioneer, something vivid and appealing that would fire children's imaginations. Her suggestion to Wilder illustrated one of the key responsibilities of a children's book editor—to help writers give their work shape and meaning. "The editor's duty is to the work itself—the story," explains Regina Griffin, vice-president and editor-in-chief at Holiday House. "I attempt to see what the book wants to be—and move on from there." In this context, there is nothing extraordinary in Fiery's initial letter to Wilder; it is exactly how children's book editors and the writers they choose to work with have communicated since the early twentieth century.[6]

Fiery leveled two specific criticisms at the "Grandma" manuscript, as well. "How do you feel," she wrote, "about the use throughout of 'Ma' and 'Pa'? It is probably more authentic, but somehow it seems a little colloquial to me." Obviously, editors can sometimes be wrong, and Fiery would eventually change her mind. "Ma" and "Pa" remained. Her second criticism concerned the title; "When Grandma Was a Little Girl" did not "convey the true character of the book." She asked for something stronger.[7] In fact, this last criticism had implications beyond the title and touched on a flaw in the "Grandma" manuscript, one that is common to writers new to the field of children's books. When Lane pieced together the manuscript from "Pioneer Girl," she recast the story from an adult point of view. "At night, when Grandma lay in her trundle bed," the short manuscript read, "she could not hear anything at all but the sound of all the trees whispering together." When a wolf howled in the night, "Grandma knew that wolves ate little girls. But Grandma was safe inside the log walls."[8] A grandma, even a grandma who appears in a story as a little girl, is not a strong leading character for young readers. It places too much distance between reader, main character, and story. The fact that the "Grandma" manuscript had a historical setting heightened the problem. Marion Fiery met with Lane in New York, where they probably discussed this issue, because Lane addressed it specifically when she wrote Wilder a few days later. "We will start right off with Laura, and not say anything about Grandma," she declared.[9]

Although Lane was a seasoned and successful writer, she had little prior experience writing fiction for children. Her only published work for young readers had appeared after

World War I in the *Junior Red Cross Magazine*.[10] Nevertheless, armed with the discussion she had had with Fiery, Lane felt sufficiently qualified to write a long editorial letter to Wilder, with more suggestions for extending the manuscript. In this letter, she tackled important artistic decisions about audience, structure, and point of view. "Marion says that we are wrong in thinking they are stories for *little* children; it is not picture book material, but must be for children from 8 to 10," Lane wrote. About structure, she suggested her own idea—that the book should cover an entire year. For point of view (the perspective from which the story would be told), she advocated, probably on Fiery's advice, that her mother write it in third person, as a young Laura Ingalls would have experienced the events. "For juveniles," she told Wilder confidently, "you can not use the first person, because the 'I' books do not sell well." With little confidence in Wilder's ability to handle the nuances of point of view, Lane added that if she found it more comfortable to write it in first person, then to go ahead and "I will change it into the third person."[11]

As extraordinary as Lane's letter may appear, it fell well within the boundaries of a typical editorial letter, which is an essential form of communication between editors and writers about the books on which they collaborate. Margery Cuyler, publisher at Marshall Cavendish Children's Books, explains that an editorial letter outlines "general revision themes," which deal with "structural weaknesses," "language and transitions," "small cuts or places that need expansion," and a "final cleaning up of all that has gone before."[12] Regina Griffin at Holiday House tailors her communication to writers individually, but "a long editorial letter" is often the best way to discuss a variety of artistic issues, dealing with structure, plot, character, and point of view. In one instance, Griffin recalls that she provided extensive structural advice on a manuscript, and after several revisions, "the author was brave enough to give up a huge amount of past work, but the novel shone from her work—it was an astonishing work of revision."[13]

What was unusual about the editorial letter Wilder received from Lane was not its content, but the fact that it came from Lane, not from Fiery. This radical distinction established the way Wilder and Lane would work together for the rest of Wilder's literary career. Lane intervened and took on the role of editor, leaving little for Wilder's actual editors to do, as Ursula Nordstrom at Harper & Brothers later observed.[14] Lane's "Grandma" editorial letter provided much more detail than Fiery's initial one, and it was much longer, covering three typewritten, single-spaced pages. Lane provided solid advice, gleaned in part from her meeting with Fiery in New York. And, after meeting with Lane, Fiery probably saw no need to write Wilder a lengthy editorial letter.

Lane's letter made another radical departure from standard editorial letters: its tone did not always express confidence in the writer. "An editor's main role," explains Cuyler, "is to bring out the best in the author. An editor and author's relationship is intimate and built on trust. It's different from any other relationship because it's a shared journey into the imagination. The imagination is fragile as is the ego, so the editor must step carefully."[15] Lane's offhand comment about Wilder's possible inability to switch points of view, for example, was insulting, as was her suggestion that she herself could better handle this critical revision. In short, Lane did not understand how to nurture her mother's creativity; she preferred to dictate this process. She had her own vision of what her mother's work should be. Yet, as Griffin points out, an editor's central responsibility is "to help the author get the story as close to the author's vision as possible."[16]

Although Lane wrote Wilder that under Fiery's direction, Knopf "will certainly make a beautiful book" out of "When Grandma Was a Little Girl," she added, "I do not think you will make a great deal of money out of the book," but "you will have those stories preserved in book form, and beautifully, which after all is the main thing."[17] Like many writers for adult readers, Lane had little respect for the artistry of children's book writers, and this lack seeped through in her first editorial letter to Wilder. She clung to this idea throughout the 1930s and even apologized to her literary agent for asking him to represent her mother. "It's really awfully decent of you to bother with this small fry . . . And I don't expect you really to bother. I want it to be nothing more than a bit of semi-annual office routine which will adequately pay for itself," she told Bye.[18] The contradictions and tensions evidenced in these exchanges reflected the larger, more pervasive conflicts between mother and daughter. The next two years would deepen the gulf between them, even as it brought their careers closer together.

Despite the tone of Lane's editorial letter, Wilder set to work making the suggested revisions. She tackled the shift in point of view herself—from the first-person narrative of her memoir to the third-person perspective of her new fictional persona, Laura. Here, for example, is an early draft of Wilder's opening for what would become *Little House in the Big Woods*: "Once upon a time, long ago, a little girl lived in the Big Woods of Wisconsin, in a little gray house made of logs." Wilder added more details, fleshing out descriptions of Pa making bullets, Ma making butter, Mary learning to sew. Wilder took Lane's advice and built the narrative for the book around a calendar year, and she wrote the story for eight- to ten-year-old readers. One of the most important characteristics of a dedicated writer is her willingness to revise; Wilder certainly passed that test.[19]

Just as she had done when she drafted "Pioneer Girl," Wilder wrote revisions for the "Grandma" manuscript on ordinary school tablets with an ordinary school pencil. She wrote in fits and starts. "The only way I can write," she explained later, "is to wander along with the story, then rewrite and re-arrange and change it everywhere."[20] Even in her rough drafts, she made notes to herself and to Lane.

She ripped a piece of paper from one of her tablets to note, "lean-to is spelled with a hyphen, but I just found it out and I may miss some that I have written without."[21] Wilder was a thoughtful, hard-working writer, who chose her words carefully. "You will hardly believe the difference the use of one word rather than another will make until you begin to hunt for a word with just the right shade of meaning, just the right color for the picture you are painting with words," she told an audience after publication of her first three books, adding, "The only stupid thing about words is the spelling of them."[22] When ideas came to her suddenly and unexpectedly, she wrote them down, even years later, on the back of fan letters.[23]

As always, Wilder respected her daughter's expertise and submitted her revised manuscript for Lane's review. By then Lane was once again back at Rocky Ridge Farm. Consistent with her journalism background, she made significant and aggressive line edits to Wilder's manuscript—shortening phrases, restructuring sentences, changing vocabulary, even shifting paragraphs around. Here, for example, is a passage near the beginning of Wilder's revised manuscript:

> Wolves lived in the Big Woods and bears and huge wildcats. Muskrats and mink and otter lived by the streams. Foxes had dens in the hills and deer roamed everywhere.
>
> But in all the miles and miles and miles of trees there were only a few little log houses scattered far apart just where the Big Woods began. And so far as the little girl could see there was only the one, little gray house where she lived with her Father and Mother and her sister Mary and baby sister Carrie. A wagon track ran before the house turning and twisting among the trees of the woods where the wild animals lived.
>
> The little girl was named Laura and she called her father Pa and her mother Ma, not Father and Mother or Papa and Mama as children do now.[24]

In the final published version of this novel, the passage reads:

> Wolves lived in the Big Woods, and bears, and huge wild cats. Muskrats and mink and otter lived by the streams. Foxes had dens in the hills and deer roamed everywhere.
>
> To the east of the little log house, and to the west, there were miles upon miles of trees, and only a few little log houses scattered far apart in the edge of the Big Woods.
>
> So far as the little girl could see, there was only the one little house where she lived with her Father and Mother, her sister Mary and baby sister Carrie. A wagon track ran before the house, turning and twisting out of sight in the woods where the wild animals lived, but the little girl did not know where it went, nor what might be at the end of it.
>
> The little girl was named Laura and she called her father, Pa, and her mother, Ma. In those days and in that place, children did not say Father and Mother, nor Mamma and Papa, as they do now.[25]

Words and phrases have changed slightly in the two passages, but Wilder's essential voice remains consistent, unique, and appealing in both.

Lane noted in her diary of May 1931 that she spent five days revising and editing the manuscript, and two days typing it. She also recorded the days on which Wilder herself was at the Rocky Ridge farmhouse, discussing the manuscript, brainstorming more ideas, and reading Lane's final edits.[26] These entries were brief and did not reveal whether Wilder questioned Lane's changes or accepted them unequivocally. Lane wrote to Marion Fiery before sending her the final draft of the revised manuscript: "I don't know just where or how I come into this, do you? But somehow I do, because my mother naturally consults me about everything concerning her writing."[27] Lane may have been trying to pre-

pare Fiery for a manuscript that would need virtually no editing; after all, Lane had done Fiery's work for her, except for
one important element: the manuscript's title.

Among the Wilder papers in the Herbert Hoover Presidential Library, a typewritten sheet of paper identified simply as "Laura Ingalls Wilder, Mansfield, Missouri, Suggested titles" lists twelve possibilities. Eight of these Lane and
perhaps Wilder herself rejected. Heavy typewritten strike-
outs make them virtually illegible, but through the lens
of a magnifying glass in good light, a few of those rejected
titles emerge: "Long Ago in the Big Woods," "The Days before Yesterday," and "Little Girl in the Wild West." The leading contenders on this list are "Trundle-bed Tales," "Little
Pioneer Girl," "Long Ago Yesterday," and "Little Girl in the
Big Woods."[28] Fiery rejected them all and settled on "Little
House in the Woods." She offered Wilder a three-book contract in September, with plans to publish the "Little House"
manuscript the following year.[29]

The fact that Fiery offered Wilder a three-book contract
does not necessarily mean she already envisioned a series; she simply hoped Wilder would write more children's
books. But it did signal Fiery's confidence in Wilder's ability to write and her department's belief that the first book
would be a strong seller. Wilder did not sign the contract
right away; instead, Lane sent it to George Bye, instructing
him to review it first, a routine request when an author is
represented by a literary agent. Then on 3 November 1931,
Lane received a handwritten letter from Fiery. "This is just
a little note to tell you that Mr. Knopf has decided to give
up the children's department the first of the year," the editor wrote. "So I shall not be there after that time." The news
came as a jolt to Wilder and Lane. Fiery explained, "My sec-
retary will run the job after I leave but just as a clerical assistant. . . . They are cutting down expenses."[30]

For books to be thus "orphaned" as editors were laid off,

fired, or moved to other publishing houses was not unusual in the 1930s or at any time. Book publishing, like any industry, is linked to the national and world economy, social and cultural trends, and the office politics unique to any business. Even a signed contract between an author and publisher does not ensure that a book will be launched successfully. Wilder, however, was uniquely blessed with a conscientious editor. Fiery cared deeply about "Little House in the Woods" and told Lane, "Under the circumstances I do not believe it would be wise for you to sign a three book contract here for your mother as heaven knows what will happen in the next three years." Fiery then made a truly extraordinary suggestion. "I should advise you to get in touch with George Bye and send your [manuscript] to Harpers or Macmillian's instead," she wrote. "I am heartbroken about the whole thing."[31]

Lane wrote back with uncharacteristic insecurity. "My mother does not know what to do and I dare not advise her, because I know nothing whatever of the juvenile field," she admitted. Her mother was "afraid that if Knopf does not publish it, she may not find another publisher for it," a fear common to many writers, especially with their first books. Above all, Lane wrote, Wilder simply wanted her book published, and "the royalties are not so much a matter of concern for her." Even though Fiery had maintained her confidence in Wilder's "Little House" manuscript, Lane had not. She hesitated to continue to consult literary agent George Bye. "I'm sure that at best there's not enough money in it to make it worth his while," she wrote Fiery. Bye was a good agent, she added, "but I don't feel like asking him to take on, as a favor to me, a lot of petty detail work on my mother's stuff; his time's too valuable."[32]

Lane's response may explain why Fiery took yet another extraordinary step. As Wilder telegraphed Knopf to delay the contract, Fiery contacted Virginia Kirkus, who headed the

Department of Books for Boys and Girls at Harper & Brothers.[33] Kirkus recalled years later that Fiery's telephone description of Wilder's book failed to ignite her interest: "'An elderly lady was writing a true story—in fictional form—about her pioneer childhood.' Well, I'd heard that tale before." Still, she agreed to meet Fiery for tea. Once she read the manuscript, Kirkus knew it was "the book no depression could stop."[34] Fiery, who had acted with unusual daring and speed on Wilder's behalf, also managed to convince Lane to keep George Bye involved with contract negotiations. On 8 December 1931, Kirkus wrote Wilder, "I am notifying Mr. Bye today that we are accepting your manuscript, LITTLE HOUSE IN THE WOODS. . . . It is so much easier to get good, colourful and dramatic material about other countries than our own, that it is always a pleasant surprise to find something that gives so graphically as does your manuscript a picture of the early days on our own frontiers."[35]

Despite its unequivocal acceptance, even Kirkus's letter contained a request for editorial changes to the manuscript. "May I take for granted your permission," she wrote, "to make certain editorial changes in the transitions between the main story and the anecdotes told within the story? There may be some other minor changes, but these seemed to me the most striking. I assure you that the pattern of the whole will not be touched, in any way."[36] Wilder responded with guarded optimism, especially concerning editorial changes. Less than a week later, Kirkus sent her another letter, explaining what she wanted. It was a question of point of view. "In some instances you have had the stories told by a person in the main story, and put into the first person, in other instances it has been thrown into the third person. This results in some confusion and shifts the emphasis inaccurately. We would not dream of making any changes that could in any way involve the very special setting of the story." Kirkus then assured Wilder that she would be able to review changes in both page and galley proofs.[37]

Wilder signed the contract with Harper & Brothers. Illustrator Helen Sewell signed on to do illustrations, and Kirkus made one last change to the title. *Little House in the Big Woods* was officially published on 6 April 1932 and debuted as a Junior Library Guild selection, which brought Wilder an additional flat royalty of $350. Wilder's first royalty check from the Bye agency came in at $529.69, a considerable sum during the Great Depression.[38]

The successful launch of *Little House in the Big Woods* fueled Wilder's desire to write its companion book about Manly and a year in the life of his family. The success of Wilder's first novel influenced Lane, as well. If her mother's stories about the frontier inspired the children of the depression, then surely those stories could be patched together for more discerning adult readers. And who was better qualified to write such a book than Lane herself? All she needed to do was rethink key episodes in "Pioneer Girl." Surely her mother would not mind.

14

Let the Hurricane Roar

1932–1933

Although Wilder's first contract with Harper & Brothers was only for one book—*Little House in the Big Woods*—she began work in late 1931 on the manuscript that would become *Farmer Boy.*[1] The three-book deal she had almost signed with Knopf may have inspired Wilder to dive right into another project. Whatever her motivation, the fact that she chose to start another book while *Little House in the Big Woods* worked its way through the publication process was not unusual. Even today, most writers are at work on a new manuscript while they await the publication of a previous one. What was significant, however, about Wilder's decision was that she chose to write something entirely new. She abandoned the source of her previous work—her own childhood experiences—and spun a story completely outside of herself. Granted, Wilder chose to focus on her husband's childhood, but she had no firsthand experience with the era and setting she chose to fictionalize. Manly was, after all, ten years older than Wilder; his family was more prosperous than hers; and his childhood story began back east, in Malone, New York.

Wilder's decision also revealed that, at this point, she had not envisioned a series of books that would showcase the American West and the frontier experience. *Farmer Boy*, like *Little House in the Big Woods,* focuses on a year in the everyday life of a nineteenth-century American farm family. Like the Ingalls clan in *Little House in the Big Woods*, the Wilders are content with their circumstances; they have no need to dream of a better future or of what lies west, just over the horizon. *Farmer Boy* was another story for the Great Depression; the book celebrates hard work, discipline, and simple home-style pleasures.

The subject also reflected Wilder's devotion to her husband. She had written about him as "the Man of the Place" with humor and affection in her *Missouri Ruralist* columns, even recreating in one a conversation about Manly's hardworking parents in Malone. "'Mother did all her sewing by hand then,'" the Man of the Place told Wilder, "'and she spun her own yarn and wove her own cloth. Father harvested his grain by hand with a sickle and cut his hay with a scythe. I do wonder how he ever got it done.'" Within the column, Wilder painted a picture of her and Manly sitting by the fire on a winter night, thinking about the past and resolving to find more pleasure in life. She ended the cosy scene with the Man of the Place lighting a lantern to make "his late round to see that everything was all right at the barns."[2] Letters she wrote to Manly when they were separated reveal a similar tenderness and intimacy. "It is cold here this morning and I have on my high shoes and a sweater," Wilder wrote her husband from Lakin, Kansas, in 1925. "Your warm underclothes are on your sock box in the closet. I can't remember whether I told you or not."[3] Wilder's new novel would honor Manly and preserve his family's stories just as *Little House in the Big Woods* had honored and preserved her father's.

Yet, her decision to choose this material for her second novel was also a shrewd one. It combined creative challenge and personal fulfillment with good business sense because it gave Wilder the chance to write a book for boys. Children's book publishers have long held that girls are more likely to read books about boys than boys are likely to read books about girls. By casting her second book about Manly—or Almanzo, as he appears in *Farmer Boy*—Wilder could conceivably broaden her audience, something vitally important during the Great Depression, when book sales were sluggish. *Farmer Boy* would at once compliment and balance *Little House in the Big Woods*.[4]

Wilder asked Lane to review the first draft of the manuscript in March 1932, a month before the publication date of *Little House in the Big Woods*. Lane edited the manuscript during May and June, then typed it in August.[5] Just a month later in September, Harper's rejected the manuscript of *Farmer Boy* as written.[6] Lane's own project, meanwhile, brought much more enthusiasm from publishers. She had started it in the fall of 1931, when it became clear that there was a market for her mother's frontier material as adult fiction, not autobiography. Belatedly, Lane came to believe that her mother's "Pioneer Girl" was "full of fascinating material about pioneer life in the Dakotas, the building of the railroads, home-steading, the coming of the grasshoppers, sod shanties, and the memorable Hard Winter of 1870 [*sic*]."[7] It just needed a writer of vision and experience to rewrite it in third person, transforming it into fiction.

A trip that Wilder and Manly took to South Dakota during the summer of 1931 may also have contributed to Lane's choice of subject matter. For Wilder, it was her first visit since Charles Ingalls's death in 1902; it was Manly's first since they left De Smet for Missouri in 1894. The memories this trip triggered for Wilder were deep and powerful. In her travel diary, she wrote, "It all makes me miss those who are gone, Pa and Ma and Mary and the Boasts and Cap Garland," who had died in 1891. A sense of sadness marked Wilder's reunion with her sisters, first with Grace Ingalls Dow, who was living in Manchester, South Dakota, a short distance from De Smet, and then a few days later with Carrie Ingalls Swanzey at her Black Hills home in Keystone, South Dakota. "Grace seems like a stranger only now and then something familiar about her face," Wilder observed. "I suppose it is the same with me." Carrie had changed, too, but Wilder had no trouble recognizing her. As always, the prairie itself stirred Wilder's emotions and inspired a wave of memories. She and Manly drove out past the Ingalls homestead across from the slough, "nearly in the place where Carrie and I walked to school and Manly used to drive Barnum and Skip as he came dashing out to take me on those long Sunday afternoon drives when I was seventeen. . . . Country looks as it used to, but there are houses and barns where the prairie used to sweep unmarked."[8] Wilder, of course, shared her impressions with Lane.

Perhaps the power of her mother's recent memories and the irrefutable interest the big markets held for a fictionalized version of "Pioneer Girl" combined to overcome Lane's initial ambivalence toward pioneer stories. Whatever her reasons, Lane also overcame her resistance to writing novels in general. Although she had written several before, she had questioned her own competency in the genre during the late 1920s.[9] By 1931, however, she had shed this insecurity; the markets had shifted and seemed to prefer fiction. The project Lane worked on that fall as Wilder wrote *Farmer Boy* was, in fact, a short novel for adult readers with the working title of "Courage." She pieced the work together using episodes, settings, and characters from "Pioneer Girl." Like *Little House in the Big Woods* and *Farmer Boy*, Lane's book would also be a novel for the depression. But Lane apparently told her mother nothing about the book's subject matter or themes. While she edited *Farmer Boy*, Lane also polished and revised her own novel, changing its title to "Let the Hurricane Roar," a hymn from Wilder's childhood. In September, at roughly the same time that Harper & Brothers refused *Farmer Boy*, the *Saturday Evening Post* accepted *Let the Hurricane Roar*, publishing it as a serial in October and November 1932. The story's main characters were named Charles and Caroline.[10]

For the first time, Wilder was deeply distressed by her daughter's success. And she felt betrayed.

Let the Hurricane Roar is set during the 1880s near a new, raw, unnamed railroad town or the western prairie. Like Charles Ingalls in *Little House in the Big Woods*, Lane's protagonist is named simply Charles—he "was laughing and bold, a daring hunter, a dancer, fiddler and fighter." Her Caroline "was a quiet person," who never loses the wonder that she had won "such a man as Charles." Both hail from the Big Woods of Wisconsin.[11] Lane melded and condensed material from the "Pioneer Girl" manuscript, which was filed upstairs in her desk at the Rocky Ridge farmhouse.[12] Her Charles and Caroline settle near a railroad camp as the real Ingalls family had. A "blowzy" woman, much like Wilder's Aunt Docia, runs the camp, and her children ride wild ponies bareback as Wilder and Lena had done. Lane described the lawlessness of the camp and included railroad riots from her mother's manuscript. When the camp breaks up for the winter, Lane's characters stay behind, just as the Ingalls family did, and like the real family, Charles and Caroline get the first shot at the best homestead site in the area.[13]

Lane's description of the homestead Charles chooses sounds like the one Charles Ingalls traded for on Plum Creek in Wilder's "Pioneer Girl." The circumstances are even similar: "On this homestead there was already a dugout and barn, and fifty acres of the sod were broken. Another man had taken the land and done all that work, yet he was giving up, he was going back east." Charles and Caroline's nearest neighbors, the Svensons, parallel the Nelsons from "Pioneer Girl." A shimmering grasshopper cloud descends and wipes out Charles and Caroline's crops. During an unusually hard winter, Charles and Caroline twist hay for fuel, and a herd of cattle, lost in a blizzard, stands motionless outside the dugout door: "Their own breath, steaming upward while they plodded before the storm, had frozen and blinded them."[14] Lane pulled out the most dramatic, most colorful elements of her mother's autobiography and distilled them into a kind of fictional pioneer elixir to fortify her readers against depression-era hopelessness.

Lane did make a few slight changes. "Wild Plum Creek," not Plum Creek, flows right outside Charles and Caroline's dugout door, and there is a slough nearby, which mirrors the setting at Silver Lake rather than Plum Creek. Throughout

Let the Hurricane Roar, Charles and Caroline are newlyweds, and their firstborn is a son, who survives. This change in the fate of the male infant is perhaps the most poignant and revealing one that Lane made to her grandparents' story— and by extension, to her mother's and her own. Baby Charles in *Let the Hurricane Roar* will someday inherit the future his parents envision for him.[15]

Lane's main characters are fictional variations of both her grandparents and her parents. In *Let the Hurricane Roar,* for example, Charles goes deeply into debt as Manly did, something the real Charles Ingalls largely avoided. Lane's Caroline eventually abandons her reserve and becomes the feminist ideal of a pioneer woman, facing adversity alone on the vast and vicious prairie. Lane's main characters share a greater intimacy than Wilder revealed in either her autobiography or her novels. The characters in *Let the Hurricane Roar* often abandon restraint; their dialogue feels modern and sometimes immature. At one point, Lane's Charles lashes out at Caroline: "'I'm not a baby! Losing a little sleep won't hurt me!'"[16]

Another major difference is the overall voice of *Let the Hurricane Roar,* which is colder, more abstract, and more overtly political than Wilder's "Pioneer Girl." In a critical scene roughly midway through the novel, Lane's Caroline rages against fate as "the angry sense of injustice welled up again. She hated the dugout . . . she hated the broken stove, the heat, the stripped, ugly prairie. She hated the wind that rasped her nerves and covered everything with dust. Her whole life seemed poor and mean. . . . They did not deserve this suffering. They had trusted and been betrayed."[17] Lane explicitly stated in 1933 that *Let the Hurricane Roar* was an affirmation of her belief in the American spirit. The novel was "a reply to pessimists," she wrote, and "written from my feeling that living is never easy, that all human history is a record of achievement in disaster."[18] Wilder never took an overtly political stance in her books, and the only time her fiction paralleled the sometimes strident and detached voice that Lane so often employed was in *The First Four Years*. And most critics and scholars criticized Wilder for it.

Let the Hurricane Roar, however, was an instant success. In 1933, less than a year after its publication in the *Saturday Evening Post*, Longmans, Green and Company produced it in book form. Critics raved. "In a way, the story is fiction; but more truly it is a thrilling chapter of American history," one reviewer enthused, "for the characters the author chooses to call Charles and Caroline might be any pair of the thousands upon thousands of hardy young pioneers who wrote with their axes and rifles and plowshares the Epic of the West."[19] Wilder, on the other hand, was dismayed by the book's success. Lane had raided her manuscript, lifted its most memorable and dramatic elements, and used them to create a bestseller. And she had done it, apparently, without Wilder's knowledge or permission. This amounts to plagiarism. If Wilder and Lane had not been mother and daughter, the case could have ended up in court, and there were those who thought it came close to doing so.[20]

Wilder must have also worried that Lane had robbed her of a literary future. The publication of *Let the Hurricane Roar* essentially killed any possibilities for "Pioneer Girl" in adult markets and perhaps even for juvenile ones. How many frontier stories about two characters named Charles and Caroline (and the grasshopper plagues and relentless blizzards they battled) could publishers afford to buy during the extraordinarily lean years of the depression? Lane was the established writer in the family. If she had covered this material in a publication as prestigious as the *Saturday Evening Post*, what could a relatively unknown writer like Wilder hope for? Already in her mid-sixties, Wilder statistically did not have a long writing future ahead of her. Furthermore, Wilder's immediate future looked dim. Harpers & Brothers, after all, had failed to embrace *Farmer Boy*. If Wilder had accepted her daughter's actions and success without any qualms, she would not have been an ambitious or discerning writer. Lane, in whom Wilder had entrusted her literary career, had dealt her a major and unexpected blow.

Lane's initial response to her mother's displeasure was remarkably naive, even insipid. She reported in her diary that she hid an advertisement promoting *Let the Hurricane Roar* from her mother out of a sense of "self-preservation," but when Wilder saw and read it "with an air of distaste," Lane remarked that her mother had effectively destroyed "the simple perfection of my pleasure."[21] Lane was apparently blind to the creative and moral implications of her actions. Perhaps it was her fatal flaw as a writer—insisting on the value of truth, honesty, and moral courage in print; yet blurring these values in her quest for publication and success. She had crossed the line earlier in her career with her biographies of Jack London and Herbert Hoover and the autobiography of Frederick O'Brien; she did it again with *Let the Hurricane Roar*, relying not on her own originality but on her mother's material for characterization, plot, and setting. In fact, even before *Let the Hurricane Roar* was finished, Lane had tried to sell her agent on another story pulled out of her mother's "Pioneer Girl" manuscript—one about "The Hard Winter." It was also during this period that she published several short stories that originated in "Pioneer Girl," including "Long Skirts" and "Object Matrimony."[22]

On some deeper level, Lane must have recognized the limitations of her own creativity and the wound she had dealt her mother, and by extension, herself. During the spring of 1933, she suffered from a deep depression. "Why am I such a monster?" she wrote in her journal. "I *am* a monster. I always have been. There is no true warmth in my nature. I have no heart."[23] A month later, she wrote: "I am mentally sick. Can't stop crying.' Lane suffered from bouts of depression throughout her life and often projected a bitter animosity toward Wilder.[24] Like her mother, Lane cared passionately about her own creativity, her worth as a writer, but she distrusted her talent. "Honest, never again. I shall never publish another book," she wrote in 1928.[25] Obviously, she changed her mind, and *Let the Hurricane Roar* solidified her reputation as a novelist. That her success had originated with her mother's work had to have undermined Lane's self-worth because, in her opinion, her mother was an inferior writer. Lane continued to undercut Wilder's value to George Bye, the literary agent they now shared. "I'm sorry to bother you about this small matter," Lane wrote in March 1933. "But I believe that over a period of years your office will make enough from my mother's work to square the account." A month later she added, "I like you and I like your business methods, and I know what my mother's books are worth to you and what they aren't." If they were too much trouble, Lane added, "it won't make a bit of difference between you and me if you'd rather not handle them."[26] Yet, Lane knew, at least subliminally, that her own recent success was directly linked to her mother's creative vision.

In retrospect, Wilder accepted the awkward situation that developed between herself and Lane during late 1932 and early 1933 with remarkable fortitude and resilience. She turned her attention away from *Let the Hurricane Roar* and back to *Farmer Boy,* beginning revisions to the manuscript. Second novels are often challenging, especially when a writer's first book is an unqualified success, as *Little House in the Big Woods* had been. What Wilder probably did not understand, and perhaps Lane did not grasp either, is that children's book publishers often ask for revisions *before* issuing a contract, even from authors they have successfully published in the past. Given Wilder's legendary reputation today, Harper's rejection of the initial *Farmer Boy* manuscript seems unfathomable, but as Ida Louise Raymond, Wilder's new editor at Harper & Brothers, would later point out, *Little House in the Big Woods* had "set a very, very high standard, quite enough to have reached once in a lifetime." Wilder's second book had to be worthy of her first.[27]

Perhaps to everyone's relief at Rocky Ridge Farm during the fall of 1932, Lane left for New York to meet with her agent, magazine editors, and publisher. She made a side trip to Malone, New York, the setting of *Farmer Boy* and, to her credit, sent Wilder extensive background information about the town, the Wilder family's old farm, and Lane's impressions of the countryside. "There is still the old stone wall on the left side of the road," she wrote. The Wilders' house was outwardly unchanged and painted white. "There are old lilac bushes in the yard, and I send you with this a twig from the balsam tree," Lane wrote.[28] The twig of balsam and the information became a kind of peace offering, on both a personal and professional level. Wilder needed more concrete details to bring her story about Manly's childhood to life, and Lane knew it, as both writer and editor. She made Malone a real, tangible place for her mother and gave her new literary material to replace what Lane herself had taken. In Malone, she searched out old-timers, who told her where to look for the old schoolhouse. "It is still the same & still a schoolhouse," she wrote to Wilder, "and we are going to see it tomorrow."[29]

Although the mother-daughter relationship remained strained when Lane returned to Rocky Ridge in 1933, they fell into their familiar roles when Wilder finished revisions of *Farmer Boy*. Lane again acted as editor before sending the typewritten manuscript to Ida Louise Raymond at Harper's. This time, she accepted the manuscript, but wrote Lane that it was "not quite another LITTLE HOUSE." She offered Wilder a contract that cut her royalties on the new book by fifty percent. Harper's had "much less money to manufacture the [second] book," Raymond wrote, because the depression was squeezing publishers even harder than the year before. Despite the extraordinary artistry of *Little House in the Big Woods*, its markets were dwindling, not from lack of interest, but from lack of disposable incomes. Other authors were already accepting the reduction in royalties,

Raymond soothed, explaining that this extraordinary measure reflected the harsh economic realities of 1933, not a lack of confidence in the book. "FARMER BOY," she assured Lane, "is excellent—different, sincere, authentic."[30]

Indeed, despite their similarities in structure and theme, *Farmer Boy* is dramatically different from *Little House in the Big Woods*. The difference hinges not so much on the setting or even the gender of the main character but on his growth and change within the story. Unlike Laura and Mary, who seem to be perpetual children, relatively unchanged by the events in *Little House in the Big Woods*, Almanzo is transformed by the end of *Farmer Boy*. He has matured, able at last to take on the responsibility he has long dreamed of: gentling a colt.[31] *Farmer Boy* has a clear forward motion: it fulfills the desires of its main character. *Little House in the Big Woods* is cyclical, ending with these lyrical, timeless lines: "She thought to herself, 'This is now.' She was glad that the cosy house, and Pa and Ma and the firelight and the music, were now. They could not be forgotten, she thought, because now is now. It can never be a long time ago."[32]

The distinction between the two books is important because it signals a shift in the way Wilder thought about her continuing career as a writer. By the spring of 1933, despite her concern that her pioneer material had been compromised, the rift between herself and her daughter, and the disappointing contract with Harper & Brothers, Wilder was at work on yet another book, one that would establish the overriding themes of her literary legacy: growth, change, and motion played out on the American frontier. "My mother is now doing another book about her childhood experiences among the Indians," Lane told their agent. It "promises to beat Little House all hollow."[33]

15

I Wish It Would Never Come to an End

1933–1935

"My teacher has read us the book of *The Little House in the Big Woods*," a fourth grader from Tipton, Iowa, wrote Wilder in 1933. "And I would like to know if you have any more books like it for I enjoyed the book very much. I wish it would never come to a [*sic*] end for it was so good."[1] This letter—and many more from enthusiastic readers across the country—certainly inspired Wilder to return to her own family story for her third novel. Wilder herself had thought the first book might be the end of her own family's recollections, but "children who read them wrote to me, begging for more," Wilder told a reporter in the 1950s. "I was amazed."[2] Yet, that fourth grader from Tipton, Iowa, would probably have been equally amazed had she known what Wilder did with her letter. It was one of perhaps a dozen that Wilder "recycled," scribbling on the other side her first attempts at an opening scene for the book she called "Indian Country." The letters Wilder recycled came from a variety of correspondents who had written her between 1931 and 1933: her daughter; *Missouri Ruralist* editor John F. Case; Ida Louise Raymond at Harper & Brothers; the State Historical Society of Missouri; and even the fourth-grade teacher from Tipton, Iowa, who wrote, "We are anxiously waiting for 'The Farmer Boy.'"[3]

The initial notes that Wilder made on the back of these letters give today's readers a glimpse into her writing process and the painstaking efforts she made to polish her manuscript before she turned it over to Lane for editing. "It was late afternoon as the white-topped covered wagon moved slowly across the prairie," Wilder's rough scribbles began. "The two black ponies seemed tired of pulling it and

Mary and Laura were tired of riding in it." A wavy line cut through these words, and Wilder began again on the next line. "A white-topped covered wagon moved slowly across the prairie drawn by two black ponies. A man and woman sat on the wagon seat in front. The man was driving, his bright blue eyes looking along the wagon trail ahead." Wilder tried several different approaches, scratching out phrases she did not like, circling words she wanted to change, and inserting whole sentences.[4]

By the time she was ready to write a more polished draft of "Indian Country," she had made even more revisions:

> A white-topped, covered wagon, drawn by two black ponies moved slowly across the prairie in Southern Kansas. A brindle bulldog trotted in the shade underneath.
>
> A man and a woman sat on the spring-seat at the very front of the wagon. The man was driving, his bright blue eyes looking ahead along the wagon trail, his brown beard blowing in the wind.[5]

Wilder was as concerned about historical accuracy as she was about choosing the right words and phrases for this version of "Indian Country." Perhaps she had learned this lesson from *Farmer Boy*, when Lane had supplied concrete details about Malone, which ultimately strengthened the historical integrity of the book. In 1933, Wilder wrote a letter to a regional expert on American Indian history. "I thought perhaps you could tell me the name of an Indian Chief that I have forgotten," Wilder wrote. She did not know which tribe he belonged to but specified the dates of 1870–1871.[6] Her contact suggested that it could have been Le-Soldat-du-Chêne, an Osage chief, who had been friendly to white people.[7] Wilder then sought confirmation with the Kansas State Historical Society, but the reply was disappointing; they could "not find any record of the story you are looking for about the Osage Chief in 1870–71."[8] After she exhausted historical sources, Wilder settled on her own interpretation of the past, for she was, after all, writing fiction, which gave her a certain amount of creative license—as long as what she wrote was true to the spirit of the times.

She finished her draft of "Indian Country" on 1 February 1934 and gave it to Lane for editing, who did not begin until May. Five weeks later, her work was finished. Among the most significant changes that Lane suggested was a new beginning, one that directly linked *Little House in the Big Woods* to "Indian Country." This new beginning provided context—an explanation why the Ingalls family, who had been content with their lives in their little log home, would suddenly abandon it. It also clarified Wilder's overriding theme. Lane recognized, perhaps as Wilder did not, that the central focus of the book was not just about Indian Country, but about moving west. In fact, Lane changed Wilder's title for the first chapter from "Going In" (to Indian Territory) to "Going West." In so doing, she helped her mother create a larger, overarching vision for this book and the ones yet to come. Again, within the context of children's book publishing, Lane's contribution, as important as it was, was not unusual. As children's book editor Regina Griffin observes, the editor's job is to work with writers to bring a shared vision to life.[9]

Lane's other major contribution to "Indian Country" was a refinement of point of view. Wilder's final draft was written in third-person omniscient. She moved freely from the thoughts of one character into another. For example, in one scene she wrote, "Mary would have been afraid but for Jack and Pa's gun that she could see hanging on the side of the wagon." This approach—shifting from Laura's into Mary's consciousness—and later into Ma and Pa's—made the voice of the author all-knowing, godlike, and less intimate. It also made it easier to manipulate plot and reveal the feelings and motivations of multiple characters. Novelists such as Charles Dickens, George Elliot, and Anthony Trollope had used this point of view. Lane, however, wisely recast the novel in third-person limited. The entire novel would be told exclusively from Laura's point of view. As a result, she could not possibly know, for example, that Mary would have been afraid. Laura could only *assume* this. This shift in point of view also meant that the man and woman on that spring seat became Ma and Pa—because that is what Laura would have called them.[10] This revision may seem subtle, but recasting the story from Laura's exclusive perspective clarified her role as the main character and gave "Indian Country," and ultimately the rest of Wilder's novels, its distinctive childlike voice, intimate and personal. Wilder continued to use this point of view (with rare exceptions) in her subsequent novels, allowing Laura's voice to mature, which, in turn, reinforced a secondary theme of the series: growth and change.

As critical as Lane's advice was on voice and point of view, it was, once again, simply part of an editor's job. Editors often ask writers to rewrite their novels from a different point of view, or they comment on the overall voice of a novel. "The voice here," editor Regina Griffin once wrote in an editorial letter, "is not yet sublime."[11] What is unusual in the context of creative writing, however, is that Lane took it upon herself to do much of the revising, a decision that, in turn, reflected both on her determination to exert control over Wilder's work and her past experience in the newspaper business. During 1935, when a sensitive, "literary" editor made gentle suggestions about Lane's own work, she wrote, "You are treating me like a New York literary lady. I am a middlewestern writer, trained in a San Francisco newspaper office by the toughest, most ruthlessly destructively critical and superlatively best of editors."[12]

After Wilder read and approved Lane's editorial changes, the two of them sent the manuscript off to Ida Louise Raymond for her approval at Harper's. Despite Lane's confidence in the strength of the story, Raymond was not sure about it. In July 1934, she wrote, "I have finished reading

'Indian Country,' and personally like it *very much* indeed, although I must confess my first reaction is: is there enough variety of detail in it to interest children of that age?" She then asked Wilder if she could send the manuscript to a midwestern librarian whose opinion Harper's valued. Roughly six weeks later, Raymond wrote Wilder again, this time to report that the librarian had liked the manuscript and "you can count on our having the book on the 1935 list." Raymond then made her own editorial decision, this time about the book's title. She and the unidentified librarian preferred "Little House on the Prairie" instead of "Indian Country." This change represented one of the rare editorial decisions Harper's would make about Wilder's books; Lane left them with little else to do.[13]

Although Wilder relied heavily on Lane and George Bye to negotiate a contract with Harper & Brothers for *Little House on the Prairie*, she had learned a great deal about the business side of publishing after working through the thorny and disappointing contract or *Farmer Boy*. Back in 1933, Wilder had initially refused to sign the *Farmer Boy* contract. Not only did Harper's cut her royalties on the book, but they initially claimed all rights to it, which would have prohibited Wilder from selling excerpts to such children's publications as *St. Nicholas*. As Lane shrewdly pointed out, "In return for the cut in royalties, Harper's should agree to keep the book actively before the trade through usual sales channels and to continue giving it publicity and Book Week displays." The only hope for extended revenue came from "its being kept actively alive on Harpers' new lists for a number of seasons."[14] The issues of copyright, royalties, ongoing publicity, and simply keeping a book in print continue to form the backbone of routine contract negotiations in children's book publishing today. Clearly, with *Farmer Boy* and even with *Little House on the Prairie*, neither Lane, Bye, Raymond, nor even Wilder herself envisioned that their contract negotiations centered on novels that would outlive most of the other children's book titles published during the 1930s. As contract negotiations for *Farmer Boy* dragged on, Bye wrote Lane, "If you can get a first class publisher to take a routine seller like a juvenile, with little chance for a flash sale, these days, at only slightly offish terms, I'd accept."[15] Even so, Wilder got at least one concession on the dismal *Farmer Boy* contract. "As far as promotion is concerned," Raymond wrote, "we have every intention of keeping the book before the trade through the usual channels until the sales drop below 200 a year." However, Harper's only agreed to display *Farmer Boy* during the all-important Book Week, where publishers unveiled their new books, in its publication year.[16]

Wilder and Lane would not accept such terms for *Little House on the Prairie*. Working with George Bye again, they successfully negotiated a more vigorous contract for it, in part because *Farmer Boy* had sold better than expected despite the depression. "Both the current books," Ida Louise Raymond wrote Wilder in 1934, "are doing very well, especially considering that January is always an extremely bad month for juveniles." During the first two months of the year, Harpers had sold 242 copies of *Farmer Boy* and 144 copies of *Little House in the Big Woods*. The same could not be said for most of the company's other juvenile books, of which they had sold only 10 to 25 copies each in the same period. "So you can see, that this is something to be quite proud of," Raymond concluded.[17] Wilder signed the contract for *Little House on the Prairie* on 26 October 1934, and the book was published the following year. But the *Farmer Boy* contract continued to trouble Wilder, even into the 1940s, when the book continued to sell well within the overall series. Harper's had not been fair in making adjustments on the novel, Lane wrote her agent. It was not so much the money that Wilder wanted as it was "the recognition of the credit due the book."[18]

Initial reviews of *Little House on the Prairie* were good,

and sales were brisk. Raymond at Harper's wrote to tell Wilder that she was free to let the next book start taking shape in her mind.[19] Wilder turned again to material from the "Pioneer Girl" manuscript, but she no longer felt inhibited or threatened by Lane's success with *Let the Hurricane Roar*. She was building a loyal readership, separate from her daughter's.

Although Lane remained at Rocky Ridge, her life had changed dramatically in 1933, when she took in a runaway teenage boy named John Turner and eventually his brother Al. She essentially became their adoptive mother, responsible for feeding, clothing, and educating the two boys. They were not the first she had taken under her wing. During the 1920s, while traveling through Albania, she had met Rexh Meta, a young Muslim boy whom she later credited with saving her life. He became Lane's first "adopted son," and she made significant contributions to his education abroad at Cambridge. She took her responsibilities to all three boys seriously, and they added significantly to her financial obligations during the Great Depression.[20] Although sales for *Let the Hurricane Roar* remained strong, Lane struggled to find markets for her short fiction and was strapped for cash. She even asked her agent to loan her money against anticipated royalties on the book. "I see no prospect of being able to meet August first bills," she wrote. 'It occurs to me that accrued royalties might justify me in asking whether you'd feel like lending me a few hundred."[21]

Lane pinned her hopes on a movie deal with Metro-Goldwyn-Mayer. She anticipated seventy-five hundred dollars if the deal went through, but Hollywood was a slippery market even in the 1930s.[22] In 1934, her agent approached Twentieth-Century Fox to buy movie rights to the book. That studio, too, was a tough sell. Movie executives there worried about the expense (and viability) of arranging for a cloud of insects. "What's this? . . . You don't mean that they are bereft of continuity writers, technicians, and actors registering terror and despair enough to put over a grasshopper invasion without an actual multitudinous cloud of veritable insects?" Lane asked incredulously. She dismissed the "grasshopper invasion" in her novel as nothing more than a detail and urged her agent to pitch *Let the Hurricane Roar* as an ideological sequel to the film *Little Women,* which had been released the previous year with Katharine Hepburn as Jo. *Let the Hurricane Roar* had, she insisted, "stronger dramatic value and a terrific punch straight to the American heart." It might even have potential as a musical.[23] Despite Lane's passionate pitch, Bye could not sustain interest in the film, and the deal fell through. In fairness to Lane, her dream that *Let the Hurricane Roar* could become an important depression-era film was not totally unrealistic. The novel was, after all, a bestseller, and one of her close friends, Catherine Brody, had landed a job as a screenwriter in the mid-1930s.[24]

Lane still had aspirations of writing the Great American Novel, and in 1933, she sketched out plans for a sweeping series of novels, as many as ten in all, that would dramatize the American spirit and its drive to populate a continent. She hoped that *Let the Hurricane Roar* would be the first novel in this ambitious series. Although Lane did write a second novel that essentially functioned as a sequel to *Let the Hurricane Roar*, she never completed the series she aspired to write. Once again, Lane's artistic vision collided with her mother's raw talent. Wilder, not Lane, would, of course, write this series.[25]

In 1935, Lane left Rocky Ridge Farm for good. She moved to Columbia, Missouri, and rented accommodations in the Tiger Hotel, named for the University of Missouri's athletic teams. Wilder and Manly moved back into the Rocky Ridge farmhouse in 1936 and eventually sold the Rock House. Suddenly, the family regained its equilibrium. The tensions between Wilder and Lane largely dissolved, and what emerged was a healthier, professional relationship based on the artistic vision the two women shared. Wilder helped Lane; Lane helped Wilder; and the correspondence between the two of them reveals how the balance of Wilder's Little House books came to be.[26]

16

The Children's Story is Now Complete

1935–1943

During the summer of 1936, Wilder completed a draft manuscript of her fourth novel and sent it to Lane at the Tiger Hotel for editing. The manuscript, which would become *On the Banks of Plum Creek,* covered many of the details and episodes Lane had borrowed from "Pioneer Girl" for *Let the Hurricane Roar*, most notably the dugout setting along Plum Creek and the grasshopper plague. At this point in Wilder's career, she no longer felt threatened by her daughter's success. After all, Ida Louise Raymond at Harper's had encouraged Wilder to follow *Little House on the Prairie* with the next book in the Ingalls family saga.[1] Lane reviewed the manuscript and sent Wilder an editorial letter on 13 June 1936. The subsequent correspondence about *On the Banks of Plum Creek* reveals the dynamics of their working relationship and Wilder's commitment to her creative work and vision.

Lane included a gift from the ten-cent store with her first letter, sending pins for her mother's hair and clips for her ears because "I thought they would be fun for you to wear," Lane wrote in the postscript. Otherwise, her letter was all business. She began, as many editors do, with a request for more concrete details: "Was school in the summer-time, in July? What school books did they have? . . . What did Pa wear when he dressed up? What were the dresses that grew too short, the ones they wore to school, when the boy called them long-legged snipes? I mean, what material, color, how made?"[2] Wilder was not intimidated by the questions and responded right away. "Our school dresses were sprigged calico made with tight waists buttoned down the back and straight skirts gathered onto the belt of the goods at the waist." Her explanation about her father's dress clothes provided the details Lane wanted and illuminated Wilder's childhood impressions of her father at the same time. "Ma made Pa's Sunday shirts of calico," Wilder recalled. "He wore a black silk tie, a coat and vest and pants. I can't describe them. Seems as though all I ever saw of Pa was his face especially his eyes, his whiskers and his hair always standing on end. And too his hands on his violin."[3]

As their correspondence continued that summer, Wilder refused to submit meekly or mindlessly to her daughter's editorial suggestions. When Lane seemed unable to grasp the geography of Plum Creek and advocated inappropriate descriptive changes, Wilder sharply corrected her. "Get these [Ozark] hills and our gorge [at Rocky Ridge Farm] out of your mind. The character of the place [Plum Creek] was altogether different." As added insurance, Wilder drew two Plum Creek diagrams in separate letters that summer, complete with notations for the dugout, stable, new home, swimming hole, tableland, fish trap, and road to town. She also sketched a map of Walnut Grove, which included the schoolhouse, church, railroad tracks, and stores.[4] Even when Wilder accepted Lane's suggestions about setting, she told her daughter what she could not tamper with. "Handle the cattle as you think best also the storm," Wilder directed, "only don't weaken nor change the character of the storm."[5]

Still, the letters reveal that Lane's editorial instincts were often right on target, especially when analyzing plot and structure. She advocated cutting an episode Wilder had adapted from her "Pioneer Girl" manuscript about Caroline Ingalls's serious illness at Plum Creek. "I think the grasshoppers are enough," Lane advised her mother. "I believe it would be better to cut out Ma's sickness altogether."[6] Wilder concurred. Lane was equally good at identifying lapses in point of view, and she directed Wilder's attention to a scene in the manuscript where Ma goes to the stable to do the chores during a blizzard while Pa is away. Wilder agreed that there was a problem, and she initially accepted Lane's suggestion that Laura could do the chores with Ma. As she thought through the scene logistically, however, she reasoned that Laura could not go along. She was too small to reach the clothesline that served as a guide to the stable, plus Ma's character would never allow Laura out in the storm nor would she have a free hand to guide her if she did. "I'm beat!" she admitted after sorting through the problem.[7]

Ultimately, Wilder worked it through and proposed the solution. "It might be that Laura could follow Ma into the barn and doing the chores, with her imagination," she suggested to Lane, "having seen Pa do the chores she would know how they would be done and how the animals would act."[8] Laura's imagined trip to the barn made it into the novel and revealed one of Wilder's growing strengths as a writer.[9] She understood her characters and their motivations far better than Lane did. With each subsequent novel in the series, Wilder exhibited a firmer grasp of her characters' personalities, desires, and motivations.

In *On the Banks of Plum Creek*, Wilder made a giant creative leap forward in her depiction of the entire Ingalls family. The previous novels in the series had emphasized how people lived in the nineteenth century and the tasks they performed. Even *Farmer Boy*, with Almanzo as a distinct central character, and *Little House on the Prairie*, with its new theme of moving west, described pioneer tasks and skills with almost how-to detail. In *On the Banks of Plum Creek,* Wilder shifted her focus from how things were done in the nineteenth century to the people who did those things. She used quick brush-stroke detail to describe how Pa builds the fish trap or Ma dries plums. And Laura is at the center of it all—learning, growing, maturing. She bickers with Mary, fights dirty with Nellie Oleson, worries about Ma in that cold dark stable doing chores.[10] *On the Banks of Plum Creek* is a character-driven novel.

The editorial letters between Wilder and Lane confirm that Wilder carefully, meticulously thought through her characters' personality traits, their motivations and aspirations, even the way they talked. When Lane suggested changes in the manuscript that ran counter to Wilder's understanding of her characters, Wilder corrected her. "But of course a lady like Ma would never use such expressions [as 'I'll be darned' or 'Great Gehosaphat']," for she "was a school teacher and well educated for her time and place, rather above Pa socially," Wilder insisted. She then used Ma as a standard for how the rest of the Ingalls family should speak in the book. Mary and Carrie spoke as Ma did, but Grace and Laura acted more like Pa, using jokes and slang. Sometimes Wilder's observations about Lane's dialogue edits were specific: "On page 12—you have Ma say, 'she vowed she didn't believe those young ones were *ever* going to sleep.' Never in the world would Ma have said such a thing." Wilder then proposed a new line using the word *children* instead and explained that "young ones" was not in Ma's vocabulary. Further, as a lady, she would never say "I vow."[11]

Wilder's fight to get the dialogue exactly right was more than a mere technical issue; dialogue goes to the heart of character. Furthermore, writing believable, character-consistent dialogue is the mark of a diligent and gifted writer. Lane herself struggled with the issue in her own fiction, where the dialogue is sometimes brilliant but more frequently awkward, artificial, or inappropriate to its characters or their settings.[12] As Wilder's talents grew, however, her understanding of dialogue and its relationship to the characters she created deepened. She also understood the essential conflicts at work in her fiction—an essential insight because, without conflict, writers have no stories to tell. When Lane appeared uncertain about the overriding conflict in *On the Banks of Plum Creek,* Wilder explained that it was about the false sense of security that the ripening wheat gave the family, "and then look what happened.

. . . enter the grasshoppers."[13] That cloud of insects robbed the Ingalls family of their dreams and aspirations and would ultimately send them moving west again—and into the next novel.

Finally, the "Plum Creek" correspondence indicates that Wilder was actively engaged with the editorial process. She did far more than write a single rough draft and leave it to Lane to revise and rewrite. Wilder made significant revisions herself. Lane apparently misunderstood the amount of revising Wilder had already done *before* sending a finished manuscript to the Tiger Hotel. "I have no copy of the thing here [the manuscript] I can go over," Wilder wrote. "If I should try to use the first scraps of scribbling I would get us all confused for I changed it so much from them." Wilder also sent her own revisions to Lane. "I think you will agree to the cuts I have made in enclosed copy," she wrote in one letter. She also made editorial suggestions to Lane, telling her to shorten sections, for example. And, finally, she refused changes that adversely affected the story. "No I think that last winter must be left as it is more or less or we spoil the effect as well as not being correct as to conditions in grasshopper times," she emphatically told Lane.[14]

Wilder submitted the finished manuscript to her literary agent on 24 September 1936 with a note directing him to negotiate for better contract terms than she had received for *Little House on the Prairie*. The text for this letter originated with Lane, who must have realized, after working with her mother on revisions that summer, that *On the Banks of Plum Creek* was an appealing and finely crafted novel.[15] Indeed, the book was a critical success, winning Wilder her first Newbery Honor Book title in 1938, the equivalent in children's book publishing of being nominated for an Oscar. In 1939, Wilder's agent remarked, "I think I told you that Miss Raymond has shown 'Plum Creek' to dozens of authors as the model for a perfect juvenile."[16]

Wilder appreciated Lane's editorial counsel and apologized to her daughter for the amount of time and effort it took her to revise and polish the book for publication. "I should think you would be so sick of this darned story, you would gag," she wrote. "Sorry it has been so troublesome."[17] No reciprocal message of thanks survives from Lane, neither for the material she had used in *Let the Hurricane Roar* and her other short fiction nor for the counsel and advice Wilder was about to provide on Lane's next novel, which would draw even more heavily on material from "Pioneer Girl" and her parents' recollections of South Dakota.

In March of 1937, Lane confessed to George Bye that she had "never written a good novel" because she had "never had time."[18] As she penned this letter to her agent, Lane was working on *Free Land*. The main character of the novel, David Beaton, is, in large part, a fictional depiction of Lane's father. His sister Eliza Jane also appears in the novel as Eliza Beaton, and the Ingalls family is recast as the Peters family. Nettie Peters, to whom David is attracted but does not marry, bears a striking resemblance to Wilder herself. Rather than work in secret on *Free Land*, as she had done with *Let the Hurricane Roar*, Lane asked her parents for help as she researched the book. She typed a set of interview questions and sent them to her father, asking about weather, food, clothing, music, and prices—details a writer of historical fiction needs to add credibility and accuracy to her story. She also asked deeper, more emotionally based questions about homesteading and conflicting attitudes between farmers, merchants, and townspeople. Manly's answers were usually short and specific. To his daughter's question about the cost of a buggy, he responded, "From $65 to $85 depending on the make." When she tried to find out if there was any antagonism between merchants and homesteaders, Manly replied, "No difference."[19] Obviously, he was a man of few words.

He did, however, write his daughter lengthier insights and descriptions for specific scenes she planned to include in *Free Land*. Early in the novel, for example, David Beaton loses a mare to bloat; Manly had lost one in the same way on his trip to Yankton, Dakota Territory, to file his homestead claim in 1879. He described the scene in detail for his daughter: "As we were driving along I notice she was bloating and pulled them down to a walk and in a few minutes large drops of sweat came out all over, . . . in about 10 minutes she lade down and stratined out dead."[20] With two writers in the family, Manly had little confidence in his own descriptive powers. "I am a poor hand to tell a Story much less to write it," he noted.[21] He sometimes resorted to illustrations; in one drawing, he illustrated the visual differences between a bobsled and a cutter, providing a list of definitions from Wilder herself.[22]

Wilder and Lane also corresponded regularly about *Free Land*. In one letter, Wilder promised to consult Lane's Aunt Grace about prairie wildflowers. In the margins of the same note, she wrote, "You remember the old saying that 'A man who won't steal from the R.R. Co isn't honest.'" Wilder went on to retell the story of how her Uncle Hi had cheated the railroad, noting, "I can't use [it] in a child's story, but you could use it if you have a place for it."[23] Indeed, Lane used much of this material. A shopkeeper in *Free Land* even tells David, "'Hell, a man that won't steal from a railroad ain't honest.'"[24] Lane also relied extensively on her mother's "Pioneer Girl" manuscript, using some of the same material Wilder would later use in *By the Shores of Silver Lake*, *The Long Winter*, *Little Town on the Prairie*, and *These Happy Golden Years*. Lane also extrapolated episodes that Wilder chose not to use, including a story about a doctor who steals the body of an American Indian baby and tries to sell it to a museum in the East.[25]

Free Land appeared as a serial in the *Saturday Evening Post* during the spring of 1938, and Longmans, Green and Company published it in book form later that same year. Like *Let the Hurricane Roar*, it became a bestseller, but this time Wilder rejoiced in Lane's success.[26] When Lane discovered that her characters in *Free Land* had threshed their wheat too early, Wilder consoled her: "Rose Dearest, Likely you need not feel so badly over the threshing in your story. Threshing *could* have been done the last of July."[27] Wilder's response was even more remarkable because as Lane wrote *Free Land*, Wilder was at work on *By the Shores of Silver Lake.* Characters, setting, plot, and themes often overlapped in the two novels. While Wilder wrote about "Big Jerry" in *By the Shores of Silver Lake,* Lane wrote about "Halfbreed Jack" in *Free Land.*[28]

Wilder clearly felt professionally secure and had good reason for her confidence. During the fall of 1937, she was invited to deliver a speech during Book Fair in Detroit, Michigan, where she would address key decision makers in the world of children's publishing: school librarians, book sellers, editors, publishers, and agents. The invitation confirmed Wilder's status as an important author of children's books, and her speech reflected her acceptance of her own literary stature. She told her audience that her intention to write a series of books for children had developed early because she "wanted the children now to understand more about the beginning of things to know what is behind the things they see—what it is that made America as they know it." By claiming this underlying sense of purpose for her career as a novelist, Wilder created a compelling backstory for herself and her books. She had been driven to write, bound by the historical significance of her own life.[29] One cannot say if she created this story consciously, but the idea took root, becoming part of established Laura Ingalls Wilder lore.

Although Wilder's skills as a writer had deepened, her next novel, *By the Shores of Silver Lake*, brought new creative challenges and a new, young adult audience, one that had not yet been formally recognized by the literary world in the 1930s. Today, the young adult, or YA, category is a well-established field in children's book publishing. Young adult fiction, which includes everything from fantasy and science fiction to contemporary and historical novels, usually focuses on a teen-aged protagonist and explores coming-of-age issues: personal identity and responsibility; social, political, or spiritual awareness; evolving relationships with family or friends; newly discovered career or occupational interests; romance and sexual awareness. In short, these books deal with more mature themes than do children's books targeting elementary-school readers. Louisa May Alcott's *Little Women*, published in 1868, is often considered the first American YA novel, but the concept of directing books specifically to teen readers did not formally emerge in this country until the 1940s. The American Library Association adopted the term YA in 1958. When Wilder began *By the Shores of Silver Lake* in 1937, she was writing in a literary category that had not formally been invented yet. She was ahead of her time, something Lane did not appreciate. When she reviewed her mother's initial draft for *By the Shores of Silver Lake,* toward the end of 1937, she worried that the book's themes—and even its main character—were too mature.[30]

Wilder, however, understood her readers and her main character. To Lane's worries, she responded that Laura was growing up. "I don't see how we can spare what you call adult stuff," she told Lane, "for that makes the story. It was there and Laura knew and understood it." Wilder trusted her readers and, on an intuitive level, knew that if they read the books in sequence, they—like Laura—would have matured. After all, Wilder's loyal readers had to wait two years for the publication of *By the Shores of Silver Lake*. "I believe children who have read the other books will demand this one," Wilder insisted, "and that they will understand and love it." Although Lane's letter on this subject does not survive, she apparently also advised her mother to switch main characters because Laura, who is twelve going on thirteen when the novel opens, seemed too old to be an appealing main character in a traditional children's book. "We can't spoil this story by making it childish!" Wilder fired back. She also insisted, "We cant change heroines in the middle of the stream and use Carrie in the place of Laura." Such a switch could spoil the story.[31]

Wilder understood her characters and her readers as Lane did not. While she was a shrewd editor who certainly strengthened her mother's writing, Lane lacked her mother's imaginative vision and essential grasp of character. She even initially advised Wilder to drop Mary's blindness from the series, but Wilder responded passionately that she could not do that because "a touch of tragedy makes the story truer to life and showing the way we took it illustrates the spirit of the times and the frontier."[32] It is hard to imagine the remaining books in Wilder's series without Mary's blindness. Again, Wilder was right. Mary's misfortune gives the later novels more resonance with young adult readers.

Mary's blindness also made the transition from *On the Banks of Plum Creek* to *By the Shores of Silver Lake* more challenging, which was another source of editorial disagreement between mother and daughter. Once again, Wilder had reverted to third-person-omniscient point of view for her original opening of the new novel: "A woman holding a small child on her arm and a small girl by the hand walked across the depot platform to the one passenger car at the end of the train. Two larger girls hand in hand followed her." On page two of the manuscript, Wilder returned to Laura's perspective.[33] The shift in point of view, though inconsistent, provided a strong, almost cinematic opening to the novel, and it let Wilder gloss over the historical fact that her family had moved from their Plum Creek farm to a house in town. Lane, however, protested that it was weak and impersonal. "It is not written from *Laura's* viewpoint," she stressed, adding, "I think your lead should be Aunt Docia driving up unexpectedly to the house on the banks of Plum Creek."[34]

Writers and editors often disagree on how a book should begin. The opening, which determines whether a reader will keep reading or set the story aside, also establishes the unique voice and tone of a novel. Wilder and Lane's heated discussion about the opening to *By the Shores of Silver Lake* reflected their mutual understanding of these issues. Lane admitted that her mother was right about the chronology but persisted with her suggestion that the novel start at Plum Creek. "It is not a fact, but it is perfectly true to take them west from the house on Plum Creek, where everything that has happened during this time might as truthfully have occurred as where it did occur," she wrote.[35] Wilder argued that it would "take the interest of the reader back to Plum Creek, instead of ahead with curiosity as to what lies ahead," and "it would begin the story with a recital of discouragement and calamities."[36] These different positions revealed each woman's unique creative strengths. Lane's editorial gifts related to structure and perspective. She saw straight through to the muscle of a sentence or paragraph and then cut away the flab with subtlety and skill, reorganizing paragraphs for clarity and drama. As she told Wilder: "I don't see how anybody could improve on your use of words. You are perfect in describing landscapes and things. What you need is more work on structure and on using points of view."[37]

Wilder's gifts went well beyond description, however. In addition to her deep understanding of character, she knew that a novel's action had to be believable; characters had to act in a credible way, consistent with a novel's time and place. Writers could not force characters to do things merely for the convenience of plot or to make the story more lively. Actions had to spring from personalities and motivations. When Lane suggested that Laura accompany Pa on a hunt, Wilder objected because Pa "loved his solitary tramps and besides it was no place for a girl."[38] When Lane suggested that the railroad crew might have been sexually interested in Laura and Mary, Wilder wrote: "Put sex and all relating to it out of your mind and think of the crowd [of railroad men] as rough and vulgar and truculent [*sic*], in camp and out, chewing and drinking and swearing and fighting. Not fit company for girls. But not degenerate."[39]

Eventually, as most writers and editors do, Wilder and Lane struck a compromise. Wilder agreed to Lane's new opening; Lane listened to her mother's arguments about character and the more adult material in the book. The opening of the published book is unforgettable and reveals an older, more mature Laura standing in the doorway of the Plum Creek house washing dishes.[40] She is also a timeless teenager, just as Wilder originally envisioned her to be—"at times, completely grown up and again just a child."[41]

By the Shores of Silver Lake was published in 1939 and became a Newbery Honor book, as did those that followed: *The Long Winter* in 1940; *Little Town on the Prairie* in 1941; and *These Happy Golden Years* in 1943. All three are also young adult novels, and they earned glowing reviews. The *New York Herald Tribune* wrote of *The Long Winter*, "For sheer gallantry, the story can't be beat. It puts iron into the imagination."[42] Wilder's agent, George Bye, was also impressed with the quality of the writing in these novels. In 1940, he wrote to tell Wilder that he sat up until two in the morning reading the manuscript for *The Long Winter* and then had trouble going to sleep "for thinking of the plight of the Ingalls family that awful winter."[43] A year later, he wrote to her about *Little Town on the Prairie*. Shortly after he read the book, he picnicked with Eleanor Roosevelt and reported that he found himself regaling her guests with stories from Wilder's novel. "If you write for children," he exclaimed to Wilder, "then I am in my second childhood."[44] When Bye read *These Happy Golden Years,* he told Wilder that the volume was beautiful and that it was "with great reluctance" that he accepted it as the last in the series.[45] Agents often flatter their clients, but Bye began his professional relationship with Wilder thinking her books were routine juvenile sellers. The strength of her young adult fiction—the last four books of the series— earned his respect.

For her part, Wilder found the last books in the series emotionally difficult to write, especially *The Long Winter*. She also suffered from memory lapses, which may explain why the last four novels in the series parallel the "Pioneer Girl" manuscript more closely than her first books. Lane had also loosened her tight editorial grip on her mother.[46] In 1941, as her mother's manuscript for *Little Town on the Prairie* neared completion, Lane told Bye, "She will send it to you without my seeing a good part of it."[47] Although Wilder valued and appreciated her daughter's assistance, she still worried that she had become a bother to Lane, that she was draining her daughter of creative energy. In effect, Wilder was also trying to loosen the editorial grip Lane held over her. "I'll try to touch it up here and there myself, to overcome some of your objections," she wrote. "If I can do it, it will give you more time for your other work."[48]

The two continued to work together as the series drew to an end. Wilder, for example, confided in Lane about her trouble finding a plot for the book on the hard winter and her concern that it was too grim for the series. Although Wilder found her own solution, making it a struggle of survival from winter to spring, she initially took Lane's suggestion to begin the book with the portent of high-flying geese. She sent Lane preliminary synopses and outlines for what she thought would be her last two books—"Hard Winter" and "Prairie Girl" ("Prairie Girl" eventually became *Little Town on the Prairie* and *These Happy Golden Years*). The two women exchanged diagrams of a railroad handcar, so that its description in *The Long Winter* would be vivid and accurate; argued over the difference between stoicism and apathy; and discussed which of Wilder's uncles should reappear in *Little Town on the Prairie*. To be historically correct, it should have been her Uncle Tom, Wilder observed, but she did not think that readers would bother "to look it up."[49] Little did Wilder know that scores of researchers would eventually do just that. As always, Wilder placed great trust in her daughter's creative talents and instincts. Before she and Manly left for their last trip to South Dakota in 1939, Wilder left instructions to Lane about her notes for "Prairie Girl." Worried that she and Manly might not survive the trip, she told Lane, "You could write the last book from them and finish the series if you had to do so."[50]

The path toward publication of Wilder's last and strongest books in the series experienced additional obstacles from her publisher. By this time, Ursula Nordstrom at Harper's had taken over from Raymond, and despite Wilder and Lane's objections, she changed "Hard Winter" into *The Long Winter*.[51] Nordstrom also nearly eliminated one of the most powerful scenes in *These Happy Golden Years*. George Bye informed Wilder, "Miss Nordstrom [is] suggesting that Mrs. Brewster's butcher knife incident be cut out."[52] This time, however, Wilder and Lane prevailed. In arguments with the editors at Harper's, blood was thicker than water. "Do not take seriously anything that publishers say," Lane advised her mother.[53]

Living apart seemed to bring Wilder and Lane closer together as mother and daughter. Their correspondence about Wilder's last novels is laced with affectionate personal observations. In a letter Wilder found waiting for her in Detroit before her big Book Fair speech, Lane wrote, "You will make a grand talk and be a lovely lion. . . . The chiffon velvet must be perfectly beautiful."[54] In 1939, as Wilder was working on *The Long Winter*, she wrote Lane that she had thought about her all day, and when she lay down on the bed that Lane had given her and looked across at Manly in his bed covered with a down quilt, all gifts from Lane, she found, "When I go to count up our comfortableness and the luck of the world we have, it all leads back to you. . . . Oh Rose my dear, we do thank you so much for being good to us."[55] Wilder accepted her daughter's gifts but simultaneously worried about her finances. "Are you short of money? . . . If you are I have a couple of hundred loose, you can have if it would help."[56]

In 1938, Lane bought property in Connecticut and decided to settle down in her own "little house." Her interest in writing fiction apparently burned itself out with *Free Land*, and she concentrated on nonfiction. In the mid-1930s, she had written a history of the state of Missouri, and, as the world plunged into World War II, she developed a keen interest in political history and its influence on current events. Perhaps, like her mother, Lane had finally recognized her niche, that indeed, as she had always suspected, she had never written a good novel.[57]

In 1942, Wilder sent her last manuscript, *These Happy Golden Years*, to George Bye, telling him, "This children's story is now complete in eight volumes."[58] He responded with the prediction that the series "will become an American fixture, something like Little Women and Little Men, but with sounder inspiration for better citizenship."[59] As he penned those lines, Wilder was fast becoming a more important client to his literary agency than her daughter.

17

To Go On from Here
1941–1957 and Beyond

In 1941, George Bye wrote Wilder with news that MayFair Togs, a national manufacturer of children's clothing, wanted to develop a merchandising program tying their products to *The Long Winter*. They planned to manufacture "children's clothes made after suggestions contained in your book," he explained, "and then offer them for sale in department stores coast to coast with a display of your book alongside."[1] Wilder liked the publicity stunt, as she called it, but only on condition that the company "pay as large a fee as they can be persuaded to pay for use of the books and my name in their advertising." As an afterthought, she added that she had never heard of the company but assumed they were first class.[2] Apparently Mayfair Togs could not be persuaded to pay a large promotional fee to Wilder because after a summer of negotiations, primarily through Ursula Nordstrom at Harper's, the project died. The episode illustrated Wilder's growing business savvy and her interest in marketing her books and herself. Furthermore, she had begun to communicate directly with her agent, relying less on Lane to mediate.

Based on the existing correspondence, Wilder was also more directly involved with book contract negotiations during the late 1930s and into the 1940s. She was beginning to understand her own worth—in dollars and cents. When Bye negotiated a profitable contract on Wilder's behalf for *By the Shores of Silver Lake*, he wrote her that he had made a gentlemen's agreement with Harper's: if the publisher lost money on the book, which awarded Wilder a straight fifteen percent on royalties, she would accept a lower percentage on the next book.[3] Wilder wrote back with the confidence of a bestselling author, "As to the 'gentlemen's agreement' to reconsider in case—I do not think we have need to expect it will be necessary."[4] Records from the Bye Agency for the first half of 1941 show that Wilder's books—the six then in print—had earned $14,444.14 since the publication of her first novel in 1932, impressive earnings for the period. Although *By the Shores of Silver Lake* had sold briskly, Wilder and Bye did not exactly win that gentlemen's agreement. Instead, they compromised: the contract for *The Long Winter* earned Wilder ten percent on the first three thousand books sold, fifteen percent thereafter.[5]

When Wilder sent the manuscript for *Little Town on the Prairie* off to Bye in July 1941, she wrote, "Harpers is, of course, expecting this book, but I think they should give me a better contract than for *The Long Winter* or else a new contract for *Farmer Boy* which I practically gave them." She added, "I am sure Harpers are making a good thing on these books taken all together and naturally I want a fair share."[6] This time she got what she wanted—an adjustment on royalties for *Farmer Boy*. It had taken her eight years to get it.[7]

Wilder was also interested in what we now call alternative media. For her, in the 1940s and early 1950s, that meant movies and radio. During contract negotiations for *The Long Winter*, Harper's asked for twenty-five percent on motion-picture rights. Wilder thought that was too much. "If by good fortune," Wilder wrote Bye, "the story should be used in pictures, it will be at no expense to Harpers, but altogether through my hard work writing and your good salesmanship." She countered with a proposal of her own. "In consideration of our accepting the 10 per cent on book sales would Harper's not be willing to take, say 15 per cent instead of 25 per cent of motion picture rights. If you are willing let's make a try for this."[8] Bye went even further than Wilder hoped; he persuaded Harper's to drop their demand for any film rights, and despite the success of Wilder's series, no motion pictures were ever made from her books. In 1944, Wilder sold Columbia Broadcasting System (CBS) one-time, limited rights to *The Long Winter* for fifty dollars. CBS planned to air the story twice as part of its radio program *Tales from Far and Near*. In 1953, radio station WMCA in New York aired *The Long Winter* on its noncommercial, educational program *Let's Listen to a Story*. Wilder gave the network rights to this material at no charge—as long as they did not rewrite or adapt her original text. The program aired again in 1958.[9] Wilder was equally generous with the many requests to translate her books into braille or "talking books" for the blind. "I shall be glad if it gives blind children any pleasure," she said in 1939. "Sister Mary had quite a small library of those books."[10]

Like most writers, Wilder was keenly interested in the design and illustration of her books. For the most part, she was pleased with Helen Sewell and Mildred Boyle's illustrations of the original series, but one illustration in *Little Town on the Prairie* annoyed her. "Have you seen the book in its published form?" she asked Bye. 'It is quite striking especially Laura's cheeks for which Miss Nordstrom apologized and promised correction in [the] next printing."[11] It was a measure of Wilder's success and clout that her editor responded to her criticism with a promise of a correction in the book's next printing. Rarely do authors have this kind of control over illustration and design, even when they write *and* illustrate their own books.

Harper's decision in the late 1930s to change the overall format of her young adult titles, beginning with *By the Shores of Silver Lake,* also concerned Wilder. She urged that her books be marketed together and have a single, cohesive design despite their broad range in readership. Harper's hoped to make the format of *By the Shores of Silver Lake* attractive to adult readers, an idea that Wilder affirmed, but she also stressed that all the books together "are *one story* and some booksellers have intended selling them in sets when the story is completed."[12] Despite her growing popularity, Wilder could not convince anyone at Harper's that she was right, but she stuck to her guns, and a few weeks later, her editor appealed to Bye. He, in turn, telegraphed Lane: "HARPERS WANT TO PUBLISH YOUR MOTHERS BOOK IN NOVEL SIZE FORMAT AS OLDER CHILDREN WONT BUY SQUARISH BOOKS BUT YOUR MOTHER OBJECTS TO CHANGE IN SERIES WHAT DO YOU SAY."[13] No record remains of Lane's reply, but *By the Shores of Silver Lake* and the remaining books in the series were published in the new format Harper's preferred.

Wilder, however, remained concerned. The following year, Bye tried to relieve her lingering reservations about the new design. He told her he had met with Helen Hoke, a children's book editor from another publishing house, and told her "of our disappointment in the Harper's change of format and she exclaimed that that was a very brilliant move on the part of Harper's." Wilder was relieved.[14] Seven years later, it finally dawned on Ursula Nordstrom at Harper's that Wilder had been right all those years before. The series did need to be marketed as a uniform set with a cohesive design. She hired Garth Williams to illustrate a new and uniform edition of Wilder's novels.[15] The new series debuted in 1953 and is the edition most readers know and love today. Once again, Wilder was ahead of her time.

In preparation for illustrating the new edition, Williams visited Wilder and Manly in September 1947. He found Wilder working in the garden when he arrived and later wrote: "She was small and nimble. Her eyes sparkled with good humor and she seemed a good twenty years younger than her age." As the illustrator prepared to head north to De Smet, Manly worried that Williams and his family would be caught in an early fall blizzard, which can "'blow for weeks.'" Wilder was eighty; Manly was ninety. Photographs from the period show Wilder in a lush garden surrounded by vegetation as tall as she was, and her husband looked frail but formidable, leaning heavily on one of his many walking canes.[16] Manly did not have much longer to live.

The Wilders sold Rocky Ridge Farm to neighbors in 1948, keeping only the land around the farmhouse and outbuildings. That year, the Detroit Public Library named one of its branches after Wilder, and she was surprised by the publicity.[17] A reporter from the *Springfield News and Leader* interviewed her, reporting, "She has been voted the most popular living writer by Chicago school children. Every mail brings her fan letters from boys and girls throughout this country and in foreign lands."[18] During this flurry of activity, Wilder wrote George Bye an important, formal letter, instructing him to assign Lane ten percent of the royalties earned on her Little House books. "I owe Rose, for helping me, at first, in selling my books and for the publicity she gave them," Wilder noted.[19] In a separate letter to Bye, she added, "This arrangement should have been made long ago."[20]

Wilder did not make it to Detroit that summer for the library's dedication ceremony, primarily because of Manly's failing health. He suffered a heart attack and died at home on 23 October 1949. He was ninety-two years old. Wilder wrote an old friend in De Smet, "It is very lonely without my husband. . . . Those dear old days seem so far away now and sometimes I am homesick for them."[21] Manly's funeral and burial were held in Mansfield. Lane came home for the funeral, her first visit there since 1937, and then returned to her own little house in Danbury, Connecticut.[22] Wilder stayed on at Rocky Ridge Farm. "There is nothing left," she observed, "but to go on from here alone."[23]

Wilder and Manly had befriended a younger couple from Mansfield, Neta and Silas Seal, who looked in on Wilder regularly after Manly's death. In an undated note to the Seals, probably from the late 1940s or early 1950s, Wilder sought to repay the kindness: "My Dears Have dinner with me. It is my turn to treat. Lots of love. Laura Wilder."[24] Between her annual visits to Rocky Ridge, Lane communicated regularly with the Seals, asking for updates about her mother's health and welfare and providing observations of her own. "You know of course that you can always reach me by telephone if my mother needs me and can't telephone herself; and I can be there within a few hours," she wrote Neta. Wilder had fallen recently and, by her own account, suffered "quite a head laceration." Lane, who was then approaching seventy, noted that she hoped her mother did not have any more accidents, adding, "I wish she did not like to live alone but there isn't much that I can say about that when I am doing the same thing myself because I like to." Lane confessed that she, too, had taken some tumbles and concluded, "We are both almost indestructible, but it is the greatest comfort to me that you are there and so loyal and good to her."[25] Indeed, Wilder remained fiercely independent. At eighty-eight, she told a reporter from the *Kansas City Star*, "'I'm not afraid to be living here by myself.'" Even so, she was cautious. "'You see,'" she told the reporter, "'I have a little gun in a cabinet by the screen door. I've got a shotgun in my bedroom and I know how to use them both.'"[26]

Although she had fought hard for her books and enjoyed their success and the publicity they brought her, Wilder projected a modest, endearing public and private image. In 1943, after she had completed *These Happy Golden Years,* she wrote George Bye, "I am still surprised at the success the books have had so far."[27] Over ten years later, she stuck to her story, telling a reporter that she was amazed at the success of the Little House books. As publicists would say today, Wilder knew how to spin her own story and give a really good sound bite. She was surprised by her success, she told the reporter in the mid-1950s, "because I didn't know how to write. I went to little red schoolhouses all over the West and I was never graduated from anything."[28] Although Wilder attended her fair share of one-room schoolhouses and even taught in a few, it is safe to assume that none were painted red.

Despite the shrewdness with which she handled the press,

Wilder's health was failing. Her sister Grace Ingalls Dow had died in 1941; Carrie Ingalls Swanzey had died in 1946, three years before Manly. Wilder had outlived her sisters. As early as 1952, she anticipated her own death and wrote Lane a letter that began, "Rose Dearest, When you read this I will be gone and you will have inherited all I have." Wilder asked Lane to give a collection of books to Mansfield's Laura Ingalls Wilder Library and hoped her daughter would leave the persimmon-wood chair and cypress stand-table, which Manly had made, to Silas Seal. Wilder encouraged Lane to keep her jewelry, the Haviland china, and her blue willow-ware, which she and Manly had loved best. Wilder signed the letter, "My love will be with you always, Mama Bess." In parentheses, she added, "Laura Ingalls Wilder."[29] She lived five years after the writing of that letter. She died in her beloved Rocky Ridge farmhouse on 10 February 1957, just three days after her ninetieth birthday. Her obituary in the *De Smet News* reported that her health had been failing for several years.[30]

Lane was at Rocky Ridge Farm when her mother died. Six years earlier, she had written her mother: "I don't know what's wrong, but I seem to have come unglued or unhinged or something. After sixty three years of practically perfect self-discipline, now suddenly I haven't any at all."[31] Wilder's death unglued Lane once again. Three weeks after the funeral, she wrote Neta Seal that she was recovering and did not feel as delirious as she had in Mansfield. "I hope after awhile to be in something like my right mind again," she wrote, apologizing for the mess she had left behind in her mother's house. "I would not have done it if I could have pulled myself together at all," she concluded, "but really I was not responsible for anything during those last weeks there. Please forgive me."[32]

Lane returned to her house in Connecticut and lived alone or with a pair of Maltese dogs. Her book *The Discovery of Freedom*, published in 1943, had influenced the emergence of the Libertarian political party. As she grew older, her interest in political theory deepened. Lane also worked closely with townspeople from Mansfield to preserve Rocky Ridge Farm and her mother's literary legacy.[33] In large part, Lane is responsible for the image most people have of her mother—the kindly old lady who started writing in her sixties and simply set down the facts of her life.

In the early 1960s, however, dedicated readers and scholars discovered that Wilder had been only three years old in Kansas, not five as Laura is in the novels. To explain the discrepancy, a contributor to *Elementary English*, a publication from the National Council of Teachers of English, reasoned: "The fact must be that Mrs. Wilder, as an author, drew on her knowledge from stories she had heard from her parents as well. As an artist working with her materials, Mrs. Wilder knew she could achieve a more artistic effect by altering the true facts occasionally."[34] Lane fired back that her mother had tampered with Laura's age only at the insistence of her publisher, who had threatened not to publish *Little House in the Big Woods* unless Wilder aged Laura by two years. "This is important only because it has been charged that my mother's books are fiction. They are the truth, and only the truth; every detail in them is written as my mother remembered it," Lane maintained. "These books are entirely the 'true stories' that they claim to be."[35]

In the same letter, Lane provided a clue that may explain why she fought so fiercely to have Wilder's novels characterized as nonfiction. "A fiction writer myself," Lane wrote, "I agree that my mother could have added to artistic effects by altering facts, but she did not write fiction."[36] And therefore, by implication, Wilder was not an artist; Lane was the artist in the family, the real writer of fiction. This depiction of Wilder and her work corresponds to George Bye's initial characterization of the "Pioneer Girl" manuscript over thirty years before—of a "fine old lady sitting in a rocking chair and telling a story chronologically."[37] Lane enlisted an ally in her subtle campaign to undermine her mother's artistic reputation by insisting that the Little House books were autobiography. In the 1940s, she informally adopted Roger MacBride, son of *Reader's Digest* editor Burt MacBride, as her "grandson." After the death of George Bye in 1957, Mac-Bride, who was a young lawyer by then, became Lane's agent and eventually her heir and literary executor. The two shared a political philosophy as well as a vision for how Wilder and her books should be remembered. MacBride was devoted to Lane. Together the two of them managed the royalties, which continued to pour in, and Wilder's literary legacy.[38]

Lane continued to write nonfiction during the late 1950s and into the 1960s. She authored the *Woman's Day Book of American Needlework* in 1963 and flew to Vietnam to cover the war for *Woman's Day* magazine in 1965, when she was seventy-eight years old. Three years later, she planned a world tour, which she would write about for the magazine. Just days before she was scheduled to sail to Europe, she died in her little house in Connecticut on 30 October 1968. Her funeral was in Mansfield, where she was buried next to her parents.[39]

After Wilder's death, most children's book scholars accepted the historical truth of the Little House books but admired their great artistry, as well. Lane's attempt to diminish her mother's reputation as a writer was not effective. Even if Wilder's work were interpreted as nonfiction, the series was unparalleled. "Until Laura Ingalls Wilder undertook the writing of her family's experiences in settling the Midwest, there were no books which really held children's interest while opening their eyes to this [the American frontier] period," praised legendary children's book expert and educator May Hill Arbuthnot. She added: "Best of all, the maturity of these books grows with the children. The first book appeals to children of eight or nine; the last is written for the almost-grown-up girl, who by this time feels that Laura is her oldest and dearest friend."[40] Illustrator

Garth Williams also praised her artistry: "She understood the meaning of hardship and struggle, of joy and work, of shyness and bravery. She was never overcome by drabness or squalor. She never glamorized anything; yet she saw the loveliness in everything."[41]

Even before Wilder's death, the American Library Association had created the Wilder Medal in 1954 to honor her and subsequent writers or illustrators who made, as Wilder's editor Ursula Nordstrom explained, "a distinguished, creative, sustained contribution to children's books." She hoped it would ultimately become more important than the Newbery or Caldecott "because it will only be awarded when it can go to some author [or illustrator] of real stature."[42] The Wilder Medal may have been, in part, a response by the American Library Association to its own failure to award Wilder a Newbery Medal. Her last five titles won Honor Book designations but never the medal itself. Nordstrom once wrote, "An influential California librarian told me 'they' [the Newbery selection committee] couldn't even consider any of the Laura Ingalls Wilder books for the Newbery 'because we don't like series books.'"[43] Wilder herself received the first Wilder Medal toward the end of her life in 1954. Garth Williams designed the medal, which was initially awarded every five years (now granted at three-year intervals). It was wonderful, Nordstrom summarized, that such an award carried Wilder's "sacred name."[44]

Still, in 1952, the first hint of a gathering storm of disapproval about Wilder's work appeared on Nordstrom's desk—a letter from a reader deeply offended by two lines in the original published text from the opening chapter of *Little House on the Prairie:* "There the wild animals wandered and fed as though they were in a pasture that stretched much farther than a man could see, and there were no people. Only Indians lived there."[45] Nordstrom responded to the letter herself, explaining that since Wilder was in her late eighties, Harper's usually answered letters on her behalf. In this instance, Nordstrom had contacted the author to discuss the complaint. "I must admit to you," Nordstrom wrote to the reader, "that no one here realized that these words read as they did. Reading them now it seems unbelievable to me that you are the only person who has picked them up and written to us about them in the twenty years since the book was published." She went on to remark that everyone at Harper's felt as strongly as the reader on the subject and that it was perhaps "a hopeful sign that though such a statement could have passed unquestioned twenty years ago it would never have appeared in anything published in recent years."[46]

According to Nordstrom, Wilder responded with this reply when she learned about the complaint: "'You are perfectly right about the fault in *Little House on the Prairie* and have my permission to make the correction you suggest. It was a stupid blunder of mine. Of course Indians are people and I did not mean to imply that they were not.'"[47] With Wilder's permission, the offensive line in the novel was changed to read, "and there were no settlers," and made its first appearance when the Little House series was re-released in 1953 with the Garth Williams illustrations.[48] In Wilder's original draft of *Little House on the Prairie*, her first chapter does not include the offensive line. In fact, there is not a single reference to Indians or Indian Country in the original draft of that chapter.[49] The line may have originated with Lane, who worked with Wilder in crafting the first chapter in *Little House on the Prairie* into a smooth transition from *Little House in the Big Woods*. Even so, the fact would make Wilder no less responsible, as she herself recognized in her response to Nordstrom.

In the late 1980s and early 1990s, the question of Wilder's depiction of American Indians in her novels took on more urgency, and the controversy continues today. American Indian writers, scholars, and critics condemn her books and urge people not to read them. Dennis McAuliffe, Jr., a member of the Osage Tribe, condemns the Ingalls family as "illegal squatters on Osage land. [Wilder] left that detail out of her 1935 children's book, *Little House on the Prairie,* as well as any mention of ongoing outrages—including killings, burnings, beatings, horse thefts, and grave robberies—committed by white settlers, such as Charles Ingalls, against Osages living in villages not more than a mile or two away from the Ingalls' little house."[50] Wilder biographer John E. Miller, on the other hand, finds Wilder's depiction subtle and complex. He contends, "A careful reading shows that Laura Ingalls Wilder was guilty of neither ignoring nor abusing American Indians in her novels."[51] The heart of this issue is not really about Wilder and her books; rather, it is about how Americans interpret the frontier experience and the clash between native cultures and the settlers that dominate this history. Wilder's Little House series, because of its enduring popularity and widespread readership, is now part of the ongoing reinterpretation of history and, by extension, of the fiction and nonfiction that explores it.

The other major controversy surrounding Wilder's books does, in fact, strike at the creative heart of the series and has been the focus of this biography: Did Wilder write her books or did Lane? Who is the real author? If Wilder *did not* write the books, that fact would compromise essential values the series celebrates: honesty, hard work, and integrity. Undoubtedly, Rose Wilder Lane played a major role in the creation of Laura Ingalls Wilder's books. She was an aggressive editor of her mother's work, probably more aggressive than most children's book editors. Within the context of children's book publishing, however, the letters and manuscripts that Wilder and Lane left behind illustrate not only where the books originated but in whose voice they were written. Wilder and Lane had unique and separate voices in their fiction, even when they covered the same material. Wilder brought warmth, engagement, and energy to her books. Lane wrote with cool detachment. Her novels about the frontier centered on ideas; Wilder's centered on characters: Laura and her family as well as the West itself. And while Wilder was indebted to Lane for her editorial expertise, Lane was indebted to her mother for the material she used in her most widely read novels, *Let the Hurricane Roar* and *Free Land*. Their artistic relationship was as deeply entwined as their familial one. Wilder, however, was the stronger novelist, Lane the stronger editor.

Devoted readers—young and old—continue to read Wilder's books and flock to the places throughout the Midwest that have a personal connection to Wilder, from Mansfield, Missouri, to De Smet, South Dakota. Many subscribe to the traditional view of Wilder's books—that they are purely autobiographical; others take a broader view. "What I love about her books is that they are true," a visitor to Rocky Ridge Farm confided to her companion. "Not true life. But true."[52] As for Wilder herself, she undoubtedly believed as Laura does in *By the Shores of Silver Lake,* when she tells Mary, "There were so many ways of seeing things and so many ways of saying them."[53]

Notes

The following abbreviations appear throughout these notes:

LIW   Laura Ingalls Wilder

RWL   Rose Wilder Lane

AJW   Almanzo James Wilder

References to Wilder's novels, published by Harper & Brothers and then Harper & Row, are taken from the revised edition with illustrations by Garth Williams, published in 1953. The first eight novels were originally published with illustrations by Helen Sewell and Mildred Boyle:

Little House in the Big Woods, 1932

Farmer Boy, 1933

Little House on the Prairie, 1935

On the Banks of Plum Creek, 1937

By the Shores of Silver Lake, 1939

The Long Winter, 1940

Little Town on the Prairie, 1941

These Happy Golden Years, 1943

After Wilder's death in 1957, several books were published by Harper & Row or HarperCollins based on her manuscripts, diaries, and letters:

On the Way Home, 1962

The First Four Years, 1971

West from Home, 1974

A Little House Traveler, 2006

I am indebted to the work of previous Wilder and Lane scholars including William T. Anderson, William Holtz, John E. Miller, and Rosa Ann Moore. Their publications on Laura Ingalls Wilder, Rose Wilder Lane, and their literary collaboration provided a solid foundation for my own interpretation of their lives and literary legacy.

Complete citations to these scholars' works appear in my endnotes for individual chapters. Various manuscript collections are also cited fully in the notes.

Introduction: Not the Whole Truth

1. LIW, Detroit Book Fair Speech, 1937, p. 8, Box 13, LIW Series, Rose Wilder Lane Papers (hereafter cited as Lane Papers), Herbert Hoover Presidential Library, West Branch, Iowa.

2. LIW to RWL, n.d. [1937], Box 13, Lane Papers.

3. LIW to RWL, 25 Jan. 1938, ibid.

4. *Springfield Leader & Press*, 9 Jan. 1949; *Springfield News/Leader*, 22 May 1949.

5. Madeleine L'Engle, *Herself* (Colorado Springs: Shaw Books, 2001), p. 322.

6. RWL to LIW, 21 Jan. 1938, Box 13, Lane Papers.

7. *Springfield News & Leader*, 1 Sept. 1974. *The First Four Years*, Wilder's ninth novel, was published in 1971, fourteen years after her death. Correspondence between Wilder and her daughter as well as Wilder's editor at Harper & Brothers indicates that LIW originally intended the book for adult readers. Although she wrote a complete first draft, she shared the manuscript with no one and did not try to publish it.

8. *Springfield News & Leader*, 22 May 1949.

9. Fred Kiewit, "Stories That Had To Be Told," *Kansas City Star*, n.d. [1955], clipping, State Archives Collection, South Dakota State Historical Society, Pierre, S.Dak.

10. LIW, *A Little House Reader: A Collection of Writings by Laura Ingalls Wilder*, ed. William Anderson (New York: HarperCollins, 1998), pp. 30–32; LIW, *These Happy Golden Years*, p. 98; RWL to LIW, 11 Apr. 1919, Box 13, Lane Papers.

11. LIW, Detroit Book Fair Speech, pp. 2–3.

Chapter 1: Once upon a Time, Years and Years Ago

1. LIW to RWL, 23 Mar. 1937, Box 13, LIW Series, Rose Wilder Lane Papers (hereafter cited as Lane Papers), Herbert Hoover Presidential Library, West Branch, Iowa.

2. LIW to Marion Fiery, n.d. [1931], Box 13, Lane Papers.

3. LIW, "Ideas for Work," Box 14, ibid.

4. LIW to Martha Carpenter, 22 June 1925, ibid.

5. Martha Carpenter to LIW, 2 Sept. 1925, ibid.

6. LIW, *Little House in the Big Woods,* p. 137; LIW, *Little Town on the Prairie,* p. 272.

7. John E. Miller, *Becoming Laura Ingalls Wilder: The Woman behind the Legend,* Missouri Biography Series (Columbia: University of Missouri Press, 1998), p. 18; Donald Zochert, *Laura: The Life of Laura Ingalls Wilder* (New York: Avon Books, 1976), p. 11.

8. Miller, *Becoming Laura Ingalls Wilder,* pp. 18–22; Zochert, *Laura,* pp. 22–23. Records are unclear about this move to Missouri in 1868. Miller mentions that, although Charles Ingalls and Henry Quiner bought property in Missouri, they may not have moved their families there. Zochert assumes that they did.

9. LIW, "Pioneer Girl," 1930, Folder 1, Laura Ingalls Wilder Home Association, Mansfield, Mo., Microfilm ed., LIW Papers, 1894–1943, Western Historical Manuscript Collection, Ellis Library, University of Missouri, Columbia, Mo. I have added punctuation where necessary to clarify meaning for modern readers; the manuscript is unpaginated. The original manuscript of this first draft of her memoir is housed at the Laura Ingalls Wilder Home Association, Mansfield, Mo. Two edited and typewritten versions of "Pioneer Girl" are part of the Rose Wilder Lane Papers at the Herbert Hoover Presidential Library in West Branch, Iowa.

10. George Bye to RWL, 6 Apr. 1931, Box 13, Lane Papers.

11. LIW, Detroit Book Week Speech, 1937, p. 3, ibid.

12. *These Happy Golden Years,* pp. 138–39.

Chapter 2: From Indian Territory to the Big Woods

1. Two typewritten and edited versions of "Pioneer Girl" are part of the Rose Wilder Lane Papers at the Herbert Hoover Presidential Library in West Branch, Iowa. Wilder's second book in the Little House series, *Farmer Boy,* is a fictionalized account of her husband's childhood in Malone, New York.

2. LIW, "Pioneer Girl," Folder 1, Laura Ingalls Wilder Home

Association, Mansfield, Mo., Microfilm ed., LIW Papers, 1894–1943, Western Historical Manuscript Collection, Ellis Library, University of Missouri, Columbia, Mo. The handwritten first draft of "Pioneer Girl" is unpaginated, but it is broken into six folders.

3. Ibid.

4. RWL to LIW, 12 Nov. 1930, Box 13, LIW Series, Rose Wilder Lane Papers (hereafter cited as Lane Papers), Herbert Hoover Presidential Library, West Branch, Iowa.

5. Virginia Kirkus to LIW, 15 Dec. 1931, ibid.

6. Many Wilder scholars and writers, most notably William T. Anderson, John E. Miller, and Donald Zochert, have commented extensively on this subject. Several chronologies published as booklets or pamphlets have also revealed inconsistencies between the facts of Wilder's life and her fiction. An example is Alma Abrahamson's "Timeline of the Little House Series," in *The Ingalls Family of De Smet* (De Smet, S.Dak.: Laura Ingalls Wilder Memorial Society, 2001), pp. 47–48.

7. U.S., Department of Interior, Bureau of the Census, *Ninth Census of the United States, 1870*, Rutland Township, Montgomery County, Kans., in *AncestryLibrary.com* (subscription required).

8. LIW, "Pioneer Girl," Folder 1.

9. Ibid.

10. LIW, "Pioneer Girl" (Brandt & Brandt manuscript), p. 6, Box 14, Lane Papers.

11. LIW, *Little House on the Prairie*, pp. 316–17.

12. John E. Miller, *Becoming Laura Ingalls Wilder: The Woman behind the Legend*, Missouri Biography Series (Columbia: University of Missouri Press, 1998), pp. 24–27.

13. LIW, *Little House on the Prairie*, pp. 332, 334–35.

14. LIW, "Pioneer Girl," Folder 1.

15. Miller, *Becoming Laura Ingalls Wilder*, pp. 26–27; Donald Zochert, *Laura: The Life of Laura Ingalls Wilder* (New York: Avon Books, 1976), p. 46.

16. LIW, "Pioneer Girl," Folder 1.

17. Ibid.

18. Ibid.

19. Ibid.

20. LIW, *Little House in the Big Woods*, pp. 131–55.

21. LIW, "Pioneer Girl," Folder 1.

22. LIW, *Little House in the Big Woods*, p. 1

23. LIW, "Pioneer Girl," Folder 1.

24. Miller, *Becoming Laura Ingalls Wilder*, p. 30; LIW, "Pioneer Girl," Folder 1.

25. LIW, "Pioneer Girl," Folder 1.

26. Ibid.

27. LIW, *Little House on the Prairie*, pp. 2, 4.

Chapter 3: A Light-Colored, Fleecy Cloud

1. LIW, "Pioneer Girl," Folder 1, Laura Ingalls Wilder Home Association, Mansfield, Mo., Microfilm ed., LIW Papers, 1894–1943, Western Historical Manuscript Collection, Ellis Library, University of Missouri, Columbia, Mo.

2. Ibid.

3. Ibid.

4. LIW, *On the Banks of Plum Creek,* pp. 10–12.

5. Ibid., p. 156.

6. LIW, "Pioneer Girl," Folder 1.

7. John E. Miller, *Becoming Laura Ingalls Wilder: The Woman behind the Legend,* Missouri Biography Series (Columbia: University of Missouri Press, 1998), p. 34.

8. LIW, "Pioneer Girl," Folder 1.

9. LIW, *On the Banks of Plum Creek,* p. 209.

10. LIW, "Pioneer Girl," Folder 2.

11. Ibid.; LIW, *On the Banks of Plum Creek,* pp. 271–75.

12. Actor and director Michael Landon set his popular television series from the 1970s, *Little House on the Prairie,* in Walnut Grove. Aside from the characters' names, the setting of Walnut Grove, and the television show's name (drawn from Wilder's novel *Little House on the Prairie,* which takes place in Kansas), the series had little in common with either Wilder's fiction or her memoir.

13. LIW, "Pioneer Girl," Folder 1.

14. Ibid., Folder 2. In this original draft of "Pioneer Girl," Wilder

recorded her age as seven shortly after describing this event in her life; in a later draft, she struck out her age. All versions of "Pioneer Girl" are episodic, and when she identified herself as seven, Wilder had just switched topics to describe memories of walking to school during the summer. This disparity in age could be one of those lapses in memory, or it could be that Wilder was referring to her age when the family first arrived at Plum Creek. She started to school during her first summer there.

15. LIW, "Pioneer Girl," Folder 2.

16. Ibid.

17. Ibid.

18. LIW, *On the Banks of Plum Creek*, pp. 335–39.

19. Miller, *Becoming Laura Ingalls Wilder*, p. 33.

20. LIW, *On the Banks of Plum Creek*, p. 6.

21. William and Mary Steadman later moved to southern Iowa. They and their children, Reuben, Thomas, and Mary, were living in Oskaloosa, Iowa, according to the 1885 Iowa State Census. *Iowa State Census Collection, 1836–1925*, in *AncestryLibrary.com* (subscription required).

22. LIW, "Pioneer Girl," Folder 2.

23. Ibid.

Chapter 4: A Story in Itself

1. LIW, "Pioneer Girl," Folder 2, Laura Ingalls Wilder Home Association, Mansfield, Mo., Microfilm ed., LIW Papers, 1894–1943, Western Historical Manuscript Collection, Ellis Library, University of Missouri, Columbia, Mo.

2. Ibid. The first names of Bisbee and the Starrs come from U.S., Department of the Interior, Census Office, *Tenth Census of the United States, 1880,* Burr Oak and West Decorah, Winneshiek County, Iowa.

3. LIW, "Pioneer Girl," Folder 2.

4. LIW to RWL, n.d. [1937], Box 13, LIW Series, Rose Wilder Lane Papers (hereafter cited as Lane Papers), Herbert Hoover Presidential Library, West Branch, Iowa.

5. LIW, "Pioneer Girl," Folder 2.

6. Ibid.

7. LIW to RWL, n.d. [1937], Box 13, Lane Papers.

8. Ibid.

9. LIW, "Pioneer Girl," Folder 2.

10. Ibid.

11. Ibid.; *Tenth Census, 1880,* Springdale, Redwood County, Minn.

12. LIW, "Pioneer Girl," Folder 2.

13. Ibid. In the original draft of "Pioneer Girl," Wilder spelled Genieve Masters's name two ways: "Jenieve" and, more frequently, "Genieve." In the typewritten versions, the spelling is "Jeneve." Since Wilder used the "Genieve" variation more often in her original manuscript, I have used that spelling.

14. LIW, "Pioneer Girl," Folder 2.

15. Ibid.; *Tenth Census, 1880,* Walnut Grove, Redwood County, Minn.

16. LIW, "Pioneer Girl," Folder 3. Lane used Wilder's story about the woman who cheated her sister in a short story titled "Object, Matrimony," published in the *Saturday Evening Post* in 1934 and reprinted in *A Little House Sampler,* ed. William T. Anderson (Lincoln: University of Nebraska Press, 1988), pp. 181–200. Lane embellished the story and changed the relationship between the two women, making them cousins rather than sisters. She also added details about character and setting that Wilder readers will recognize from the Little House books. Lane incorporated the story of the neighbor into a short story for the *Ladies Home Journal,* titled "Long Skirts," which later became part of her larger work, *Old Home Town* (New York: Longmans, Greene & Co., 1935), pp. 121–58.

17. LIW, "Pioneer Girl," Folder 3.

18. LIW to RWL, n.d. [1937], Box 13, Lane Papers.

19. LIW, "Pioneer Girl," Folder 2.

20. Ibid.

21. Ibid., Folder 3.

22. Ibid. *See also* John E. Miller, *Becoming Laura Ingalls Wilder: The Woman behind the Legend,* Missouri Biography Series (Columbia: University of Missouri Press, 1993), p. 43.

23. LIW, "Pioneer Girl," Folder 3. *See also* LIW, *By the Shores of Silver Lake,* pp. 3–4.

Chapter 5: The Great New Country: Dakota Territory

1. LIW, "Pioneer Girl," Folder 3, Laura Ingalls Wilder Home Association, Mansfield, Mo., Microfilm ed., LIW Papers, 1894–1943, Western Historical Manuscript Collection, Ellis Library, University of Missouri, Columbia, Mo.

2. Ibid.

3. RWL to LIW, n.d. [1931], Box 13, LIW Series, Rose Wilder Lane Papers (hereafter cited as Lane Papers), Herbert Hoover Presidential Library, West Branch, Iowa.

4. Wilder misspelled Brookings in both her memoir and her novels. *See* LIW, *By the Shores of Silver Lake*, p. 223, for example. She regretted the error and told an old family friend in De Smet that the books contained "several typographical errors in the spelling, besides leaving the 'g' out of Brookings." She added that at one point in the novel, "Mother's name is misspelled" (LIW to Aubrey Sherwood, 18 Nov. 1939, James Oliver Brown Collection, Rare Book and Manuscript Library, Columbia University, New York).

5. LIW, "Pioneer Girl," Folder 2. Lena and Gene were Hiram Forbes's children from a previous marriage.

6. LIW, *By the Shores of Silver Lake*, p. 54.

7. LIW, "Pioneer Girl," Folder 2.

8. Ibid. The chapter on Big Jerry occurs in LIW, *By the Shores of Silver Lake*, pp. 57–69.

9. LIW to RWL, n.d. [1932], Box 13, Lane Papers.

10. LIW, *By the Shores of Silver Lake,* p. 69.

11. LIW, "Pioneer Girl," Folder 3.

12. LIW, *By the Shores of Silver Lake,* p. 76.

13. LIW, "Pioneer Girl," Folder 3.

14. Ibid.

15. Rachel Clendenin, curator, Laura Ingalls Wilder Memorial Society, Inc., De Smet, S.Dak., to the author, 12 June 2007. Wilder's vivid descriptions of the house can be found in LIW, *By the Shores of Silver Lake*, pp. 141–45.

16. LIW, *By the Shores of Silver Lake*, p. 152

17. LIW, "Pioneer Girl," Folder 3.

18. LIW to RWL, n.d. [1932], File 13, Lane Papers.

19. John E. Miller, *Becoming Laura Ingalls Wilder: The Woman behind the Legend,* Missouri Biography Series (Columbia: University of Missouri Press, 1998), p. 50; LIW, *By the Shores of Silver Lake*, pp. 224–37.

20. LIW to Sherwood, 18 Nov. 1939.

21. LIW, "Pioneer Girl," Folder 3.

22. Ibid.; Herbert S. Schell, *History of South Dakota,* 4th ed., rev. John E. Miller (Pierre: South Dakota State Historical Society Press, 2004), pp. 158–74.

23. LIW, *By the Shores of Silver Lake,* p. 237.

24. Quoted in Kenneth M. Hammer, "Come to God's Country: Promotional Efforts in Dakota Territory, 1861–1889," *South Dakota History* 10 (Fall 1980): 305.

25. Schell, *History of South Dakota,* p. 159; Robert F. Karolevitz, *Challenge: The South Dakota Story* (Sioux Falls, S.Dak.: Brevet Press, 1975), pp. 159–60.

26. LIW, "Pioneer Girl," Folder 3.

27. LIW, *By the Shores of Silver Lake,* p. 234.

28. LIW, "Pioneer Girl," Folder 3. The fictional account of these events occurs in LIW, *By the Shores of Silver Lake,* pp. 224–31.

29. LIW, "Pioneer Girl," Folder 3.

30. LIW, *By the Shores of Silver Lake,* pp. 250–51.

31. LIW, "Pioneer Girl," Folder 3.

32. Ibid. For more about De Smet, *see* John E. Miller, *Laura Ingalls Wilder's Little Town: Where History and Literature Meet* (Lawrence: University Press of Kansas, 1994), esp. pp. 16–34.

33. LIW, "Pioneer Girl," Folder 3. The fictional murder can be found in LIW, *By the Shores of Silver Lake,* p. 257, and in RWL, *Free Land* (New York: Longmans, Green & Co, 1938), pp. 89-92. Many episodes in *Free Land* originated either from "Pioneer Girl" or from stories and information Lane gleaned from her parents.

34. LIW, "Pioneer Girl," Folder 3.

Chapter 6: A Malignant Power of Destruction

1. LIW, "Pioneer Girl," Folder 4, Laura Ingalls Wilder Home Association, Mansfield, Mo. Microfilm ed., LIW Papers, 1894–1943, Western Historical Manuscript Collection, Ellis Library, University of Missouri, Columbia, Mo.

2. RWL to George Bye, 5 June 1940, James Oliver Brown Collection, Rare Book and Manuscript Library, Columbia University, New York.

3. LIW, "Pioneer Girl," Folder 4.

4. RWL to George Bye, 30 July 1932, Brown Collection.

5. RWL, *Free Land* (New York: Longmans, Green & Co., 1938), pp. 153–65.

6. LIW to George Bye, 7 May 1940, Brown Collection.

7. LIW, "Pioneer Girl," Folder 4.

8. LIW to RWL, 7 Mar. 1938, Box 13, LIW Series, Rose Wilder Lane Papers (hereafter cited as Lane Papers), Herbert Hoover Presidential Library, West Branch, Iowa.

9. LIW, "Pioneer Girl," Folder 4. For more on the winter of 1880–1881, *see* Richard Maxwell Brown, "The Enduring Frontier: The Impact of Weather on South Dakota History and Literature," *South Dakota History* 15 (Spring/Summer 1985): 32. Pioneer memoirs and newspapers of this period contain accounts of the winter of 1880–1881, but a comprehensive history of the winter has not been written. The melting of the snow in the spring of 1881 caused disastrous floods on the Missouri River and its tributaries. *See* Herbert T. Hoover, John Rau, and Leonard R. Bruguier, "Gorging Ice and Flooding Rivers: Springtime Devastation in South Dakota," *South Dakota History* 17 (Fall/Winter 1987): 181–201.

10. LIW, "Pioneer Girl," Folder 4. *See also* LIW, *The Long Winter*, p. 237.

11. LIW, "Pioneer Girl," Folder 4.

12. Ibid.

13. LIW to RWL, 7 Mar. 1938.

14. LIW, "Pioneer Girl," Folder 4.

15. LIW to RWL, 7 Mar. 1938.

16. LIW, *The Long Winter*, pp. 249–50.

17. LIW to RWL, 7 Mar. 1938.

18. LIW to Martha Carpenter, 22 June 1925, Box 14, Lane Papers.

19. LIW, *Farmer Boy,* pp. 1–2.

20. Ibid, pp. 87–88.

21. John E. Miller, *Becoming Laura Ingalls Wilder: The Woman behind the Legend,* Missouri Biography Series (Columbia: University of Missouri Press, 1998), pp. 72–73. Lane built the opening sequence of her novel *Free Land* around her father's experiences filing a homestead with his sister Eliza. *See* RWL, *Free Land,* pp. 15–36.

22. LIW, "Pioneer Girl," Folder 4.

23. Ibid.

Chapter 7: Bessie and Manly

1. LIW, "Pioneer Girl," Folder 5, Laura Ingalls Wilder Home Association, Mansfield, Mo., Microfilm ed., LIW Papers, 1894–1943, Western Historical Manuscript Collection, Ellis Library, University of Missouri, Columbia, Mo.

2. Ibid.

3. Ibid. For more about Cap Garland, who died in a farm machinery accident in 1891, *see* Mary Fugate, "Grandma Garland," in *The Best of the* Lore (De Smet, S.Dak.: Laura Ingalls Wilder Memorial Society, 2007), pp. 88–91.

4. LIW, *These Happy Golden Years,* pp. 60–66.

5. LIW, "Pioneer Girl," Folder 5.

6. Ibid. *See also* LIW, *These Happy Golden Years*, pp. 69–77.

7. LIW, "Pioneer Girl," Folder 5.

8. Ibid. *See also* LIW, *These Happy Golden Years*, pp. 89–94.

9. LIW, "Pioneer Girl," Folder 4.

10. LIW, "Pioneer Girl: More Stories from the 'Little House,'" p. 236, File 1997.001.145, Laura Ingalls Wilder Memorial Society, Inc., De Smet, S.Dak. This manuscript in De Smet, a third unpublished but typewritten and edited copy of Wilder's autobiography, contains additional information. *See also* LIW, *Little Town on the Prairie,* pp. 35–46, 108–23.

11. LIW, "Pioneer Girl," Folder 4.

12. LIW, "Pioneer Girl" (Brandt & Brandt manuscript), p. 114, Box 14, LIW Series, Rose Wilder Lane Papers (hereafter cited as Lane Papers), Herbert Hoover Presidential Library, West Branch, Iowa.

13. LIW, "Pioneer Girl," Folder 6.

14. Ibid.

15. Ibid. The fictional version of this story can be found in LIW, *These Happy Golden Years*, p. 237.

16. LIW, "Pioneer Girl," Folder 5; LIW, *These Happy Golden Years*, p. 98.

17. LIW, *These Happy Golden Years*, p. 136.

18. LIW, "Pioneer Girl," Folder 5.

19. LIW, "The Difference," in *A Little House Reader*, ed. William Anderson (New York: HarperCollins, 1998), pp. 39–40.

20. RWL to LIW, 11 Apr. 1919, Box 13, Lane Papers. These children's stories do not appear to survive; Lane found them "not so important as the articles" Wilder was writing at the time.

21. LIW, "Pioneer Girl," Folder 5. A selection of Wilder's *Missouri Ruralist* writings can be found in *Little House Reader*, ed. Anderson, pp. 69–92.

22. LIW, *These Happy Golden Years*, pp. 157–63.

23. LIW, "Pioneer Girl," Folder 5.

24. LIW to RWL, 5 Feb. 1937, Box 13, Lane Papers.

25. LIW, "Pioneer Girl," Folder 5.

26. LIW, *Little House in the Big Woods*, p. 140.

27. LIW, "Pioneer Girl," Folder 6.

28. Ibid., Folders 5 and 6. The fictional version of the hat episode appears in LIW, *These Happy Golden Years*, pp. 248–50.

29. LIW, "Pioneer Girl," Folder 5.

30. LIW, *These Happy Golden Years*, pp. 172–77.

31. LIW, "Pioneer Girl," Folder 5.

32. LIW, *These Happy Golden Years*, p. 214.

33. LIW, "Pioneer Girl," Folder 6; LIW, *These Happy Golden Years*, pp. 279–89.

Chapter 8: A Faint Air of Disillusion

1. LIW to "Dear Children" (publisher's promotional letter),

Harper & Row, LIW Folder, State Archives Collection, South Dakota State Historical Society, Pierre, S.Dak.

2. LIW, "Pioneer Girl," Folder 6, Laura Ingalls Wilder Home Association, Mansfield, Mo., Microfilm ed., LIW Papers, 1894–1943, Western Historical Manuscript Collection, Ellis Library, University of Missouri, Columbia, Mo.

3. LIW, *The First Four Years,* pp. 23, 49–50, 57; John E. Miller, *Becoming Laura Ingalls Wilder: The Woman behind the Legend,* Missouri Biography Series (Columbia: University of Missouri Press, 1998), p. 74; Herbert S. Schell, *History of South Dakota,* 4th ed., rev. John E. Miller (Pierre: South Dakota State Historical Society Press, 2004), pp. 187–88.

4. LIW, *Farmer Boy,* pp. 370–71.

5. LIW, *The First Four Years,* p. 54; Miller, *Becoming Laura Ingalls Wilder,* pp. 79–89. Homesteaders could file on, or claim, an additional 160 acres if they planted ten acres in trees. Miller, *Becoming Laura Ingalls Wilder*, p. 73.

6. LIW, *The First Four Years,* pp. 68–72; William Anderson, comp., *Laura's Album: A Remembrance Scrapbook of Laura Ingalls Wilder* (New York: HarperCollins, 1998), p. 28; Donald Zochert, *Laura: The Life of Laura Ingalls Wilder* (Chicago: Contemporary Books, 1976), p. 211.

7. LIW, *The First Four Years,* pp. 71–72.

8. Miller, *Becoming Laura Ingalls Wilder,* p. 80.

9. LIW, *The First Four Years,* p. 88.

10. RWL, Introduction to LIW, *On the Way Home: The Diary of a Trip from South Dakota to Mansfield, Missouri, in 1894* (New York: Harper & Row, 1962), p. 2. During the 1880s, diphtheria killed hundreds of people, mostly children, in Dakota Territory. Survivors of the disease often suffered long-term paralysis and other complications. *See* Paula M. Nelson, "'In the Midst of Life We Are in Death': Medical Care and Mortality in Early Canton," *South Dakota History* 33 (Fall 2003): 216–18.

11. LIW, *The First Four Years,* p. 89.

12. Ibid.

13. RWL, Introduction to *On the Way Home,* p. 4.

14. LIW, "Pioneer Girl," Folder 6.

15. LIW, "So Far and Yet So Near," in *A Little House Reader: A Collection of Writings by Laura Ingalls Wilder,* ed. William Anderson (New York: HarperCollins, 1998), p. 48.

16. LIW, *The First Four Years,* p. 93; Miller, *Becoming Laura Ingalls Wilder,* pp. 81–82.

17. LIW, *The First Four Years*, pp. 125, 127.

18. Grace Ingalls Diary, 27 Aug. 1889, in *Little House Reader,* ed. Anderson, p. 27.

19. Ibid.

20. RWL, "I, Rose Wilder Lane, Am the Only Truly Happy Person I Know and I Discovered the Secret of Happiness on the Day I Tried to Kill Myself," *Hearst's International/Cosmopolitan* (June 1926): 42.

21. Ibid.

22. Grace Ingalls Diary, 18 May 1890, p. 28.

23. Miller, *Becoming Laura Ingalls Wilder,* pp. 86–88; William T. Anderson, ed., *A Little House Sampler* (Lincoln: University of Nebraska Press, 1988), pp. 40-41; William Holtz, *The Ghost in the Little House: A Life of Rose Wilder Lane,* Missouri Biography Series (Columbia: University of Missouri Press, 1993), pp. 23–24.

24. LIW, "Laura Ingalls Wilder," in *Junior Book of Authors,* 2d. ed., rev. Stanley J. Kunitz and Howard Haycroft (New York: Wilson, 1951), p. 299.

25. RWL, Introduction to *On the Way Home,* p. 1. Using the profits from the sale of sheep in 1890, Almanzo had purchased his tree claim outright, but he was apparently unable to hold onto it in the national financial panic of 1893. Miller, *Becoming Laura Ingalls Wilder*, p. 85.

26. LIW to RWL, n.d. [1937], and Ida Louise Raymond to LIW, 18 Dec. 1937, Box 13, LIW Series, Rose Wilder Lane Papers (hereafter cited as Lane Papers), Herbert Hoover Presidential Library, West Branch, Iowa. When Wilder actually wrote her handwritten draft of *The First Four Years* is unclear, but it is unlikely that she wrote it in 1937 when she first told Lane and Ida Louise Raymond about her idea for the story. Wilder was then working on *By the Shores of Silver Lake* and already thinking about *The Long Winter.* In 1940, she

wrote her literary agent George Bye that a story to follow her eighth book and "telling of what next happens is taking shape slowly in my mind, but it is to[o] soon to say if it will crystalize into a completely adult novel. I can only say perhaps it may do so" (LIW to Bye, 21 June 1940, James Oliver Brown Collection, Rare Book and Manuscript Library, Columbia University, New York). Three years later, Wilder wrote Bye again: "I don't know what to say about my writing more. I have thought that "Golden Years" was my last; that I would spend what is left of my life in living, not writing about it, but a story keeps stirring around in my mind and if it pesters me enough I may write it down and send it to you sometime in the future" (LIW to Bye, 10 May 1943, Brown Collection).

27. LIW, *The First Four Years*, pp. 3–4.

28. Ibid., pp. 4–5.

29. LIW, "Pioneer Girl," Folder 6.

30. Ursula Nordstrom to Virginia Haviland, 8 Apr. 1969, in *Dear Genius: The Letters of Ursula Nordstrom*, ed. Leonard S. Marcus (New York: HarperCollins, 1998), pp. 267–63.

31. Nordstrom to Zena Sutherland, 18 Nov. 1969, ibid., p. 289.

32. This argument is the entire premise of William Holtz's biography of Rose Wilder Lane, *The Ghost in the Little House.*

33. RWL to LIW, 20 Dec. 1937, Box 13, Lane Papers.

34. LIW to RWL, n.d. [1937], ibid. It is interesting that while the manuscript was apparently not written yet, this time period in Wilder's life was already known as "The First Three Years." Lane's extensive use of her mother's material from "Pioneer Girl" for both *Let the Hurricane Roar* and *Free Land* is discussed more fully in chapter 14.

35. LIW, "Our Little Place in the Ozarks," in *Little House in the Ozarks: The Rediscovered Writings*, ed. Stephen W. Hines (New York: Galahad Books, 1991), p. 27.

36. RWL, *Let the Hurricane Roar* (New York: Longmans, Green & Co., 1933), p. 6.

37. LIW, *The First Four Years*, pp. 9–10.

38. RWL, *Let the Hurricane Roar*, pp. 18–19.

39. LIW, *The First Four Years,* pp. 70–71.

40. RWL, *Let the Hurricane Roar*, p. 152.

41. LIW, *The First Four Years*, pp. 133–34.

42. LIW to RWL, n.d. [1937], Box 13, Lane Papers.

43. RWL, "A Word about Herself," *Free Land* (New York: Longmans, Green & Co, 1938), jacket copy.

44. Eloise Jarvis McGraw, "Welcome to the Club," in unpublished manuscript (author's copy), pp. 4–5.

45. LIW, *The First Four Years*, p. 134.

46. RWL, Introduction to *On the Way Home*, pp. 4, 6.

47. Wilder described Wright County as the "Land of the Big Red Apple" in a 1923 newspaper column titled "Our Little Place in the Ozarks," reprinted in *Little House in the Ozarks*, ed. Hines, p. 26.

48. RWL, Introduction to *On the Way Home*, pp. 8–10; Miller, *Becoming Laura Ingalls Wilder*, pp. 89–90.

Chapter Nine: The Sky Seems Lower Here

1. *Mansfield Mirror*, 2 May 1957, clipping, Box 17, LIW Series, Rose Wilder Lane Papers (hereafter cited as Lane Papers), Herbert Hoover Presidential Library, West Branch, Iowa.

2. LIW, *On the Way Home: The Diary of a Trip from South Dakota to Mansfield, Missouri, in 1894* (New York: Harper & Row, 1962), pp. 10–11.

3. LIW, *On the Way Home*, p. 15.

4. RWL, Introduction to ibid., pp. 11–12.

5. Ibid., pp. 8, 10. *See also* John E. Miller, *Becoming Laura Ingalls Wilder: The Woman behind the Legend*, Missouri Biography Series (Columbia: University of Missouri Press, 1998), p. 92.

6. LIW, *On the Way Home*, pp. 24, 62.

7. Ibid., pp. 18–23, 31, 33, 36–37, 51, 59.

8. Ibid., pp. 23–24.

9. Ibid., pp. 17, 41–42.

10. Ibid., p. 37.

11. Ibid., pp. 65, 67–69.

12. Ibid., pp. 71–74. Wilder summarized the first six weeks of her journal in a short letter that summer for the *De Smet News*. The text of this letter appears on pages 87–88 in *A Little House Sampler*, ed.

William Anderson (New York: HarperCollins, 1995).

13. RWL, Afterword to *On the Way Home*, pp. 76–79.

14. Ibid., pp. 79, 81.

15. RWL to LIW, Correspondence 1908-ca. 1914, Box 13, Lane Papers.

16. RWL to LIW, ibid.

17. RWL, "Rose Wilder Lane by Herself," *Sunset Magazine* 41 (1918): n.p.

18. RWL to Guy Moyston, 27 July 1925, Box 13, Lane Papers.

19. *Mansfield Mirror*, 2 May 1957, clipping. Box 17, ibid.

20. Miller, *Becoming Laura Ingalls Wilder*, p. 96.

21. LIW, "Rocky Ridge Farm," *Missouri Ruralist*, July 1911, in *Writings to Young Women from Laura Ingalls Wilder: On Life as a Pioneer Woman*, ed. Stephen W. Hines (Nashville: Tommy Nelson, 2006), p. 21.

22. *Mansfield Mirror*, 5 May 1949, clipping, State Archives Collection, South Dakota State Historical Society, Pierre.

23. RWL, Afterword to *On the Way Home*, pp. 91–95; LIW, "Rocky Ridge Farm," in *Writings to Young Women*, ed. Hines, pp. 22–23; Miller, *Becoming Laura Ingalls Wilder*, p. 98.

24. Miller, *Becoming Laura Ingalls Wilder*, p. 99.

25. RWL, "An Autobiographical Sketch of Rose Wilder Lane," n.d., Box 5, Lane Papers.

26. Lynn Morrow and Linda Myers-Phinney, *Shepherd of the Hills Country: Tourism Transforms the Ozarks, 1880s to 1930s* (Fayetteville: University of Arkansas Press, 1999), pp. 78, 82, 96.

27. LIW, "My Apple Orchard," June 1912, *Missouri Ruralist;* reprinted in *Writings to Young Women*, ed. Hines, p. 15.

28. John F. Case, "Let's Visit Mrs. Wilder," *Missouri Ruralist*, Feb. 1918, reprinted in *A Little House Sampler,* ed. Anderson (Lincoln: University of Nebraska Press, 1988), p. 9.

29. LIW, "Pioneer Girl," Folder 5, Laura Ingalls Wilder Home Association, Mansfield, Mo., Microfilm ed., LIW Papers, 1894–1943, Western Historical Manuscript Collection, Ellis Library, University of Missouri, Columbia, Mo.

30. Miller, *Becoming Laura Ingalls Wilder*, p. 100.

31. LIW, "Rocky Ridge Farm," p. 25.

32. "Laura Ingalls Wilder," *Wilson Library Bulletin* 52 (Apr. 1948): 582, clipping, Box 17, Lane Papers.

33. Miller, *Becoming Laura Ingalls Wilder*, pp. 109, 111. *See also* William Holtz, *The Ghost in the Little House: A Life of Rose Wilder Lane,* Missouri Biography Series (Columbia: University of Missouri Press, 1993), pp. 41–42. Wilder also made several references to the increasing acreage of Rocky Ridge Farm in her columns for the *Missouri Ruralist.*

34. RWL, "I, Rose Wilder Lane, Am the Only Truly Happy Person I Know and I Discovered the Secret of Happiness on the Day I Tried to Kill Myself," *Hearst's International/Cosmopolitan* (June 1926): 42.

35. RWL, Introduction to *On the Way Home*, p. 3.

36. RWL, Afterword, ibid., p. 95.

37. RWL to Clarence Day, 26 June 1928, Box 5, Lane Papers.

38. RWL to Berta and Elmer Hader, ca. 1919, ibid.

39. LIW, "Pioneer Girl," Folder 4.

40. LIW, *Little Town on the Prairie*, pp. 172–73.

41. RWL, "An Autobiographical Sketch of Rose Wilder Lane," in *Saturday Evening Post*, clipping, p. 9, Box 5, Lane Papers.

42. RWL, Diary, 1927–1930, 11 Feb. 1929, Lane Papers.

Chapter 10: The Result of Evolution

1. LIW, "The Building of a Farm House," in *A Little House Reader: A Collection of Writings by Laura Ingalls Wilder*, ed. William Anderson (New York: HarperCollins, 1998), p. 52.

2. RWL, Afterword to *On the Way Home: The Diary of a Trip from South Dakota to Mansfield, Missouri, in 1894* (New York: Harper & Row, 1962), p. 97.

3. LIW, "Building of a Farm House," p. 52. *See also* RWL, Afterword to *On the Way Home*, pp. 100–101.

4. LIW, "My Dream House," in *Little House in the Ozarks: The Rediscovered Writings*, ed. Stephen W. Hines (New York: Galahad Books, 1991), p. 34.

5. LIW, "Building of a Farm House," pp. 53–54.

6. Quoted in Fiona MacCarthy, *William Morris: A Life for Our Time* (New York: Alfred A. Knopf, 1995), p. 185.

7. LIW, "Building of a Farm House," p. 60.

8. Janice Bennet, tour guide, Rocky Ridge Farmhouse, 25 May 2006.

9. LIW, "Building of a Farm House," pp. 60-61.

10. LIW, "My Dream House," p. 35.

11. LIW, "Ideas for Work," Box 12, LIW Series, Rose Wilder Lane Papers (hereafter cited as Lane Papers), Herbert Hoover Presidential Library, West Branch, Iowa.

12. Willam Anderson, comp., *Laura's Album: A Remembrance Scrapbook of Laura Ingalls Wilder* (New York: HarperCollins, 1998), p. 42.

13. Quoted in John F. Case, "Let's Visit Mrs. Wilder," in *A Little House Sampler*, ed. William Anderson (New York: HarperPerennial, 1988), p. 7.

14. John E. Miller, *Becoming Laura Ingalls Wilder: The Woman behind the Legend*, Missouri Biography Series (Columbia: University of Missouri Press, 1998), p. 115; Billy C. Brantley, "History of the *Missouri Ruralist*, 1902 through 1955" (M.A. thesis, University of Missouri, 1958), pp. 9–10, 18, 43, 74.

15. Case, "Let's Visit Mrs. Wilder," p. 7.

16. LIW, "The Home Beauty Parlor," pp. 65-69; "Rocky Ridge Farm," pp. 21-26, and "My Apple Orchard," pp. 11-17; all in *Writings to Young Women from Laura Ingalls Wilder: On Life as a Pioneer Woman*, ed. Stephen W. Hines (Nashville, Tenn.: Tommy Nelson, 2006).

17. LIW, "Rocky Ridge Farm," p. 26.

18. LIW, "This and That—a Neighborly Visit with Laura," ibid., p. 70.

19. LIW, "The Man of the Place," in *Little House in the Ozarks*, ed. Hines, pp. 66-67.

20. LIW, "New Day for Women," in *Writings to Young Women*, ed. Hines, p. 74.

21. LIW, "Shorter Hours for the Farm Home Manager," in *Little House in the Ozarks*, p. 196.

22. Brantley, "History of the *Missouri Ruralist*," pp. 1, 118. The

online address for the *Missouri Ruralist* is www.missouriruralist. com.

23. Miller, *Becoming Laura Ingalls Wilder*, p. 116; LIW, "Laura's Land Congress Speech," in *Little House Sampler*, ed. Anderson, p. 97.

24. Quoted in Case, "Let's Visit Mrs. Wilder," p. 10.

25. Brantley, "History of the *Missouri Ruralist*," p. 94. Under Case's editorial direction, the *Missouri Ruralist* also increased its coverage of women's issues, something which could only deepen Wilder's value to the newspaper (p. 103). Case and Wilder also shared early memories of Dakota Territory. When he was five, his family crossed into present-day South Dakota from Minnesota during the land boom and remained there until he was twelve (pp. 78-79).

26. William Holtz, *The Ghost in the Little House: A Life of Rose Wilder Lane,* Missouri Biography Series (Columbia: University of Missouri Press, 1993), pp. 51–52.

27. RWL to LIW, Correspondence 1908-ca. 1914, Box 13, Lane Papers.

28. Ibid., n.d.[1911–1914].

29. Ibid., n.d. [1914].

30. LIW to AJW, 21 Aug. 1915, in LIW, "West from Home," in *A Little House Traveler: Writings from Laura Ingalls Wilder's Journeys across America* (New York: HarperCollins, 2006), pp. 134–36. Wilder closed this first letter, "I'll get back before you get to learn how to get on without me."

31. LIW to AJW, 11 Sept. 1915, ibid., p. 190.

32. Ibid., 29 Aug. 1915, p. 152.

33. Ibid., 4 Sept. 1915, p. 178.

34. Ibid., 29 Aug. 1915, p. 163.

35. Ibid., 21 Sept. 1915, p. 208.

36. Ibid., 13, 15 Sept. 1915, pp. 195, 201.

37. Ibid., 21 Sept. 1915, p. 212.

38. Ibid., 4 Oct. 1915, p. 242–43.

39. Ibid., 21 Sept., 14, 22 Oct. 1915, pp. 212, 248, 271; Miller, *Becoming Laura Ingalls Wilder*, pp. 127–28.

40. LIW to AJW, 22 Oct. 1915, in "West From Home," p. 271.

41. Ibid., 22 Oct. 1915, pp. 268–69.

42. Case, "Let's Visit Mrs. Wilder " p. 11.

43. Miller, *Becoming Laura Ingalls Wilder*, pp. 123, 128–29.

44. LIW, "Tuck'em In Corner," Box 14, Lane Papers. Some of the poems carry Lane's byline, and some are unsigned. The few that Wilder wrote have been collected as *Laura Ingalls Wilder's Fairy Poems*, comp. Stephen W. Hines (New York: Doubleday, 1998).

45. Holtz, *Ghost in the Little House*, p. 93.

46. RWL to LIW, n.d. [Nov. 1924], Box 13, Lane Papers.

Chapter 11: No Opportunity in Children's Stories

1. LIW, "Whom Will You Marry?," reprinted in *A Little House Reader: A Collection of Writings by Laura Ingalls Wilder*, ed. William Anderson (New York: HarperCollins, 1998), p. 131.

2. Ibid., pp. 134, 140.

3. RWL to LIW, 11 Apr. 1919, Box 13, LIW Series, Rose Wilder Lane Papers (hereafter cited as Lane Papers), Herbert Hoover Presidential Library, West Branch, Iowa.

4. Ibid., Nov. [1924], ibid.

5. Ibid., 11 Apr. 1919.

6. Ibid., Nov. [1924].

7. "The Heart and Home of Rose Wilder Lane," *Kansas City Star,* reprinted in *Springfield Leader & Press*, 5 July 1925, clipping, RWL File, Greene County Local History Library Collection, Mansfield, Mo.

8. William Holtz, *The Ghost in the Little House: A Life of Rose Wilder Lane,* Missouri Biography Series (Columbia: University of Missouri Press, 1993), p. 150.

9. "Heart and Home of Rose Wilder Lane."

10. LIW, "The Hard Winter," in *Writings to Young Women from Laura Ingalls Wilder: On Life as a Pioneer Woman*, ed. Stephen W. Hines (Nashville, Tenn.: Tommy Nelson, 2006), pp. 30–33.

11. LIW, "The Friday Night Literary," in *Little House in the Ozarks: The Rediscovered Writings*, ed. Stephen W. Hines (New York: Galahad Books, 1991), p. 150.

12. John E. Miller, *Becoming Laura Ingalls Wilder: The Woman behind the Legend,* Missouri Biography Series (Columbia: University of Missouri Press, 1998), p. 165.

13. RWL to LIW, 11 Apr. 1919, Box 13, Lane Papers.

14. Ibid.

15. Ibid.

16. LIW, "Home for Christmas," in *A Little House Sampler*, ed. William Anderson (Lincoln: University of Nebraska Press, 1988), p. 37.

17. LIW, "First Memories of Father," *Little House Reader*, ed. Anderson, pp. 159–60.

18. "Mother Passed Away," in *Little House in the Ozarks*, ed. Hines, p. 313.

19. Miller, *Becoming Laura Ingalls Wilder*, p. 164.

20. RWL to LIW, 12 Nov. [1924], Box 13, Lane Papers.

21. RWL to LIW, Nov. [1924]. Lane did not like to have someone rewrite her work any better than Wilder did. A few years later, Lane complained to her agent that a magazine had printed a story with her name on it, but "they not only cut all the story out of it, but wrote in a little; it's a horrible mess, stupid and meaningless" (RWL to George Bye, 12 Aug. 1932, James Oliver Brown Collection, Rare Book and Manuscript Library, Columbia University, New York).

22. E-mail interview with Margery Cuyler, 3 Mar. 2007.

23. RWL to LIW, 12 Nov. [1924].

24. Miller, *Becoming Laura Ingalls Wilder*, pp. 128, 163–64, 178; John F. Case, "Let's Visit Mrs. Wilder," in *A Little House Sampler*, ed. Anderson, p. 7. In 1911, Wilder wrote about the up-to-date farm woman, who stayed informed via new technologies. *See* LIW, "The March of Progress," in *Writings to Young Women*, ed. Hines, pp. 43–50.

25. "Heart and Home of Rose Wilder Lane."

26. Holtz, *Ghost in the Little House*, pp. 66, 90, 145, 153.

27. Ibid., pp. 103, 160.

28. RWL to Mr. Broun, 8 July 1929, Box 10, Lane Papers.

29. RWL to Mr. Colcord, 8 July 1929, ibid.

30. Holtz, *Ghost in the Little House,* p. 180.

31. RWL to Clarence Day, 26 June 1928, Box 5, Lane Papers.

32. Holtz, *Ghost in the Little House,* pp. 176–77.

33. LIW to RWL, 19 Feb. 1938, Box 13, Lane Papers.

34. Miller, *Becoming Laura Ingalls Wilder,* pp. 171–72; Holtz, *Ghost in the Little House,* p. 217.

Chapter 12: Interesting Pioneer Reminiscences

1. RWL to Fremont Older, 31 Oct. 1928, Box 13, LIW Series, Rose Wilder Lane Papers (hereafter cited as Lane Papers), Herbert Hoover Presidential Library, West Branch, Iowa.

2. House plans, Box 10, ibid.

3. Eugene F. Johnson to RWL, 28 Dec. 1928, ibid.

4. Furniture company invoices, ibid.

5. Johnson to RWL, 28 Dec. 1928; William Holtz, *The Ghost in the Little House: A Life of Rose Wilder Lane,* Missouri Biography Series (Columbia: University of Missouri Press, 1993), p. 195. Lane had met Helen Boylston, known as Troub (short for Troubles, a family nickname) in 1920, when they were both working on assignment in Europe with the Red Cross. Boylston was a registered nurse, who—after encouragement from Lane—turned to writing. Boylston is remembered today for her Sue Barton novels. The first book, *Sue Barton, Student Nurse,* published in 1936, essentially launched the career-series genre for girls. Wilder first met Troub in 1925, when she visited Rocky Ridge with Lane, and the three of them had taken a road trip together to California in Isabelle, the 1923 Buick sedan. Holtz, *Ghost in the Little House,* pp. 149, 157–58; Michael Cart, *From Romance to Realism: 50 Years of Growth and Change in Young Adult Literature* (New York: Harper Collins, 1996), pp. 14–15.

6. RWL to Older, 31 Oct. 1928

7. LIW, "My Dream House," in *Little House in the Ozarks: The Rediscovered Writings,* ed. Stephen W. Hines (New York: Galahad Books, 1991), p. 34.

8. RWL to Fremont Older, 16 Nov. 1928, Box 10, Lane Papers.

9. Eugene F. Johnson to RWL, 21 Dec. 1928, ibid.

10. Ibid., 28 Dec. 1928.

11. RWL to Fremont Older, 23 Jan. 1929, ibid.

12. Spread sheet, 20 Dec. 1928, ibid.; Johnson to RWL, 28 Dec. 1928.

13. RWL to George Bye, 9 Jan. 1932, James Oliver Brown Collection, Rare Book and Manuscript Library, Columbia University, New York.

14. John E. Miller, *Becoming Laura Ingalls Wilder: The Woman behind the Legend,* Missouri Biography Series (Columbia: University of Missouri Press, 1998), pp. 180–81; Holtz, *Ghost in the Little House*, pp. 219–27; William T. Anderson, "Laura Ingalls Wilder and Rose Wilder Lane: The Continuing Collaboration," *South Dakota History* 16 (Summer 1986): 94–95; RWL to Bye, 9 Jan. 1932.

15. Carrie Ingalls Swanzey to LIW, 15 Oct. 1928, Laura Ingalls Wilder Historic Home and Museum, Mansfield, Mo.

16. LIW, "Pioneer Girl," Folder 2, Laura Ingalls Wilder Home Association, Mansfield, Mo., Microfilm ed., LIW Papers, 1894–1943, Western Historical Manuscript Collection, Ellis Library, University of Missouri, Columbia, Mo.

17. LIW, "Pioneer Girl" (Brandt & Brandt manuscript), p. 1, Box 14, Lane Papers.

18. LIW, "Pioneer Girl," Folder 1.

19. Ibid., Folder 2.

20. LIW, "Pioneer Girl" (Brandt & Brandt manuscript), pp. 27–28.

21. Phillip D. Bennet, *Laura's Pathway to Home* (Mansfield, Mo.: By the Author, 2004), p. 29.

22. LIW to RWL, 25 Jan. 1938, Box 13, Lane Papers. A more complete discussion of correspondence about the Little House series appears in Chapters 14–16.

23. William Holtz in his biography of Rose Wilder Lane, *Ghost in the Little House*, maintains that not only did Wilder passively submit to her daughter's editorial suggestions, but that Lane essentially wrote all the books in the Little House series. Other scholars share this view.

24. RWL, Diary, 1927–1930, 31 July 1930, Box 21, Lane Papers.

25. George T. Bye to RWL, 22 Apr. 1931, Box 13, ibid.; Miller, *Becoming Laura Ingalls Wilder*, pp. 181–82; Holtz, *Ghost in the Little House*, pp. 219–23.

26. RWL to LIW, 12 Nov. 1930, Box 13, Lane Papers.

27. *Country Home* to LIW, 1 May 1931, ibid.

Chapter 13: Not a Great Deal of Money

1. George T. Bye to RWL, 6 Apr. 1931, RWL to George Bye, 25 Sept. 1931, and Jasper Spock to RWL, 24 Feb. 1933, all in Box 13, LIW Series, Rose Wilder Lane Papers (hereafter cited as Lane Papers), Herbert Hoover Presidential Library West Branch, Iowa.

2. RWL/LIW, "When Grandma Was a Little Girl," p. 1, ibid.

3. RWL to LIW, 16 Feb. 1931, ibid.

4. Marion Fiery to LIW, 12 Feb. 1931, ibid.

5. Ibid.

6. E-mail interview with Regina Griffin, New York City, 22 May 2007.

7. Marion Fiery to LIW, 12 Feb. 1931.

8. RWL/LIW, "When Grandma Was a Little Girl," p. 1. The first page of this manuscript is reproduced in William T. Anderson, "The Literary Apprenticeship of Laura Ingalls Wilder," *South Dakota History* 13 (Winter 1983): 322.

9. RWL to LIW, 16 Feb. 1931.

10. William Holtz, *The Ghost in the Little House: A Life of Rose Wilder Lane,* Missouri Biography Series (Columbia: University of Missouri Press, 1993), p. 99.

11. RWL to LIW, 16 Feb. 1931.

12. E-mail interview with Margery Cuyler, New York City, 22 Mar. 2007.

13. E-mail interview with Regina Griffin.

14. Ursula Nordstrom to Doris K. Stotz, 11 Jan. 1967, in *Dear Genius: The Letters of Ursula Nordstrom*, ed. Leonard S. Marcus (New York: HarperCollins, 1998), p. 234.

15. E-mail interview with Margery Cuyler.

16. E-mail interview with Regina Griffin.

17. RWL to LIW, 16 Feb. 1931.

18. RWL to George Bye, 5 Oct. 1931, Box 13, Lane Papers.

19. LIW, draft of *Little House in the Big Woods*, Folder 7, Laura Ingalls Wilder Home Association, Mansfield, Mo., Microfilm ed.,

LIW Papers, 1894–1943, (hereafter cited as LIW papers), Western Historical Manuscript Collection, Ellis Library, University of Missouri, Columbia, Mo.

20. LIW to RWL, 17 Aug. 1938, Box 13, Lane Papers.

21. LIW, Correspondence and Notes, *On the Banks of Plum Creek,* Folder 19, LIW Papers.

22. LIW, "My Work," in *A Little House Sampler: A Collection of Early Stories and Reminiscences*, ed. William Anderson (New York: Harper Perennial, 1988), p. 179.

23. Marjorie Vitense to LIW, 22 Feb. 1933, Folder 14, LIW Papers.

24. LIW, draft of *Little House in the Big Woods*, Folder 7.

25. LIW, *Little House in the Big Woods*, pp. 2–3.

26. John E. Miller, *Becoming Laura Ingalls Wilder: The Woman behind the Legend,* Missouri Biography Series (Columbia: University of Missouri Press, 1998), p. 184; Holtz, *Ghost in the Little House*, p. 225.

27. RWL to Marion Fiery, 27 May 1931, Box 13, Lane Papers.

28. LIW/RWL, "Suggested Titles," 1931, ibid.

29. Miller, *Becoming Laura Ingalls Wilder,* p. 185; William T. Anderson, "How the 'Little House' Books Found a Publishing Home," *Language Arts* 58 (Apr. 1981): 439; Marion Fiery to RWL, 3 Nov. 1931, Box 13, Lane Papers.

30. Marion Fiery to RWL, 3 Nov. 1931.

31. Ibid.

32. RWL to Marian Fiery, n.d. [1931], Box 13, Lane Papers.

33. Marion Fiery to George T. Bye, 28 Nov. 1931, ibid.; Anderson, "How the 'Little House' Books Found a Publishing Home," p. 440.

34. Virginia Kirkus, "The Discovery of Laura Ingalls Wilder," *The Horn Book Magazine* 29 (Dec. 1953): 428–29.

35. Virginia Kirkus to LIW, 8 Dec. 1931, Box 13, Lane Papers.

36. Ibid.

37. Virginia Kirkus to LIW, 15 Dec. 1931, Box 13, Lane Papers. Galley proofs, sometimes simply called galleys, are loose, typeset pages of a manuscript. What will eventually become two pages of the printed book usually run down the length of each galley page;

margins are wide so that writers and editors can easily make corrections on each page. Page proofs usually come later in the publication process and show two pages side by side as they will look in the finished book.

38. Virginia Kirkus to LIW, 18 Dec. 1931, and Jasper Spock, George T. Bye Agency, 17 Jan. 1933, both in Box 13, Lane Papers.

Chapter 14: Let the Hurricane Roar

1. William Holtz, *The Ghost in the Little House: A Life of Rose Wilder Lane,* Missouri Biography Series (Columbia: University of Missouri Press, 1993), p. 230; John E. Miller, *Becoming Laura Ingalls Wilder: The Woman behind the Legend,* Missouri Biography Series (Columbia: University of Missouri Press, 1998), p. 190.

2. LIW, "The Man of the Place," reprinted in *Little House in the Ozarks: The Rediscovered Writings,* ed. Stephen W. Hines (New York: Galahad Books, 1991), p. 66–67.

3. LIW to AJW, 21 Sept. 1925, Box 13, LIW Series, Rose Wilder Lane Papers (hereafter cited as Lane Papers), Herbert Hoover Presidential Library, West Branch, Iowa.

4. A prime example of the application of this gender-based publishing adage in today's market is J. K. Rowling's Harry Potter series. It is hard to imagine that the series would have had such universal appeal among young (and adult) readers of both sexes if the main character were an orphaned witch rather than an orphaned wizard. On the other hand, the only other children's book series that even remotely parallels Harry Potter's almost unprecedented popularity among boys as well as girls appeared in the early twentieth century, and its most enduring and widely known main character was indeed a girl: Dorothy Gale of L. Frank Baum's Oz books. As Wilder returned to autobiographical fiction after the publication of *Farmer Boy,* she worried that her books would appeal only to girls. She was delighted when she received fan letters from boys. LIW to RWL, 19 Feb. 1938, Box 13, Lane Papers.

5. Holtz, *Ghost in the Little House,* p. 230; Miller, *Becoming Laura Ingalls Wilder,* p. 190.

6. LIW, Diary, 1931–1935, 22 Sept. 1933, Box 22, Lane Papers;

William T. Anderson, "Laura Ingalls Wilder and Rose Wilder Lane: The Continuing Collaboration," *South Dakota History* 16 (Summer 1986): 131. Lane wrote in her diary that Harper's "refused" the manuscript; whether or not the editor also suggested revisions or pinpointed its problem areas is unknown.

7. RWL to Marion Fiery, 3 Oct. 1931, Box 13, Lane Papers.

8. LIW, "The Road Back," in *A Little House Traveler: Writings from Laura Ingalls Wilder's Journeys across America* (New York: Harper-Collins, 2006), pp. 307, 311, 314. Grace Ingalls Dow married Nate Dow in De Smet on 16 October 1901. Before settling in Manchester with her husband, she was a schoolteacher. Carrie Ingalls married David Swanzey, a widower, on 1 August 1912. Before her marriage at the age of forty-two, Carrie homesteaded in western South Dakota, learned the printing business, and managed several newspapers in the southern Black Hills. Neither Carrie nor Grace had children of their own. *The Ingalls Family of De Smet* (De Smet, S.Dak.: Laura Ingalls Wilder Memorial Society, 2001), pp. 21–28.

9. RWL to Clarence Day, 26 June 1928, Box 5, Lane Papers.

10. William Holtz, *Ghost in the Little House,* pp. 230, 232; Miller, *Becoming Laura Ingalls Wilder,* pp. 190, 195; Anderson, "Laura Ingalls Wilder and Rose Wilder Lane," pp. 104–5.

11. RWL, *Let the Hurricane Roar* (New York: Longmans, Green & Co., 1933), pp. 3–4, 7.

12. RWL to LIW, 16 Feb. 1931, Box 13, Lane Papers.

13. RWL, *Let the Hurricane Roar*, pp. 7–8, 10–11.

14. Ibid., pp. 10, 14–16, 22–23, 40–43, 136, 151–52.

15. All three generations of women, Caroline Ingalls, Wilder, and Lane, lost infant sons. Lane, however, maintained that she had not known anything about her little brother until after her mother's death in 1957. Holtz, *Ghost in the Little House*, pp. 341, 414n.6. It seems unlikely, however, that her parents kept the loss a secret, especially since Wilder included it in her story of their early marriage. Lane herself wrote vividly about her memories of her parents' battle against diphtheria, which predated the birth of her little brother, and about her role in the De Smet house fire, which took place shortly after his death. It seems odd that Lane would have no

memory of a family tragedy that occurred between two others that she explicitly recalled.

16. RWL, *Let the Hurricane Roar*, pp. 37, 50, 132–52.

17. Ibid., p. 67.

18. RWL to Eleanor Hubbard Garst, n.d., reproduced in *Better Homes & Gardens* (Dec. 1933): 19.

19. Review of "Let the Hurricane Roar," *Saturday Evening Post* (4 Mar. 1933): 22. During the late 1970s, *Let the Hurricane Roar* was retitled *Young Pioneers* and adapted into a made-for-television movie, also called *Young Pioneers*. The renewed interest in Lane's work coincided with the premier of the television series *Little House on the Prairie*. As *Young Pioneers*, Lane's novel is now usually classified as young adult fiction. For modern readers, *Let the Hurricane Roar* and much of Wilder's later fiction—from *By the Shores of Silver Lake* to *The First Four Years*—appeal to the same audience. If Wilder's later work had not eclipsed her daughter's, Lane's appropriation of material from "Pioneer Girl" would certainly have undercut her mother's career. What no one envisioned in 1932 and 1933, however, was that Wilder's literary legacy would be stronger than Lane's.

20. Anderson, "Laura Ingalls Wilder and Rose Wilder Lane," pp. 108–10.

21. RWL, Journal, 25 Jan. 1933, Box 23, Lane Papers. Lane's journal entry suggests that Wilder may also have been distressed by the blurring of generations in *Let the Hurricane Roar*. As a blend of both her parents' story and her own, it may have lost its grounding in historical truth from Wilder's point of view.

22. RWL to George Bye, 30 July 1932, James Oliver Brown Collection, Rare Book and Manuscript Library, Columbia University, New York.

23. RWL, Journal, 19 Feb. 1933, Box 23, Lane Papers.

24. RWL, Diary, 1931–1935, March Memo 1933, Box 22, ibid. *See also* Miller, *Becoming Laura Ingalls Wilder*, p. 201.

25. RWL to Day, 26 May 1928.

26. RWL to George Bye, 20 Mar., 27 Apr. 1933, Brown Collection.

27. Ida Louise Raymond, quoted in RWL to Bye, 20 Mar. 1933.

28. RWL to LIW, n.d.[postcard, 1932], Box 13, Lane Papers.

29. RWL to LIW, 7 Oct. 1932, ibid.

30. Raymond, quoted in RWL to Bye, 20 Mar. 1933.

31. LIW, *Farmer Boy*, p. 372.

32. LIW, *Little House in the Big Woods*, p. 238.

33. RWL to Bye, 20 Mar. 1933.

Chapter 15: I Wish It Would Never Come to an End

1. Marjorie Vitense to LIW, 22 Feb. 1933, Folder 14, Laura Ingalls Wilder Home Association, Mansfield, Mo., Microfilm ed., LIW Papers, 1894–1943 (hereafter cited as LIW Papers), Western Historical Manuscript Collection, Ellis Library, University of Missouri, Columbia, Mo.

2. Fred Kiewit, "Stories That Had to be Told," *Kansas City Star*, n.d. [1955], clipping, Laura Ingalls Wilder Folder, State Archives Collection, South Dakota State Historical Society, Pierre, S.Dak.

3. Tipton Consolidated Schools Fourth Grade Teacher [signature missing] to LIW, 25 Apr. 1933, Folder 14, LIW Papers. *See also* Ida Louise Raymond to LIW, 13 July 1934, Box 13, LIW Series, Rose Wilder Lane Papers (hereafter cited as Lane Papers), Herbert Hoover Presidential Library, West Branch, Iowa.

4. Miscellaneous correspondence and rough manuscript notes, Folder 14, LIW Papers.

5. LIW, *Little House on the Prairie* manuscript, p. 1, Folder 15, ibid.

6. LIW to Dear Sir [R. B. Selvidge], 26 June 1933, Folder 14, ibid.

7. R. B. Selvidge to LIW, 5 July 1933, ibid.

8. Kansas State Historical Society to LIW, 10 Jan. 1934, ibid.

9. William Holtz, *The Ghost in the Little House: A Life of Rose Wilder Lane,* Missouri Biography Series (Columbia: University of Missouri Press, 1993), p. 253; John E. Miller, *Becoming Laura Ingalls Wilder: The Woman behind the Legend,* Missouri Biography Series (Columbia: University of Missouri Press, 1998), pp. 205–7; LIW, *Little House on the Prairie* manuscript, p. 1; LIW, *Little House on the Prairie*, p. 1; e-mail interview with Regina Griffin, New York City, 22 May 2007.

10. LIW, *Little House On The Prairie* manuscript, p. 11. *See also* LIW, *Little House on the Prairie*. Wilder did make effective shifts in

point of view in her later novels, most notably in *The Long Winter,* when she described scenes exclusively from Almanzo's perspective. This change freed Wilder to develop Almanzo as an important character and to contrast the Ingalls family's situation with the Wilders' more secure and less desperate one.

11. Regina Griffin to author, 27 Aug. 1997.

12. RWL to Mr. McBride, 19 Dec. 1935, James Oliver Brown Collection, Rare Book and Manuscript Library, Columbia University, New York.

13. Ida Louise Raymond to LIW, 13 July, 27 Aug. 1934, Box 13, Lane Papers.

14. RWL to George Bye, 17 Apr. 1933, Brown Collection. Wilder and Lane had already negotiated serialization. *See St. Nicholas Magazine* to RWL, 23 Sept. 1932, Folder 14, LIW Papers.

15. George Bye to RWL, 24 Mar. 1933, Box 13, Lane Papers.

16. Ida Louise Raymond to RWL, 27 Apr. 1933, ibid.

17. Ibid., 23 Mar. 1934.

18. LIW to George Bye, 1 Aug. 1941, Brown Collection.

19. Ida Louise Raymond to LIW, 27 Aug. 1934, Box 13, Lane Papers.

20. Holtz, *Ghost in the Little House*, pp. 109, 198, 248–49; Miller, *Becoming Laura Ingalls Wilder*, p. 205.

21. RWL to George Bye, 23 June 1934, Brown Collection.

22. RWL to George Bye, 2 July 1933, ibid.

23. Ibid., 14 Oct. 1934.

24. Holtz, *Ghost in the Little House,* p. 254.

25. William T. Anderson, "Laura Ingalls Wilder and Rose Wilder Lane: The Continuing Collaboration," *South Dakota History* 16 (Summer 1986): 114–16.

26. Miller, *Becoming Laura Ingalls Wilder*, pp. 208–13.

Chapter 16: The Children's Story Is Now Complete

1. Ida Louise Raymond to LIW, 27 Aug. 1934, Box 13, LIW Series, Rose Wilder Lane Papers (hereafter cited as Lane Papers), Herbert Hoover Presidential Library, West Branch, Iowa.

2. RWL to LIW, 13 June 1936, Folder 19, Laura Ingalls Wilder

Home Association, Mansfield, Mo., Microfilm ed., LIW Papers, 1894–1943 (hereafter cited as LIW papers), Western Historical Manuscript Collection, Ellis Library, University of Missouri, Columbia, Mo.

3. LIW to RWL, n.d. [1936], ibid.

4. LIW to RWL, n.d. [1936, two letters with diagrams], ibid.

5. LIW to RWL, 2 July 1936, ibid.

6. RWL to LIW, 13 June 1936, ibid.

7. LIW to RWL, n.d. [1936], ibid.

8. LIW to RWL, 2 July 1936, ibid.

9. LIW, *On the Banks of Plum Creek,* pp. 304–8.

10. Ibid., pp. 63–64, 134–35, 174–76, 304–8.

11. LIW to RWL, 6 Aug. 1936, Folder 19, LIW Papers.

12. Lane usually gives her best dialogue to secondary characters, who provide color, contrast, and background in her short stories and novels. In *Let the Hurricane Roar* and her later novel, *Free Land,* her main characters appear to give voice to Lane's own thematic ideas, which makes the dialogue stiff and flat and the characters archetypal.

13. LIW to RWL, 6 Aug. 1936, Folder 19, LIW Papers.

14. Ibid., n.d. [1936] and 6 Aug. 1936.

15. LIW to George Bye, 24 Sept. 1936, James Oliver Brown Collection, Rare Book and Manuscript Library, Columbia University, New York; RWL to LIW, 21 Sept. 1936, Box 13, Lane Papers.

16. George Bye to LIW, 31 May 1939, Brown Collection.

17. LIW to RWL, n.d. [1936], Folder 19, LIW Papers.

18. RWL to George Bye, 12 Mar. 1937, Brown Collection.

19. RWL, Interview with AJW, in *A Little House Sampler: A Collection of Early Stories and Reminiscences*, ed. William Anderson (New York: Harper Perennial, 1988), pp. 204, 209.

20. AJW to RWL, 25 Mar. 1937, Box 17, Lane Papers.

21. Ibid., 20 Mar. 1937.

22. LIW and AJW to RWL, 12 May 1937, ibid.

23. LIW to RWL, 5 Feb. 1937, ibid.

24. RWL, *Free Land* (New York: Longmans, Green & Co., 1938), p. 107.

25. LIW, "Pioneer Girl," Folder 3, LIW Papers; RWL, *Free Land*, pp. 109–30.

26. Holtz, *Ghost in the Little House* p. 280; Miller, *Becoming Laura Ingalls Wilder*, pp. 221–22.

27. LIW to RWL, 15 Feb. 1938, Box 13, Lane Papers. *See also* RWL to LIW, n.d. [1938], ibid.

28. LIW, *By the Shores of Silver Lake,* pp. 64–65; RWL, *Free Land*, p. 130.

29. LIW, Detroit Book Fair Speech, 1937, pp. 3–4, Box 13, Lane Papers.

30. Michael Cart, *From Romance to Realism: 50 Years of Growth and Change in Young Adult Literature* (New York: Harper Collins, 1996), pp. 4–6; Miller, *Becoming Laura Ingalls Wilder*, p. 224.

31. LIW to RWL, 26 Jan. 1938, Box 13, Lane Papers.

32. Ibid., n.d. [1932]. *See also* RWL to LIW, 19 Dec. 1937, ibid.

33. LIW, *By the Shores of Silver Lake* manuscript, pp. 1–2, Folder 25, LIW Papers. J. K. Rowling, author of the Harry Potter series, occasionally makes a similar shift in point of view. Contrast the opening of *Harry Potter and the Goblet of Fire* (New York: Arthur A. Levine Books, 2000), p. 1, with the opening chapters of other books in the series.

34. RWL to LIW, 19 Dec. 1937, Box 13, Lane Papers.

35. Ibid., 21 Jan. 1938.

36. LIW to RWL, 25 Jan. 1938, ibid.

37. RWL to LIW, 19 Dec. 1937.

38. LIW to RWL, n.d. [1937], ibid.

39. Ibid., 25 Jan. 1938. *See also* RWL to LIW, 21 Jan. 1938, ibid.

40. LIW, *By the Shores of Silver Lake,* p. 1.

41. LIW to RWL, n.d. [1937], Box 13, Lane Papers.

42. *New York Herald Tribune,* 10 Nov. 1940, clipping, Box 15, ibid.

43. George Bye to LIW, 30 Apr. 1940, Brown Collection.

44. Ibid., 25 July 1941.

45. Ibid., 5 May 1943.

46. LIW to George Bye, 17 May 1940, ibid.; Miller, *Becoming Laura Ingalls Wilder*, p. 223.

47. RWL to George Bye, 30 June 1941, ibid.

48. LIW to RWL, 28 Jan. 1938 and n.d. [1937–1938], Box 13, Lane Papers.

49. LIW to RWL, 19 Feb. 1938, 7 Mar. 1938, 3 June 1939, and n.d., Box 13; LIW, "Prairie Girl" outline, Box 16; "The Last Mile" manuscript notes and resource material, Box 15; RWL/LIW, "Would it be possible to substitute . . . " n.d., Box 15, all in Lane Papers.

50. LIW to RWL, 3 June 1939, Box 13, ibid.

51. RWL to George Bye, 5 June 1940, Brown Collection.

52. George Bye to LIW, 29 Sept. 1942, ibid.

53. RWL to LIW, 20 Dec. 1937, Box 13, Lane Papers.

54. Ibid., RWL to LIW, 11 Oct. 1937.

55. LIW to RWL, n.d. [1939], ibid.

56. LIW to RWL, 10 Jan. 1939, ibid.

57. RWL to LIW, 20 Dec. 1937, ibid. Lane's book on the history of Missouri was never published. Although she signed a contract, received an advance, and completed a draft of the entire book, she and the publisher at McBride Publishing Company disagreed on its content and focus. Holtz, *Ghost in the Little House,* pp. 258–59; Miller, *Becoming Laura Ingalls Wilder*, p. 208.

58. LIW to George Bye, 28 Sept. 1942, Brown Collection.

59. George Bye to LIW, 5 May 1943, ibid.

Chapter 17: To Go On from Here

1. George Bye to LIW, 9 May 1941, James Oliver Brown Collection, Rare Book and Manuscript Library, Columbia University, New York.

2. LIW to George Bye, 19 May 1941, ibid.

3. George Bye to LIW, 7 July 1939, and Jasper Spock to RWL, 8 July 1941, ibid.

4. LIW to George Bye, 10 July 1939, ibid.

5. Jasper Spock to RWL, 8 July 1941, and LIW to George Bye, 21 June 1940, Brown Collection.

6. LIW to George Bye, 3 July 1941, Brown Collection.

7. George Bye to LIW, 11 July 1941, and LIW to Bye, 15 July 1941, ibid.

8. LIW to George Bye, 21 June 1940, ibid.

9. LIW to George Bye, 5 July 1940, George Eye to LIW, 6 June 1944, LIW to George Bye, 10 June 1944, Dorothea Howley to Miss Okum, 11 Dec. 1953, and John Van Bibber to RWL, 16 Dec. 1958, all ibid.

10. LIW to George Bye, 2 Oct. 1939, ibid. *Little House on the Prairie*, the television series loosely based on Wilder's books, premiered in the late 1970s. It is impossible to know, of course, what Wilder would have thought of the television series, but if she insisted on no changes from her original text when she granted rights for *The Long Winter*, it is tempting to suspect that Wilder would not have approved of Michael Landon's television adaptation.

11. LIW to George Bye, 19 Nov. 1941, Brown Collection. It is not clear which illustration Wilder is objecting to, but it is probably the dust jacket illustration in which Laura's cheeks appear to be highly rouged. Illustrator Mildred Boyle began assisting Helen Sewell with illustrations for the original Little House series early in 1937. Sewell had suffered a severe car accident and needed help with research and backgrounds to meet publication deadlines for *On the Banks of Plum Creek*. Ida Louise Raymond to LIW, 22 Dec. 1936, File 13, LIW Series, Rose Wilder Lane Papers (hereafter cited as Lane Papers), Herbert Hoover Presidential Library, West Branch, Iowa.

12. LIW to George Bye, 10 July 1939, Brown Collection.

13. George Bye to RWL, Western Union Telegram, 25 June 1939, ibid.

14. George Bye to LIW, 8 Feb. 1940, ibid. *See also* LIW to George Bye, 14 Feb. 1940, ibid.

15. John E. Miller, *Becoming Laura Ingalls Wilder: The Woman behind the Legend,* Missouri Biography Series (Columbia: University of Missouri Press, 1998), p. 257.

16. Garth Williams, "Illustrating the Little House Books," *Horn Book* (Dec. 1953), reprinted in *The Horn Book's Laura Ingalls Wilder,* ed. William Anderson (Boston: Horn Book, 1987), pp. 26–28.

17. Miller, *Becoming Laura Ingalls Wilder*, p. 250; LIW to George Bye, 16 July 1949, Brown Collection.

18. Lucille Morris Upton, "True Stories That Read Like Fiction," *Springfield News & Leader*, 22 May 1949.

19. LIW to "Dear Sir" [George Bye], 16 July 1949, Brown Collection.

20. LIW to George Bye, 16 July 1949, ibid.

21. LIW to Mrs. E. F. Green, 11 Nov. 1949, Laura Ingalls Wilder Memorial Society, Inc., De Smet, S.Dak. (hereafter cited LIW Memorial Society).

22. William Holtz, *The Ghost in the Little House: A Life of Rose Wilder Lane,* Missouri Biography Series (Columbia: University of Missouri Press, 1993), p. 335; Miller, *Becoming Laura Ingalls Wilder*, p. 252.

23. LIW to Mrs. E. F. Green, 11 Nov. 1949.

24. LIW to Silas and Neta Seal, n.d., LIW Memorial Society; Fred Kiewit, "Stories That Had to Be Told," *Kansas City Star*, n.d. [1955], clipping, Laura Ingalls Wilder Folder, Archives Collection, South Dakota State Historical Society, Pierre.

25. RWL to Neta Seal, 23 Apr. 1955, LIW Memorial Society. *See also* Miller, *Becoming Laura Ingalls Wilder*, pp. 258–59.

26. Quoted in Kiewit, "Stories That Had to Be Told."

27. LIW to George Bye, 10 May 1943, Brown Collection.

28. Quoted in Kiewit, "Stories That Had to Be Told."

29. LIW to RWL, 30 July 1952, Box 13, Lane Papers.

30. "Laura Ingalls Wilder Succumbed Monday," *De Smet News*, 17 Feb. 1957.

31. RWL to LIW, 9 July 1951, LIW Memorial Society.

32. RWL to Neta Seal, 2 Mar. 1957, ibid.

33. Holtz, *Ghost in the Little House*, pp. 340, 373.

34. Louise Hovde Mortensen, quoting herself, in "Idea Inventory," *Elementary English* (Apr. 1964): 428.

35. RWL to Louise Hovde Mortensen, 31 Dec. 1963, ibid.

36. Ibid.

37. George Bye to RWL, 6 Apr. 1931, Box 13, Lane Papers.

38. Holtz, *Ghost in the Little House,* p. 343; James Oliver Brown to Raymond T. Benedict, 31 Mar. 1959, Brown Collection. When Lane and MacBride terminated their relationship with the George Bye Agency in 1957, an advocate for the agency reported that the earn-

ings from the Laura Ingalls Wilder estate were one of the largest sources of income for the agency. The termination was not cordial, but the Bye Agency could not afford to take legal action. The Bye Agency advocate characterized Lane as "a peculiar old lady" from Connecticut and reported that dealing with her had been "difficult" (James Oliver Brown to Howard O. Hill, 14 Sept. 1959, Brown Collection).

39. Holtz, *Ghost in the Little House*, pp. 370–71; Amy Mattson Lauter, *The Rediscovered Writings of Rose Wilder Lane: Literary Journalist* (Columbia: University of Missouri Press, 2007), p. 1; "Rose Lane Dies at 82," *Springfield News & Leader*, 31 Oct. 1968.

40. May Hill Arbuthnot, "Laura Ingalls Wilder," *Children and Books* (Chicago: Scott, Foresman & Co., 1957), p. 441.

41. Garth Williams, "Illustrating the Little House Books," p. 36.

42. Ursula Nordstrom to Garth Williams, 11 Feb. 1954, in *Dear Genius: The Letters of Ursula Nordstrom*, ed. Leonard S. Marcus (New York: HarperCollins, 1998), pp. 74–75. The Caldecott Award, sponsored by the American Library Association, is given annually to the illustrator of the most distinguished American picture book.

43. Ursula Nordstrom to Ethel Heins, ibid., p. 365.

44. Nordstrom to Jim Blake, 9 Feb. 1954, ibid., p. 2.

45. LIW, *Little House on the Prairie*, 1st ed. (New York: Harper & Bros., 1935) p. 1.

46. Ursula Nordstrom to unidentified reader, 14 Oct. 1952, in *Dear Genius,* pp. 53–54.

47. LIW, quoted ibid., p. 54.

48. LIW, *Little House on the Prairie*, new ed., p. 2.

49. LIW, *Little House on the Prairie* manuscript, pp. 1–13, Folder 16, Laura Ingalls Wilder Home Association, Mansfield, Mo., Microfilm ed., LIW Papers, 1894–1943 (hereafter cited as LIW papers), Western Historical Manuscript Collection, Ellis Library, University of Missouri, Columbia, Mo.

50. Dennis McAuliffe, Jr., "Little House on the Osage Prairie," *Oyate,* www.oyate.org/books-to-avoid, accessed 7/17/07.

51. John E. Miller, "American Indians in the Fiction of Laura

Ingalls Wilder, *South Dakota History* 30 (Fall 2000): 303.

52. Unidentified visitor to Laura Ingalls Wilder Home and Museum, Mansfield, overheard by author, 25 May 2006.

53. LIW, *By the Shores of Silver Lake,* p. 58.

Selected Bibliography

Anderson, William T., ed. *The Horn Book's Laura Ingalls Wilder*.
Boston: Horn Book, 1987.

_____. "Laura Ingalls Wilder and Rose Wilder Lane: The
Continuing Collaboration." *South Dakota History* 16 (Summer
1986): 89–143.

_____, comp. *Laura's Album: A Remembrance Scrapbook of
Laura Ingalls Wilder*. New York: HarperCollins, 1998.

_____. "The Literary Apprenticeship of Laura Ingalls Wilder,"
South Dakota History 13 (Winter 1983): 285–331.

_____, ed. *A Little House Reader: A Collection of Writings by
Laura Ingalls Wilder*. New York: Harper Collins, 1998.

_____, ed. *A Little House Sampler*. Lincoln: University of
Nebraska Press, 1988.

Arbuthnot, May Hill. *Children and Books*. Chicago: Scott, Foresman
& Co., 1957.

Bennet, Phillip D. *Laura's Pathway to Home*. Mansfield, Mo.: By the
Author, 2004.

The Best of the Lore. De Smet, S.Dak.: Laura Ingalls Wilder
Memorial Society, 2007.

Cart, Michael. *From Romance to Realism: 50 Years of Growth and
Change in Young Adult Literature*. New York: Harper Collins,
1996.

Hines, Stephen W., comp. *Laura Ingalls Wilder's Fairy Poems*. New
York: Doubleday, 1998.

_____, ed. *Little House in the Ozarks: The Rediscovered
Writings*. New York: Galahad Books, 1991.

_____, ed. *Writings to Young Women from Laura Ingalls Wilder:
On Life as a Pioneer Woman*. Nashville: Tommy Nelson, 2006.

Holtz, William. *The Ghost in the Little House: A Life of Rose Wilder
Lane*. Missouri Biography Series. Columbia: University of
Missouri Press, 1993.

The Ingalls Family of De Smet. De Smet, S.Dak.: Laura Ingalls Wilder
    Memorial Society, 2001.

Karolevitz, Robert F. *Challenge: The South Dakota Story.* Sioux Falls,
    S.Dak.: Brevet Press, 1975.

Kunitz, Stanley J., and Howard Haycroft, eds. *Junior Book of
    Authors.* 2d. ed., rev. New York: Wilson, 1951.

L'Engle, Madeleine. *Herself.* Colorado Springs: Shaw Books, 2001.

Lauter, Amy Mattson. *The Rediscovered Writings of Rose Wilder Lane:
    Literary Journalist.* Columbia: University of Missouri Press, 2007.

Marcus, Leonard S., ed. *Dear Genius: The Letters of Ursula
    Nordstrom.* New York: HarperCollins, 1998.

Miller, John E. "American Indians in the Fiction of Laura Ingalls
    Wilder." *South Dakota History* 30 (Fall 2000): 303–20.

_____. *Becoming Laura Ingalls Wilder: The Woman behind the
    Legend.* Missouri Biography Series. Columbia: University of
    Missouri Press, 1998.

_____. *Laura Ingalls Wilder's Little Town: Where History and
    Literature Meet.* Lawrence: University Press of Kansas, 1994.

Moore, Rosa Ann. "Laura Ingalls Wilder and Rose Wilder Lane: The
    Chemistry of Collaboration." *Children's Literature in Education*
    11 (Sept. 1980): 101–9.

_____. "Laura Ingalls Wilder's Orange Notebooks and the Art
    of the Little House Books." *Children's Literature* 4 (1975): 105-19.

Morrow, Lynn, and Linda Myers-Phinney. *Shepherd of the Hills
    Country: Tourism Transforms the Ozarks, 1880s to 1930s.*
    Fayetteville: University of Arkansas Press, 1999.

Schell, Herbert S. *History of South Dakota.* 4th ed. Rev. John E.
    Miller. Pierre: South Dakota State Historical Society Press, 2004.

Zochert, Donald. *Laura: The Life of Laura Ingalls Wilder.* New York:
    Avon Books, 1976.

Index

The following abbreviations appear throughout this index:

LIW   Laura Ingalls Wilder

RWL   Rose Wilder Lane

AJW   Almanzo James Wilder

Page numbers in **bold** indicate photographs.